T0305769

# Complex Management Systems and the Shingo Model

## Foundations of Operational Excellence and Supporting Tools

# Complex Management Systems and the Shingo Model

## Foundations of Operational Excellence and Supporting Tools

Author: Professor Rick L. Edgeman

Contributor: Shaun Barker

A PRODUCTIVITY PRESS BOOK

First edition published in 2019

by Routledge/Productivity Press
52 Vanderbilt Avenue, 11th Floor New York, NY 10017
2 Park Square, Milton Park, Abingdon, Oxon OX14 4RN, UK

International Standard Book Number-13: 978–1–138–62622–5 (Hardback)
International Standard Book Number-13: 978–1–3152–2963–8 (e-Book)

# Contents

## PART I   Brick-by-Brick: Building the
## Complex Management Systems Model

## PART II   Elaboration of Key
## Components of the Complex Management
## Systems Model

# List of Figures

# List of Tables

# Acknowledgments

A few of the words from the 1970s hit song "Lucky Man" by the band Emerson, Lake and Palmer are "oh, what a lucky man he was." In the end, I believe that my epithet will be "oh, what a blessed man he was." It is here that I would like to acknowledge a small fraction of parties responsible for this blessing.

I have many to thank who have gone before or have walked beside me: family and friends, mentors and colleagues, and forebears in the various fields that have been integrated to yield what now goes by many names, among which are operational excellence, performance excellence, enterprise excellence, organizational excellence, and business excellence.

My wife, Julie, is, to me, ideal in every way. Without her patience and encouragement, I could not have completed this volume. When I was lost, she found me. She loves me. She is patient with me—far more patient than I deserve. She forgives me yet holds me accountable—what a rare and valuable combination. I have learned so much from her, have much more left to learn, look forward to *almost* every minute of the learning, and owe her far more than I can ever repay. Instead, I will simply and eternally love her.

I continue to aspire to be like my mother and father, Eunice and Howard Edgeman. They instilled values by modeling them for myself and my siblings and will ever be my heroes. Among those values are honesty and the importance of truth, sacrifice, persistence, a sense of adventure, curiosity to ask and seek answers to "why" and "how," to esteem wisdom more than knowledge, to acquire experience, and to thirst for excellence. One day I hope to master these. They taught me that opportunities are a gift and not to be taken lightly. They taught me how to think and not what to think—and hence, how to think for myself, to understand that the cost of kindness is far lower than that of cruelty, and that a few important words and phrases spoken often but genuinely will take one far in life: thank you, please, I apologize, how can I help, I forgive you, I love you. They forgave, inspired, and loved me day upon day upon day.

I have learned much from my children—now young adults—and my step-daughter, and I continue to do so. I have a very long way to go but hope that one day they will be able to legitimately think of me as I do my own parents and that in turn their children will think the same of them, generation upon generation.

Similarly, I have had many thousands of students in the U.S., Denmark, Sweden, Switzerland, and from around the globe, and I have learned more from them than they have from me. Still, they are part of my legacy, and I hope I have and will continue to serve them well. I will not slight any by naming a few.

With advance apologies to the many exceptional mentors, colleagues, and collaborators not mentioned below, "thank you." Still, I will highlight a few: Gopal Kanji, H. James Harrington, Harry Hertz, Greg Watson, Bob Hogg, and John Hromi. I hope that I can do for others what these mentors did or are doing for me. Equally, a few of the *giants of quality* upon whose foundations we have built must be recognized: Shigeo Shingo, W. Edwards Deming, Joseph M. Juran, Val Feigenbaum, Masaaki Imai, and Peter Drucker.

An unorthodox last few whom I wish to thank are authors, adventurers, and a few others who have inspired me to imagine and explore what is possible and what is right: all the courageous astronauts who circled or walked on the moon; C.S. Lewis; J.R.R. Tolkien; Mark Twain; Jules Verne; Edgar Rice Burroughs; H. Rider Haggard; H.G. Wells; James Fennimore Cooper; Davy Crockett; Daniel Boone; Billy Graham; Mother Teresa of Calcutta; Martin Luther King, Jr.; James Ryle; Rick Olmstead; Elon Musk; and Ann Makosinksi. Their influence spans generations and they have been responsible for changed lives.

The Shingo Institute's Amy Sadler is especially to be thanked for "smoothing out the roughness" herein.

Finally, while there are many to credit for anything of value in this book, any shortcomings belong to the authors alone.

**Rick L. Edgeman—Hays, Kansas, USA**

# About the Authors

**Rick L. Edgeman** is Professor and Chair of the Management Department in the Robbins College of Business & Entrepreneurship at Fort Hays State University (Kansas) and Research Fellow in the Shingo Institute at Utah State University, where he previously served as Research Director and Professor of Management Practice. He is also concurrently Professor of Sustainability & Enterprise Performance in the Business Development & Technology Department at Denmark's Aarhus University and Honorary Professor of Engineering Operations Management in the Department of Technology & Innovation at Denmark's Southern Denmark University.

Past or occasional service includes roles as Visiting Professor in the Executive MBA program at the University of Lugano, which serves as the University of Lugano (Switzerland); Professor of Quality Management in the Quality Sciences Division at Uppsala University (Sweden); Visiting Professor in the Faculty of Management and Economics at Tomas Bata University in the Czech Republic; Visiting Professor in the Quality and Environmental Management Division at Luleå University (Sweden; QUEST Professor & Executive Director of the QUEST Honors Fellows Program in the Robert H. Smith School of Business at the University of Maryland; Professor & Chair of the Statistical Science Department at the University of Idaho; and Professor & Director of the Center for Quality & Productivity Improvement at Colorado State University. He has provided numerous keynote addresses and other invited lectures, including ones at Oxford University, Cambridge University, the University of Versailles (France), Chalmers University (Sweden), and the Royal Melbourne Institute of Technology.

Rick has authored more than 250 publications on quality management, sustainability, six sigma, leadership, innovation, and statistics. He formerly co-edited the journal *Measuring Business Excellence* and is presently associate editor of *Total Quality Management & Business Excellence*. He has also edited special issues of several journals, and on the editorial review boards of numerous journals, including the *Six Sigma Forum* and *Quality Engineering.* He earned the Ph.D. in Statistics from the University of Wyoming and was cited by the American Society for Quality in 2000 as one of *21 Voices of Quality for the 21st Century*—one of only six academics worldwide included among the 21.

 **Shaun Barker** has been the assistant executive director for the Shingo Institute since 2001 where he is responsible for such organizational operations as finance, human resources, information technology, marketing and development. He is also responsible for the assessment value stream and its pool of approximately 160 examiners from industries around the world. He has personally participated in dozens of comprehensive site assessment visits to business and government organizations worldwide that have challenged for the Shingo Prize. Shaun participates in the development of Shingo educational offerings and is a contributor to both the world-renowned *Shingo Model* and the Shingo Prize Application Guidelines—the international standard of operational excellence. He was also a key participant in the creation of a Lean certification program sponsored by AME, SME, and the Shingo Institute.

Shaun is an engaging speaker and instructor for the Shingo Institute and trains companies on the *Shingo Model* and *Shingo Guiding Principles,* teaching how to apply principle-based leadership to their own operations and to use assessment tools to foster continuous improvement within their organizations. As a result of his expertise, Shaun has delivered presentations and workshops to professionals in various parts of the world including the United States, Canada, China, Mexico and Europe.

Shaun's professional industry background in retail management operations included 14 years of work with Sav-On Drugs, Wal-Mart and Dollar General. He has experience with profit and loss responsibility for multi-million dollar operations in high growth environments.

He earned a bachelor's degree in marketing with a minor in economics from Utah State University in 1984 and an MBA with an emphasis in entrepreneurship in 1999. As an instructor for the Jon M. Huntsman School of Business at Utah State University, Shaun has taught courses in organizational change management, marketing and introduction to business.

Shaun spent his childhood in the Philippines where he lived for 13 years, and he speaks Tagalog fluently. At the age of 15 he began his working career as a wrangler at a ranch in Jackson Hole, Wyoming. He would fly to the United States from the Philippines to work during the summer and then return home in August each year. In 1978, the same year he returned to the United States permanently, he worked on a commercial fishing boat in the Gulf of Mexico. While attending college, he worked for Del-Monte Corp., E.A. Miller Beef and Trans-Western Airlines. Shaun has a rich variety of life and work experiences that he is eager to expand.

# Introduction

## ON A TREASURE HUNT

In what follows, the word *enterprise* is used in a very broad sense as substitutable for such other choices as *business, company,* or *organization* without regard to whether the enterprise is a for-profit one, a governmental entity, an NGO, or a for-benefit entity that seeks to "do well by doing good" (Sabeti, 2011).

Virtually all enterprises hope to improve—but only some enterprises manage to routinely improve and prosper year-upon-year. Those enterprises experiencing such success tend to have cultivated cultures founded on unity of purpose—that is, "what they are all about." Complementary to this, a critical mass of the enterprise's human ecology buys into a shared vision for the future of the enterprise and understands the means and necessity and value of their contributions to advancing that vision.

While unity of purpose and shared vision are critical to prolonged year-upon-year success, these must be supported by well-defined means by which the enterprise formulates and executes strategy that delivers specific results that are aligned with enterprise purpose and vision. More formally, we regard strategy as a description of how the enterprise intends to create value for its varied stakeholders (Kaplan and Norton, 2004).

Such organizations are "purpose-driven" and fulfilling their purpose and vision is a matter of intention, rather than accident.

It is translation of intention into fulfillment that is challenging. The precise recipe for successful translation varies from organization to organization, yet various commonalities can be identified and from those commonalities, models—maps, if you will—can be formed that can provide general guidance to other organizations seeking to be predictably successful year-upon-year.

Such models may be referred to as "*X Excellence Models*" where "*X*" has been variously described as operational, business, performance, organizational, or enterprise. Herein, we will most commonly equate X with operational, though of course any of the other near-synonyms cited might have been selected.

In almost all cases, the core motivations behind such models are identical—that via successful implementation thereof, the organization will be rendered more sustainable, more resilient, more robust, and will routinely deliver more positive performance and impacts in areas critically important to the enterprise and its varied stakeholders.

*X Excellence Models* fundamentally treat an organization or relevant subset thereof (e.g., plant, division, etc.) as a complex adaptive system. This macro view regards the overall structure or architecture of the organization as a complex macroscopic collection of relatively similar and partially connected microstructures. Complex adaptive system (organizational) architectures are formed with the intent of making the organization more adaptive to environmental changes, thereby increasing the survivability at the macrostructural (organizational) level. The ability to adapt to environmental changes, as broadly construed, simultaneously renders the organization more resilient, more robust, and hence more sustainable.

The approach pursued herein is to identify and elaborate the elements of an organizationally relevant complex adaptive systems model, after which these will be assembled into a coherent architecture that will be referred to as a complex management systems model. More to the point, the goal herein is not simply to derive such a model—of which many are possible— but to produce one that is an *X Excellence Model* useful to organizations pursuing excellence. Ultimately then, our model is a complex (adaptive) management systems for operational excellence model.

Once constructed, this model will be correlated with the *Shingo Model*™. The *Shingo Model* is core to the globally relevant Shingo Prize for Operational Excellence award and has served as a key enabler for many enterprises that are on a quest for ongoing operational excellence. In the end, it will be seen that not only does the *Shingo Model* work from a pragmatic perspective but that it is supported by a sound theoretical foundation. These facts should be comforting since their combined implication is that proper and persistent use of the *Shingo Model* can set an enterprise on a path that progresses predictably toward excellence. Further, once on the path, adherence to the Model and its principles— duly adapted to specific enterprise context—can help the enterprise to become sustainably operationally excellent.

The principles and criteria upon which the *Shingo Model*, along with the more general complex (adaptive) management systems for operational excellence model are founded, provides a means by which an enterprise can assess its progress toward operational excellence. As such—though more comprehensive tomes on the topic of enterprise self-assessment or third-party assessment can be found—some attention will be dedicated to assessment.

Enterprise assessment can be highly nuanced for those enterprises lacking experience in this realm and, for that reason, expert external assessors can often provide excellent insight. Properly conducted, enterprise assessment regularly (usually annually), rigorously, and systemically evaluates all relevant enterprise strategies, processes, activities, and results against a specified model. The aim of doing this is to provide the enterprise with insight into its recent "health," along with foresight or direction into what more or what else to do to improve its short-term and long-term future health.

Recalling that a model is a map of sorts, our complex (adaptive) management systems for operational excellence model in the general sense and the *Shingo Model* more specifically can provide an enterprise with an "X-marks-the-spot treasure map" where the spot marked by X is operational excellence. Indeed, organizations should regard operational excellence and its sustainable, resilient, and robust constituents as treasure. Well implemented, such models support enterprise adaptability and can deliver treasure year-upon-year to the enterprise and its stakeholders.

Let's construct a map and set out on a treasure hunt. Unlike most treasure maps, however, we will find as we proceed that "there is treasure everywhere."

Recall that maps are abstractions of reality and are hence inherently flawed. That is true of the maps provided by Figures I.1 and I.2—treasure maps that provide many "X-marks-the-spot" opportunities—where each "X" is a chapter detailing where specific types of operational excellence treasure can be found. Each "X" is imprecisely marked since the precise location of any of these is partially governed by enterprise context.

Figure I.1 maps the complex management systems model, whereas Figure I.2 maps the *Shingo Model*. Chapter numbers in Figures I.1 and I.2 are indicated by small solid circles.

Figure I.1 describes the topography of the complex management systems model. This model will be addressed in detail as it is built and explained in a brick-by-brick manner. The present objective is merely to highlight the primary chapter(s) in which various model components are addressed.

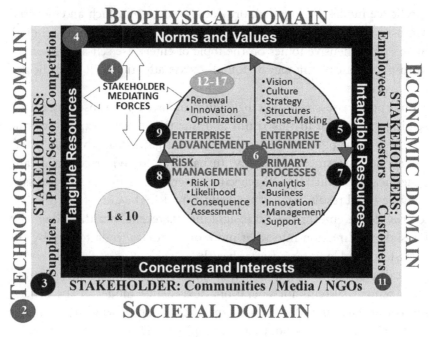

**FIGURE I.1**
Complex management systems model treasure (chapter) map.

Most model elements are also discussed in multiple other chapters—either in lesser detail—or in relation to the *Shingo Model*.

We see that the model is addressed abstractly in Chapter 1 and holistically in Chapter 10. So-called Chapter 2 discusses the BEST environmental domains that are recorded on the perimeter of Figure I.1—biophysical, economic, societal, and technological—as they relate to the enterprise. Stakeholder segments that are recorded just inside the BEST domains are addressed in varying levels of detail in Chapter 3, with customers receiving additional, detailed consideration in Chapter 11. Chapter 4 addresses mediating forces that fundamentally address the rules of engagement the enterprise must navigate in its interactions with the BEST domains and its stakeholder segments. Mediating forces are recorded in the black, inner perimeter of Figure I.1. Chapters 5 and 7 through 9 deal with four main areas of concern that enterprises must confront—how the enterprise achieves alignment, its primary processes, how it manages risk, and how it develops and advances. Chapter 6 discusses the PDSA (Plan–Do–Study–Act) Cycle both in terms of general use and as a sort of mortar that joins the various enterprise bricks comprising other model elements together.

**FIGURE I.2**
*Shingo Model* treasure (chapter) map.

Chapters 12 to 17 are generally more tools-based than most other chapters, with content that can be categorized in multiple ways. Fundamentally these chapters deal with generations of products and service offerings that satisfy stakeholder wants and needs. While it is most certainly possible to link these considerations and methods directly to customers—the prime stakeholder segment for a majority of enterprises—it is also true that these contribute substantially to innovation, renewal, and optimization—means by which the enterprise develops and advances.

Chapters 18 through 26 explore the *Shingo Model*, both in isolation and in relation to the complex management systems model with Figure I.2 positioning the *Shingo Model* in an enterprise context.

Discussion of this model begins in Chapter 18 where three key insights into operational excellence that, to an extent, frame the thinking behind the *Shingo Model* are presented. These insights appear on the outer circle of Figure I.2, as does the issue of sustainment (enterprise sustainability).

In some cases, Figure I.2 content reveals linkages between the *Shingo Model* and the complex management systems model. As a few examples of this, vision and objectives—integrally related to enterprise alignment—are discussed in Chapter 5, strategy and processes are discussed in Chapter 7, and various activities are discussed in Chapters 6, 8, and 13 through 17.

Relative to the complex management systems model developed earlier, these insights guide not only the ways and reasons the enterprise behaves and performs as it does internally, but consequentially—the ways in which it engages its various stakeholders—hence these might be thought of as mediating forces.

Enterprise culture and cultural enablers are discussed in Chapter 19, whereas Chapter 20 addresses key drivers of continuous improvement. Chapter 21 deals with the important issue of enterprise alignment, an issue also addressed in Chapter 5 relative to the complex management systems model.

Chapter 22 deals explicitly with the creation of stakeholder value, especially for customers. This topic is fundamental to operational excellence and is, whether directly or indirectly, related to all elements of both the *Shingo Model* and the complex management systems model. Chapter 17, which focuses on quality function deployment, addresses one mechanism that aids delivery of stakeholder value, whereas the content of Chapters 12 to 16 addresses in detail how the concept for that which generates stakeholder value is conceived and vetted prior to being handed over for development and deployment.

The content of Chapters 12 through 17, as just noted, addresses generation of stakeholder value; but as previously discussed, they are also strongly related to enterprise advancement and hence its sustainability. Key to enterprise (and momentum) sustainment is management of the risk environment so that the methods discussed in Chapters 12 through 17 also provide means of managing risk while simultaneously helping to facilitate enterprise success relative to implementation of the *Shingo Model*. Chapters 8 and 9 deal with the topic of sustainment first from a risk management perspective (Chapter 8) and then from an enterprise advancement perspective (Chapter 9).

Chapter 23 assembles the *Shingo Model* whereas Chapter 24 integrates the complex management systems model and the *Shingo Model*. Chapter 25 discusses the use of the *Shingo Model* relative to assessment of enterprise progress toward operational excellence, while Chapter 26 identifies specific enterprises that have been awarded the Shingo Prize, Shingo Silver Medallion, or Shingo Bronze Medallion from 2010 to 2017.

Finally, Chapter 27 deals explicitly with the integration of the *Shingo Model* and the complex management systems model. Challenges are addressed in the afterword.

It's time to hunt for treasure!

# Part I

# Brick-by-Brick

*Building the Complex
Management Systems Model*

# 1

# Complex Management Systems Modeling of Operational Excellence

Anyone venturing to forecast a future scenario or result is, whether implicitly or explicitly, engaged in modeling. The question is not whether to model, but rather whether to develop an explicit model as a means of forecasting or—stronger—guiding future performance.

In stating that "all models are wrong, but some are useful," Box and Draper (1987) capture the essence of a longer comment on the matter by quality management guru, W. Edwards Deming, that: "Any theorem (theory) is correct in its own world, but which world are we in? Which of several worlds makes contact with ours? That is the question" (Deming, 1994). In accepting these as reasonable observations, the objective herein is to construct a useful operational excellence model of the enterprise, noting simultaneously that there are several commonly used near synonymous expressions for the term *operational excellence* that will be used interchangeably in this tome. Among these terms are *business excellence, enterprise excellence, organizational excellence,* and *performance excellence.*

Determination of whether our model is useful will depend on various factors, not least among which is that it must connect with this world both generally and, more particularly, in competitive landscapes in which reasonable enterprise application of the model must yield an organization that performs at elevated levels in relevant domains over a relevant period—a point that will be revisited in due course. The phrase *reasonable application* intends, at the least that:

- Enterprise leadership adequately embraces and promotes the model,
- The model is implemented either directly or is logically adapted throughout an appropriate swath of the enterprise,
- Its use is reinforced through practice, and

- Sufficient effort is devoted to embedding the model and its accompanying foundation of thinking in enterprise culture or appropriate segments thereof.

As a contextually framed version of the familiar adage that "a tree is known by the fruit it bears," model value should be determined only after its implementation has been reasonably approached and it has been provided with a fair opportunity to succeed or fail on its own merits, as measured by the results it has produced.

This approach is one that is in stark contrast to the natural tendency toward implementation failure that is associated with enterprise impatience. In enterprise cultures marked by an unhealthy level of impatience, a "flavor of the month" culture emerges and "initiatives" routinely come and go without having been given proper opportunity to achieve the promise that led to their initial adoption, thereby establishing the expectation that there is no need to truly adopt the model and embed it in enterprise culture, because "it too shall pass."

## MODELS AS MAPS

A model is fundamentally a map. Maps are abstractions or reductions of reality that emphasize only selected essential features. Features regarded as essential depend on the purpose of the map and the perspective of the mapmaker.

A single reality can usually be seen or interpreted from several perspectives, with a given map representing one or more of those perspectives. The usefulness of a map depends largely on the match between the needs of its users, features emphasized by the map, its level of resolution, and the flexibility or adaptability offered by the map relative to perturbations in its corresponding landscape, whether that landscape is a geological, political, or competitive one.

Our goal is to provide a map for management of enterprises that are willing to relentlessly and rigorously pursue excellence. Given that enterprises are fundamentally complex systems, management is understood in this context to entail mastering the complexity of designing, controlling, and developing the strategies, activities, and relationships of purpose-oriented entities.

Excellence is here broadly construed to include socially, ecologically, and economically relevant, responsible, and superior performance and impacts, paths to such performance and impacts, and the strategy and governance that identifies possible such paths and selects from among them.

In taking this approach, we acknowledge the now clear obligations, or privileges, that enterprises should serve as responsible stewards of social, environmental, economic, and technological change. To serve in such ways necessitates better understanding and management of social trends and processes. In part, this implies that enterprises must attend to more stakeholders than past circumstances dictated, when shareholder expectations were paramount, customers were royalty, and little else—including the natural environment—mattered.

Additionally, advanced intelligence gathering and analytic capabilities are becoming increasingly synchronized with decision-making, thus aiding the effort to respond to changes in the competitive, political, or other relevant landscapes in as near to real-time as possible. This trend generates greater pressure to accurately forecast production and service demands along with innovation and design directions, all with the intention of positioning enterprises to lead or get in front of change, rather than lag change. This does not, of course, imply that an enterprise must always be first to market or must always be highly innovative relative to its product or service offerings portfolios, but it does imply that the value of any enterprise's strategy will, to an extent, depend on the accuracy with which it forecasts or anticipates changes on its horizon.

Successful and sustainable management for excellence will require the creation and cultivation of a sustainable culture of excellence. These require attention to the preceding issues, and hence to the development of an enterprise culture necessary to pursue excellence.

Resulting from successful management for excellence will be enterprises that are not only socially, ecologically, and economically relevant and responsible, but that are also resilient and robust in the face of perturbations in their competitive landscapes. This perspective implies that such perturbations are beyond the direct control of the enterprise, but not beyond its ability to address via appropriate risk management and other approaches. Such enterprises are more likely than others to generate *next* best practices and sources of sustainable competitive advantage that derive from the sort of sustained superior performance and impacts ordinarily associated with excellence. Given this formulation, we will deem (Edgeman, 2015a; Edgeman et al., 2015) the enterprise to be:

- *Sustainable* to the extent it is able to create and maintain economic, ecological, and social value for itself, its stakeholders, society at large, and policy makers;
- *Resilient* to the extent that it possesses the capacity to self-renew over time through innovation by adapting its responses to negative shocks and challenges;
- *Robust* to the degree that the enterprise is highly resistant or immune to a critical subset of such shocks and challenges; and
- *Excellent* when its governance, leadership, and strategy as deployed through people, processes, partnerships, and policies deliver sustained superior performance and impact in enterprise critical areas that might include, e.g., the human ecology of the enterprise, innovation, financial, social, ecological, enterprise intelligence gathering, analytics, and supply chain management.

The phrase *human ecology* employed above is used in preference to the more familiar forms of human capital or human resource. This choice is intentional and means to convey both the continuous development of the knowledge, experience, skills, and abilities of people resident in the enterprise (the typical meaning of human capital), as well as people with relevant impact on the strategy, activities, and results of the enterprise, but who themselves are not part of the enterprise. These may include individuals who are part of the (external) supply chain, policy makers, and others.

In creating our map or model, the above considerations will be integrated. First identified will be a more general management model, with management as described above. This will be followed by the creation of a more specific management for excellence model, more commonly referred to as an operational excellence model, after which the *Shingo Model* that is associated with the Shingo Prize for Operational Excellence will be examined in a way that identifies its correlations with enterprise excellence.

While this book is not intended to be a "tools" book, selected strategic or tactical tools will be introduced where necessary or helpful, with explanation of those tools provided as needed. Many excellent and comprehensive resources exist for the reader seeking to become more knowledgeable or a more adept user of tools, including an edited volume by DeFeo (2017) and works by Gerst (2001) and Voehl et al. (2014).

## TOWARD A MODEL: ENTERPRISES AND COMPLEX SYSTEMS

Enterprises are complex systems. A system is an integrated entirety or unity of elements that is distinguishable from its environment (Ackoff, 1981, 1994; Gharajedaghi and Ackoff, 1984). To quote systems guru Peter Senge (1990),

> Vision without systems thinking ends up painting lovely pictures of the future, with no deep understanding of the forces that must be mastered to move from here to there . . . Business and human endeavors are systems . . . we tend to focus on snapshots of isolated parts of the system and wonder why our deepest problems never get solved.

Relative to management models: a system is a path employed by the enterprise as it strives to fulfill its objectives. The system or path is comprised of a set of principles and procedures to which the enterprise is subject and by which its actions are governed.

This implies that a system and hence an enterprise has borders. Borders could include institutional borders such as membership or borders of identity. Demarcating the borders of an enterprise is generally challenging as they are commonly perceived rather than physical and may be constrained by such shifting influences as legislative actions that limit, enhance, or otherwise affect the ways in which the enterprise competes. This is increasingly so as modes of communication and forms of cooperation, collaboration, and competition multiply (Gloor, 2005).

A system is complex when its elements interact and interrelate with one another in specific and dynamic ways. As such, enterprises are fundamentally dynamic, complex, adaptive systems that have been formed in part with the objective of maximizing both the short- and long-term survivability of the enterprise and that are hence in constant development where, ideally, development is synonymous with advancement (Checkland, 1994).

System elements may be immaterial or material (object-like). Material elements could include, for example, buildings, equipment, infrastructure, information technology, documents, employees, and so on. Immaterial elements have no objective physical embodiment with examples including events such as *kaizen* blasts or conferences, communication patterns, relationships, processes, teams, departments, divisions, principles or codes of conduct, routines, strategies, and so on.

The word *kaizen* as used above is of Japanese origin and is typically used to convey continuous attention to and improvement of all processes, all products, and all functions by all enterprise personnel, ranging from the newly added or most junior associate to the executive level. Kaizen is traditionally interpreted and manifested as improvement that is incremental in magnitude. The true intent of kaizen is one that includes improvement and innovation of any magnitude accomplished at any pace, including improvement or innovation that is monumental in scope or impact and abrupt in emergence.

Additionally, enterprises have many characteristics. Included among these:

- *Enterprises are purpose-driven and multifunctional.* They must perform functions for other systems through their own specific value creations, and hence must simultaneously satisfy the demands/ interests of multiple stakeholders.
- *Enterprises are economic systems* that must be profitable over contextually-driven time horizons so that revenues must surpass expenditures. This is fundamental to enterprise survival and anticipates consideration of enterprise risk management strategies.
- *Enterprises are sociotechnical systems* defined by groups of people that are united by common purpose, shared expertise, and are channeled or organized into communities of practice (Wenger and Snyder, 2000). Communities of practice are supported by technical means and have the aim of benefiting diverse stakeholders. This is done through complex processes that require division of labor as a means of executing specific tasks intended to yield specific results.

Further, enterprises compete economically with one another. The rules of engagement in this competition, especially with respect to customers, are to:

- Remove scarcity with minimum resource use, yet without creating undue surplus or super-abundance, and to

- Identify and leverage new or latent needs and demands that lead to new areas of real or perceived scarcity. This is done through creative discovery, innovation, and invention (of new needs and demands). Customers do not simply desire products or services only; they want solutions to their perceived needs (Teece, 2010).

In highly competitive environments, enterprises able to repeatedly discover and leverage value creation opportunities better than their competition tend to be among the most successful enterprises. These enterprises experience comparatively superior value creation for diverse stakeholders (an effectiveness advantage) while operating in more resource-efficient and cost-efficient ways (an efficiency advantage). Taken together, these can enable the enterprise to both generate and sustain competitive advantage.

The continuing viability of a complex system requires reliance on a means of enterprise alignment and ordering (structuring) forces. Effective leadership is essential to enterprise alignment.

Complex system structures emerge via repeated and similar executions of processes and are revealed by patterns of interactions and communication, in development of mutual expectations (e.g., roles), which in time are relatively constant or stable. Complex systems are also characterized by a degree of order through repeatedly emerging patterns in day-to-day communication, decision-making, leadership, cooperation, and collaboration. These patterns are often subtle and can be aided by formal sense-making and analytics processes (Burton, Obel, and DeSanctis, 2011; Evans and Lindner, 2012; Kurtz and Snowden, 2003). Patterns in regularly occurring events express the predominant order created through these structuring processes—a phenomenon aimed at the formation of order (Rüegg-Stürm, 2005).

We see then that a management model can be formed from the following categories, where, again, by management we mean a system of complex tasks that together are used to design, control, and further develop purpose-oriented sociotechnical systems:

- Environmental domains (BEST),
- Stakeholders,
- Mediating factors,
- Alignment means,
- Processes,

- Risk management, and
- Advancement means.

These categories will next be elaborated in a one-by-one or "brick-by-brick" fashion with a brief chapter dedicated to each "brick." After elaborating the various elements of the model, it will be presented in fully assembled form and described briefly.

# 2

## Brick-by-Brick: BEST Environmental Domains

In Chapter 1, several building blocks or bricks of the complex systems-based management model for operational excellence were cited. In this and several subsequent chapters, these will be elaborated brick-by-brick. Once this process is complete, our bricks will be assembled into an initial model, after which some of its most critical components will be elaborated more fully. Finally, the correlation of this initial model with the *Shingo Model* will be addressed.

### BEST ENVIRONMENTAL DOMAINS

Environmental domains represent the enterprise's external context that constrains the enterprise in sometimes visible and invisible ways. This external context will ordinarily exert significant influence on the enterprise since it often defines competitive, legal, and other boundaries or constraints within which the enterprise operates. This context is in near continual flux and defines boundaries, some of which are fixed and semi-permanent, and others are soft or permeable and perhaps temporary.

Equally, the context often has embedded un- or under-exploited opportunities as well as areas that may well be saturated. Un- or under-exploited areas correspond loosely to so-called *blue oceans* where uncontested market space may be carved out, whereas saturated areas represent *red oceans* where there is already "blood in the (competitive) waters" (Kim and Mauborgne, 2005).

In light of this, trend-spotting (or futuring) relative to these domains can be an important enterprise activity wherein generation of sufficient and targeted foresight can aid timely and targeted change (Drucker, 1988; Petrakis and Konstantakopoulou, 2015; Rohrbeck and Gemünden, 2011). Such trend-spotting is central to reliably formulating effective strategy and the strategy selected may be of various natures, depending on enterprise goals and the mindset of the strategist since, surely, the overall direction of strategy may range from highly guarded or conservative to highly aggressive, and from passive to highly active.

As an example, consider an enterprise that has a principal aim of becoming more robust and resilient by becoming more immune to disruptions in the environmental domains. Such an enterprise may use trend-spotting to inform its strategy, policies, practices, product and service portfolio innovation and diversification, or supply chain security, as well as the means by which these may be approached (Edgeman and Wu, 2015).

The most obvious such domains have been referred to as the BEST Environmental Domains (Edgeman, 2000; Edgeman and Hensler, 2005) where *B* represents the biophysical (natural or ecological) environment, *E* represents the economic or financial environment, *S* is the societal domain, and *T* is the technological domain. These domains can be described as follows:

## B: THE BIOPHYSICAL ENVIRONMENT DOMAIN

The biophysical or ecological domain addresses the external impact of the natural environment on the enterprise. How this manifests strongly depends on current social discourses—especially in relation to sometimes controversial ecological concerns such as whether and, if so, how much impact humanity has on the earth's climate. Organizations that consume more natural resources, produce more waste or pollution (e.g., carbon emissions, effluents, soil contaminants, etc.), or whose core business is driven by the natural environment (e.g., energy companies) may be particularly sensitive to changes in this domain.

Shifts or disruptions in this domain can cause short-term, long-term, or permanent changes that impact the enterprise and its stakeholders. Such shifts or disruptions can be caused by local, regional, or widespread events—any of which may reverberate on a global level. This may be especially important to multinational enterprises as the social discourse in such cases can vary dramatically from country to country, culture to culture, and across social and economic contexts (Rueda-Manzanares et al., 2008) as it does, for example, with respect to means of energy generation, energy distribution, and the by-products thereof.

The biophysical domain can interact substantially with shifting political winds. This is perhaps nowhere more evident than in the pre- versus post-2016 United States of America presidential election wherein national environmental energy and environment priorities shifted significantly, and, almost literally so, overnight. In some cases, the impact of this shift on business decisions that influence both the U.S. and global economies was nearly equally as swift.

## E: THE ECONOMIC ENVIRONMENT DOMAIN

The economic environment domain includes procurement, commercial, labor, and financial markets and is the soil in which an enterprise flourishes or withers. Governmental shifts in economic policy, actions by the Federal Reserve, economic upturns or downturns, seasonal spending patterns, energy and fuel cost fluctuations, and so on can have profound effects on overall enterprise health and financial performance.

Some elements in this domain, such as the sort of seasonable pricing and purchasing associated with the Black Friday and Cyber Monday phenomena in the United States, are predictable. Still other elements in this domain, such as changes in the prime interest rate, come with relatively sufficient warning associated, with signals to the Federal Reserve. Each of these first two cases better enable relevant enterprise strategy formulation compared to instances where changes in the economic domain are simultaneously large and abrupt.

## S: THE SOCIETAL ENVIRONMENT DOMAIN

The societal domain is the most comprehensive of the BEST external environmental domains. It represents the social discourse that impacts (for example) how the natural domain is perceived, how technological developments progress, and how economic value creation should occur

(Hull' and Rothenberg, 2008). Although many societal norms are the result of slow, evolutionary changes, sudden societal paradigm shifts can at times dramatically impact enterprises, as we have seen, for example, with respect to enterprises that generate environmental pollutants and the impact of environmental and labor legislation, carbon trading, how those enterprises source their energy, and so on. Similarly, the magnitude of, and increase in, extremist terror attacks throughout Europe, North America, and elsewhere have impacted numerous elements that affect businesses, including immigration policies and hence access to labor costs, security requirements, and more.

Paradigm shifts may fundamentally affect an enterprise's product and service portfolio, supplier selection, and more and hence may clearly interact with the economic domain relative to, e.g., procurement, supplier network, and trade partners.

## T: THE TECHNOLOGICAL ENVIRONMENT DOMAIN

Technology is strongly influenced by social discourses regarding the perception of relative risk vs. reward, as, for example, in determination of whether and in what measure to develop electric or hybrid vehicles as alternatives to vehicles that rely solely on gasoline or diesel fuel. As a second case in point, consider regional vs. global discourses and how they may vary with respect to energy development in coal- or oil-rich areas, versus hydro- or thermal-rich areas, versus areas with high solar or wind energy generation potential.

The technological domain is also closely linked to economic forces. Enabling conditions such as high densities of types of enterprises or resident expertise can be critical as these have been central to the formation of technology incubators or innovation clusters such as those in California's Silicon Valley, North Carolina's Research Triangle Park, or those in Boston, Cambridge (UK), and elsewhere. Additional examples of industries where the technological domain and the influence of social discourse can be critical include biotechnology, genetic engineering, chemical and process industries, food production, communication, and technology (Orlikowski, 2010).

Equally, geographic concentration of selected knowledge bases has, in some areas, stimulated regional contagion-like spread of that knowledge together with whatever advantages are associated with that knowledge as, for example, in Ireland. Localized operational excellence knowledge in Ireland has spread across various industries. Partially stimulating this contagion has been a several-year cycle where an Irish enterprise or facility has been acknowledged of either the Shingo Prize, Shingo Silver Medallion, or Shingo Bronze Medallion, along with concurrent or subsequent sharing of that knowledge, thus stimulating additional Irish entities to embark on their operational excellence journey.

The technological domain can be subject to substantial influence that is exerted by governmental policies that manifest in the forms of legislation, tax incentives, or as funded research and development.

## INTERSECTING DOMAINS AND WICKED CHALLENGES

Differentiating enterprise domains from one another is quite often difficult, if not impossible, since domains commonly intersect. This is especially true when boundary-crossing wicked challenges that involve legal, ethical, moral, or broad humanitarian dilemmas are present (Edgeman, 2015b). *Wicked* here does not refer to *evil*, but rather is used to describe complex problems, issues, or challenges that are resistant to resolution due to incomplete, contradictory, changing, or boundary-spanning requirements (Churchman, 1967).

Example cases of wicked challenges are provided by genetically modified food production, stem cell research, or legal compliance—all of which may involve legal, moral, or ethical elements that may limit financial gains. Strategy formulation and subsequent deployment in the face of wicked challenges can be daunting and will almost certainly involve deep consideration of trade outs or compromises that often fail to fully satisfy any of the various impacted stakeholders (Camillus, 2008).

One well-known example of a profound situation where domains intersected is provided by the 2004 Indian Ocean earthquake and tsunami. This event led to rapid global mobilization of humanitarian relief that involved technology to aid complex logistical challenges (Van Wassenhove, 2006); significant and costly supply chain disruptions for many enterprises that led to short-term opportunities for other unaffected or less affected suppliers; and widespread societal impacts (Ratick, Meacham, and Aoyama, 2008).

A second familiar example is provided by the Great East Japan earthquake of 2011 that produced a 1.2 percent decline in Japan's gross output in the year following the earthquake. So significant was this disruption that it sent shockwaves up and down the supply chains of hundreds if not thousands of enterprises globally (Carvalho et al., 2016) and created significant and long-lasting physical and mental health threats to much of the Japanese populace (Kukihara et al., 2014; World Health Organization, 2013).

A third familiar and related example is provided by the Fukushima nuclear disaster caused by the Great East Japan earthquake of 2011. The damage at Fukushima was so devastating that it stimulated announced reform in Japan's nuclear energy policy with a shift away from nuclear power toward renewable energy, although there are significant indications at the time of this writing that there may be little in the way of significant and lasting change in the face of ever-shifting political winds and the relative paucity of natural resources in Japan (Joskow and Parsons, 2012).

Many other examples of situations associated with intersecting BEST domains to wicked challenges are readily available. Familiar among such situations are the Chernobyl and Three-Mile Island nuclear disasters (Friedman, 2011; Poortinga, Aoyagi and Pidgeon, 2013), the Deepwater Horizon oil platform explosion (Clarke and Mayer, 2017; Kellar et al., 2017), and the Exxon Valdez oil spill that caused extreme environmental damage while also exposing firm stakeholders to risk resulting from Exxon hiding

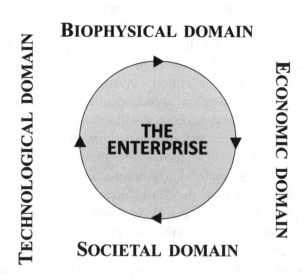

**FIGURE 2.1**
The enterprise positioned with the BEST environmental domains.

company performance deficits prior to the disaster (Shabana, Buchholtz, and Carroll, 2016; Wiens, 2013).

The BEST domains in many ways form the contextual borders within which the enterprise competes. As such, these are portrayed as the perimeter of the complex management systems model for operational excellence that will be developed progressively over the ensuing chapters, the beginning of which is displayed in Figure 2.1.

The enterprise itself appears as a circle within the perimeter of Figure 2.1. The arrowheads on the boundary of the enterprise (circle) are intended to communicate that the enterprise is in constant evolution. The velocity of evolution will be more rapid at some times than at others. An enterprise in decay could be represented by counterclockwise-pointing arrowheads, whereas one that is poorly aligned or in chaos could be presented by using a mixture of clockwise- and counterclockwise-pointing arrowheads.

The description of our complex management systems operational excellence model will be systematically expanded at the conclusion of the following few brick-*by*-brick chapters, then summarized in a brick-*upon*-brick chapter. Afterward, a critical subset of model elements will be elaborated. Finally, the correlation of this model to the *Shingo Model* will be addressed.

# 3

## *Brick-by-Brick: Stakeholder Perspectives*

Enterprises generate social benefit via active interaction with stakeholders. While many stakeholders manifest at the perimeter of the enterprise and its environment, others, such as the human ecology of the enterprise, are internal stakeholders. A single entity may simultaneously belong to several stakeholder segments, for example, an individual may be employed by an automobile manufacturer, may be a customer of the company in the sense that they are the driver of a vehicle produced by the company, and may hold shares of company stock. Decisions made and actions taken by the company will affect such stakeholders in multiple and generally unequal ways relative to the stakeholder segment considered. For example, a car manufacturer may introduce a new model or a significant innovation that does not impact employee salary, but may increase customer costs in the form of, e.g., purchase price or may cause increased depreciation in value of a car already owned by the individual that was produced by the company; and may also drive up share value. For the hypothetical individual described, they are affected in a financially neutral way as an employee, in a financially negative way as a consumer, and positively as a shareholder.

Stakeholders such as competitors, suppliers, and public sector entities provide or define enterprise operating conditions or resources. Other stakeholders such as investors, customers, and employees are more directly affected by enterprise value creation. Still, other stakeholders that could include communities, media, or NGOs may serve in observational or watchdog roles that may range from passive to active in nature.

Stakeholder relationships require the establishment of give-and-take balance between the stakeholder(s) and the enterprise. How this occurs often depends on the enterprise's dominant stakeholder perspective, of which the two most common are the strategic stakeholder value approach

(Freeman, 2010) and the ethically critical stakeholder value approach (Carroll, 1991; McVea and Freeman, 2005).

## STRATEGIC, ETHICALLY CRITICAL, AND SHAREHOLDER VALUE PERSPECTIVES

The strategic stakeholder value approach bases enterprise selection of stakeholders primarily on the impact of their concerns, interests, and demands on securing the future of the enterprise. The strategic management of stakeholders is expressed in creating or maintaining the willingness of all participants to cooperate in securing the agreement or goodwill of influential stakeholders.

In contrast, the ethically critical stakeholder value approach fundamentally acknowledges as stakeholders all parties impacted by the enterprise's actions, whether positively or negatively so. This view embraces the belief that the humanity of said stakeholders entitles them to dignity and moral rights. Equally, this view legitimizes the inclusion of the "voice of the natural environment," albeit through surrogate means, as well as the "voice of society." Ethically critical stakeholder management is hence concerned with consensus-oriented resolutions of conflicts of interests. The obligation of management in deriving such resolutions is to assume the role of a respectful, impartial, responsible citizen.

A third perspective is the highly utilitarian shareholder value approach which holds that, within legal limits, the social responsibility of the enterprise is confined to profit maximization—that is, to Adam Smith's so-called "invisible hand" wherein adherents to this approach assume that it optimizes the public welfare (Bevan and Werhane, 2015).

## AN EMERGING PARADIGM: THE STAKEHOLDER VALUE PERSPECTIVE

A somewhat tamer alternative to the shareholder value approach is the stakeholder value approach. This approach pursues long-term balanced consideration of all stakeholders that leads to maximum shareholder value. This perspective is countered by the idea that ethically justifiable and morally imperative decisions can arise that favor some stakeholders over others, while foregoing any long-term positive impact on shareholder value. This implies that, under select conditions, investors will be willing to consciously ignore their own interests in favor of the interest of other stakeholders.

Increasingly, this approach is being rejected, with a trend instead toward embracing a view of *profit* as *that which remains after all obligations are met.*

Enterprises vary with respect to what they regard as obligations, but more and more enterprises, whether willingly or unwillingly, are including ecological and social values and considerations such as social justice, among the obligations they are committed to meeting (Corbera, 2015; Sanford, 2011; Soyka, 2012). Thoughtfully approached, many such enterprises have experienced enhanced financial performance as an artefact of attracting increasing numbers of so-called ethical investors who positively value such considerations (Gibson-Graham et al., 2013; Koomey, 2012).

In contrast to this perspective, a study spanning a large number of enterprises in diverse business sectors found that financial performance of more socially and ecologically committed enterprises is similar to that of enterprises with more conventional approaches to business (Revelli and Vivian, 2014). Ethical investors tend to be more patient and loyal investors, willing to wait longer to see and receive the fruit of their investment (Matulis, 2014; Peifer, 2014) whereas more conventional investors and enterprises tend to surrender to the tyranny of the present in the sense of seeking more rapid returns on their investments.

Whether by choice, due to consumer pressure, or to legislative requirements, the generally emerged view in the developed world is that these stakeholder positions are increasingly less viable. Bearing witness to this claim is the growth of the United Nations Global Compact (UNGC) and the Global Reporting Initiative (GRI).

There are more than 9,000 UNGC signatory companies and 3,000 non-businesses from more than 160 nations that pledge adherence to and annually communicate their progress toward ten principles that address human rights, the natural environment, labor rights, and anti-corruption (Rasche et al., 2013). Similarly, the GRI is an international independent standards organization that helps businesses, governments, and other organizations understand and communicate their impacts on issues such

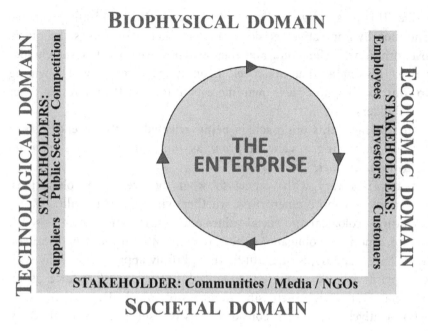

**FIGURE 3.1**
The enterprise, key stakeholders, and the BEST environmental domains.

as human rights, corruption, and climate change (Milne and Gray, 2013) while also considering business performance.

Figure 3.1 portrays varied enterprise stakeholders in the developing complex management systems model for operational excellence as residing between the BEST domains and the enterprise itself. This positioning in the model is intended to communicate that many stakeholder segments form a sort of bridge or synapse between the enterprise and the environment that is defined by the BEST domains.

# 4

## Brick-by-Brick: Stakeholder Mediating Forces

Stakeholder mediating forces, hereafter referred to simply as mediating forces, refer to what stakeholders are able to contribute to the enterprise; what they provide the enterprise access to; or what elements, aspects, or activities of the enterprise they deem objectionable. Mediating forces thus refer to issues to which the enterprise must respond.

Mediating forces can be either principle-based or intangible, or material and tangible. Tangible or material elements include infrastructure, commercial goods, disposable goods, or other physical resources as well as non-physical elements such as legal or contractual rights or limitations. Principle-based and intangible mediating forces include personal and cultural ones such as interests, norms, concerns, and values.

Concerns for the welfare of children have led to legislation restricting child labor. Similarly, interest in level competitive playing fields has fueled international anti-corruption enforcement, while values for environmental stewardship are behind carbon emissions limitations. Cultural value for social equity can be found at the heart of many enterprise diversity efforts and a combination of interests, norms, concerns, and values typically provide enterprises with the initiative needed to operate in socially responsible ways.

Personal values have driven the impressive philanthropic efforts of leading business executives such as Bill Gates of Microsoft, Warren Buffett of Berkshire Hathaway, Mark Zuckerberg of Google, and James Goodnight of the SAS Institute—the world's largest, privately held software company. The efforts of these leaders have ranged from local to regional or global in scale and have generated goodwill and positive notoriety for their organizations.

## INTERACTING MEDIATING FORCES AND STAKEHOLDERS

The individuals, communities, societal segments, special interest groups, organizations, or institutions that influence or are influenced by the enterprise are counted among its stakeholders. This is true whether they are affected by the activity of the business directly or indirectly, whether through benefits or risks, or either short-term or long-term promotion or limitation of their quality of life or potential for development.

As can already be surmised, just as the BEST environmental domains often interact, so also mediating forces may interact as in cases where the legal environment intersects principle-driven activities. These are areas of potential friction between the enterprise and selected stakeholder segments. Indeed, a few such cases have already been cited relative to child labor, anti-corruption, and environmental legislation.

As such, stakeholders can appropriate demands from the BEST environmental domains and assert their interests in realizing these demands. The ways in which stakeholders assert their interests may range from passive to forceful, with strategies that range from open to more covert, and with results that may range from mutually damaging, to tit-for-tat, to mutually beneficial. A challenge faced by many enterprises then, often in collaboration with their stakeholders, is to identify and deploy win-win solutions in those areas where friction would otherwise erode relationships between the enterprise and its stakeholders.

It is of course at least partially up to the enterprise to ascertain how or if they will respond to stakeholder interests. In some instances, the enterprise may be forced to respond to stakeholder interests due to legislation, or may be pressured to do so through organized stakeholder actions such as boycotts or some other manner of attracting negative attention to or otherwise damaging the enterprise. Regardless of enterprise response, it is generally in the best interest of the enterprise to consider public perception of any visible interactions.

We see then that "norms and values" play an important social role (Oliver, 1997; Tushman and Nadler, 1986). Legitimizing the enterprise's orienting or guiding purpose and core practices relative to stakeholder norms and values, concerns, and interests hence requires respectful consideration, constant ethical reflection and legitimization, carefully reasoned evaluation, and explanation for the final decisions and subsequent actions of the enterprise, along with assurance that these are well understood by the stakeholders in the enterprise (Cooke and Rousseau, 1988; Wry et al., 2011).

Further demanded is that the enterprise should be accountable for the results and impacts of its decisions and actions. Accountability is at least partially addressed via transparency with one role of an enterprise's governance structure being to assure such transparency.

The issue of transparency provides an example of changing societal norms, values, concerns, or interests that have made their way into legislation to which enterprises must respond. This trend was fueled in part by high-level ethical failures by enterprises that chose not to communicate significant risks to shareholders that in turn contributed to significant shareholder losses. Such failures ultimately led to, e.g., the Sarbanes–Oxley Act (Coates, 2007) that legally mandated appropriate levels of transparency and hence accountability.

Other changes or trends impacting enterprises include increased and legislatively enforced respect for diversity in various forms that include but are not limited to ethnicity or national origin; gender and gender identity; sexual orientation; religious persuasion; and mental, physical, or emotional conditions (Barak, 2013; Bond and Haynes, 2014). Similarly, it

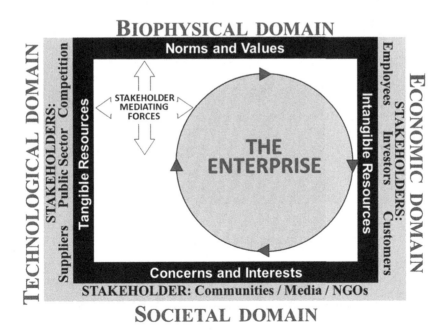

**FIGURE 4.1**
The enterprise, key stakeholders, mediating forces, and BEST environmental domains

is now common to expect or demand that an enterprise will be sensitive to the needs of all stakeholder segments and not merely those able to exert financial or regulatory sway over the enterprise (Ackermann and Eden, 2011; Fassin, 2012; Werther and Chandler, 2010).

In the developing complex management systems operational excellence model of Figure 4.1, stakeholder mediating forces appear between the BEST environmental domains and the enterprise itself.

# 5

## Brick-by-Brick: Enterprise Alignment

Ongoing strategic management requires enterprise leadership to both derive and implement strategy. It is dynamic and involves content and process, planning and action (Freeman, 2010). An enterprise's strategy is key to its agility and ability to renew its business models in a timely manner (Doz and Kosonen, 2010). Further, enterprise strategy is often emergent in the sense that while much of it may be intentional in nature, other aspects develop as reactions to unanticipated side effects of the implementation of intentionally formed and deployed strategy. Strategic management should also thoughtfully consider the BEST environmental domains, mediating forces, and should identify and challenge constraints originating within the enterprise.

## UNITY OF PURPOSE AND SHARED VISION: PROS AND CONS

Clear understanding of enterprise identity and purpose is core to the formulation of strategy that differentiates the enterprise from its competitors. Similarly, awareness of enterprise competences, capacity, resources, collaboration and cooperation opportunities, supply chain capability, market opportunities and potential, the risk environment, and its knowledge reservoir are essential to the determination of value-creating enterprise offerings (Hamel and Prahalad, 1994; Porter, 1985; Prahalad and Hamel, 1990).

Over longer periods, processes related to strategy formulation, culture establishment, and development of structure tend to become relatively constant and stable. This promotes constancy of purpose (Deming, 1985;

Spencer, 1994) which is here expressed as unity of purpose resulting from continuous commitment to fulfilling a shared vision.

This fact tends to mitigate the need, or at least urgency, for an enterprise to radically reinvent or renegotiate many things as these instead become routinized and familiar to people, manifesting in behavioral habits, habitualized focus, and habitualized ways of sensing or perceiving the goings on of the enterprise (Salvato, 2009). Advantages of routinization include increased efficiency (processing speed) and reduction of errors. These advantages are primary generators of both cost reduction and quality improvement (Burt, 1989).

As a perhaps obvious watchword, it is crucial that the habits formed are the right habits: doing wrong things better does not make things better, instead, it is doing right things better that makes things better (Berry et al., 1990; Edmondson, 2008). When right habits are formed, an additional advantage of routinization accrues: being able to direct focus toward non-routine areas that require higher degrees of innovation or invention.

We see then that routinization may not be uniformly positive. A threat of a thing becoming "too routine" is that it becomes so habitual that it disappears from our consciousness, creating a so-called blind spot. Further, over-routinization can in some cases lead to unswerving— dare we say "mindless"—adherence to that which is routine. When this happens, the natural consequence is that we fail to question the suppositions or reasoning behind routines, even when changing conditions suggest a need to change the routine. Stated differently, vigilance should be exercised in order to ensure that constancy of purpose does not produce the sort of stagnation consequential to the failure to probe and challenge the status quo, an alternative expression for which is Latin for "the mess we're in."

Unchecked preference for the status quo is a common and often insidious cognitive bias that can hinder rational decision-making and action-taking (Kahneman, Lovallo, and Sibony, 2011). Failure to probe and challenge norms can transform innovative market leaders into enterprises with cemeteries full of dead ideas that leave innovation to others and teeter on the precipice of becoming insolvent zombie firms, peopled by zombie workers, with portfolios of zombie products and services (Leavy and Sterling, 2010; Nonaka, 2008; Quiggin, 2012).

Economically sustainable enterprises routinely generate superior stakeholder benefits in an efficient and enduring manner. Relative to strategic management, this requires an enterprise to derive strategic foresight that consistently contributes to its ongoing renewal (Crossan et al., 1999). This is a rigorous endeavor that, like many other key leadership and management responsibilities and activities, is aided by analytics-driven sense-making that provides a sort of trend-spotting on steroids in order to drive better decisions and actions (Chen, Chiang, and Storey, 2012; Lycett, 2013; Sharma, Mithas and Kankanhalli, 2014).

A chief thrust of this effort is that of correctly orienting the enterprise and aligning its strategy with its purpose and vision via planning, policies, practices, partnerships, and processes (Collins and Porras, 1996). This is done in order to better ensure that actual performance and impacts match intended performance and impacts (Katzenbach, 2000). This process provides the enterprise with the clarity necessary to move forward with unity and a sense of shared purpose in a dynamic landscape where the flux rate may range from calm to volatile (Andreadis, 2009; Pentland and Feldman, 2007).

Unity and a sense of shared purpose begin to approach, in a non-robotic way, the hive mind of Hegel (1807) in which the enterprise's human ecology possess both individually and collectively nonlocal and atemporal awareness of all aggregates, components, constituents, entities, personalities, relationships, technologies, processes, and cycles of the enterprise (Edgeman and Eskildsen, 2012). This does not exclude individualism.

It is precisely this unity and shared purpose that enables the enterprise and its people to collectively act, react, and adapt appropriately when unforeseen turbulence arises (Miles et al., 1978). A sense of shared purpose is of particular importance relative to engendering positive attitudes toward enterprise change (Shin et al., 2012). Further, a shared sense of purpose is central to creating and maintaining successful cooperation and collaboration, positive financial performance, and a healthy social environment (Lee et al., 2012). In all then, we see that sense-making, adaptability, and shared purpose are key drivers of increased enterprise resilience, robustness, and sustainability (Antunes, 2011; Limnios et al., 2014), not to mention enterprise excellence.

Equally important is the ability to successfully navigate, both individually or collectively, critical changes in conditions impacting the enterprise wholly or in part. Vital to this ability is that people must have the competence, confidence, and freedom to adapt and act within turbulent or ill-defined operational conditions—often in the absence of any clear enterprise directive—and do so in ways that remain within the business activity as a whole. In other words, people must be appropriately empowered to decide and act in a manner that balances accountability for the results and consequences of these with forgiveness for honest mistakes—mistakes generally attributable more to process and system inadequacies or to the degree of environmental volatility than to human failing.

These issues are formative to enterprise culture, where at a crude level we may regard culture as "the way we do things around here." That said, it is predictable that any enterprise of any size will have micro-political issues that are driven by motivations as diverse as the whole of the enterprise's human capital. Included among the array of micro-political concerns are pursuit of self-interest, power, or greed rather than constant and uniform exercise of altruism or enterprise stewardship. We here define stewardship as the conscious decision and consequent action of subordinating self-interests to better serve enterprise interests (Block, 2013; Haynes et al., 2015). Figure 5.1 is intended to summarize this.

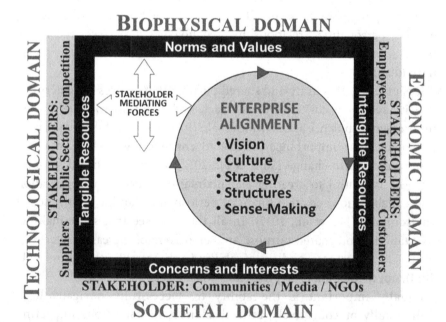

**FIGURE 5.1**

Enterprise alignment in relation to key stakeholders, mediating forces, and the BEST environmental domains.

## ENTERPRISE ALIGNMENT: FROM STRATEGY TO EXECUTION THROUGH HOSHIN KANRI

Prior to World War II, the U.S. share of the world export market was approximately 30%. In the aftermath of World War II, this share grew to more than 70%, a result of a generally healthy and educated workforce, as well as a U.S. infrastructure that remained largely untouched by the war. In contrast, many European and Asian nations were left to deal with infrastructure devastation and human tragedy alike, often with less-educated workforces using antiquated equipment.

Given that context, American manufacturers were generally able to sell all they were able to manufacture, even if production was of superior, average, or inferior quality. It is simple but inaccurate to assume, especially in the aftermath of World War II victory, that American superiority was responsible for this growth in market share and consequent relative prosperity.

Relatively unnoticed was the role instruction played in the active spread of quality control methods in American industry during World War II by such luminaries as Joseph M. Juran and W. Edwards Deming, as well as other, usually uncredited, individuals. Those methods proved fundamental to, for example, production of superior quality military equipment such as tanks. This is not intended to imply that quality control methods were solely responsible for the Allied victory over the Axis powers in World War II, but only that these were an important factor.

Many Americans trained in quality control and related methods during World War II were women. Subsequent to WWII, many soldiers and other personnel returned from the European and Pacific theaters of conflict, at which time many of the women trained in these methods left the workforce and returned to the home, taking their valuable expertise and accompanying lessons learned with them.

Over the next decades, many of the lessons learned were lost. This was one of at least two things happening concurrently with a second being that the same "quality gurus" largely responsible for teaching quality methods to approximately 30,000 members of America's World War II workforce were exposed to the post-WWII plight of the Japanese people and, out of resulting empathy, began to teach those same quality methods in Japan, with the belief that those methods could significantly aid the long climb Japan would need to make to recover from the devastation of World War II.

What Juran, Deming, and others found in Japan was a highly talented, highly motivated collection of business and engineering leaders who embraced these methods with near "tent revival" zeal, and who not only widely and expertly adapted and deployed these methods, but who added new and highly pragmatic approaches. This was done with the sort of efficiency that extreme resource scarcity can motivate, augmented by the effectiveness that dedication to precision can birth.

Just as Juran, Deming, Armand Feigenbaum, Philip Crosby, H. James Harrington, Walter Shewhart, and other American quality luminaries wielded significant influence, a new constellation of Japanese "quality stars" arose, the names and developments of whom have been and remain integral to contemporary expressions of quality in its many forms. These forms include but are not limited to Lean enterprise methods and Six Sigma—individuals such as Shigeo Shingo and single minutes exchange of die (SMED or quick changeover); Taiichi Ohno together with Shigeo Shingo and the Toyota Production System (TPS) that resides at the heart of the Lean manufacturing movement; Masaaki Imai and kaizen (continuous improvement); Kauro Ishikawa and cause-and-effect diagrams; Yoji Akao and quality function deployment; Genichi Taguchi and robust product design; Noriaki Kano and the customer needs model; and hoshin kanri—development of which is not attributed to any single individual, but rather the first use of the term appears to have originated at Japan's Bridgestone Tire company in 1965 (Watson, 2003).

Hoshin kanri as developed in Japan integrated the work of W. Edwards Deming and Joseph M. Juran with Management by Objectives (MBO) elements out of Peter Drucker's now classic tome, *The Practice of Management*. *The Balanced Scorecard*, by Robert S. Kaplan and David P. Norton reinforces the Plan–Do–Study–Act (PDSA) nature of the process by providing focus on the four key performance perspectives of financial, customer, internal processes, and learning and growth, along with the development of a scorecard that is used to track progress and support the governance system.

This combination of zeal, expertise, methodological innovation and application, and relentless pursuit of perfection began to erode the American share of the world export market. This effect was scarcely noticed until American manufacturers surrendered consumer electronics and automotive markets to Japanese manufacturers—victims not only of Japanese drive and ingenuity, but of their own inflated sense of accomplishment that cultivated the belief that it was "impossible" for anyone else to out-perform, out-create, or out-innovate American enterprises.

The result of this was that, by 1990, the U.S. share of the world export market had fallen to its pre-World War II level of about 30%. Today that share ranges between 10% and 15% and the U.S. has become by far the world's greatest debtor nation.

Much has been and continues to be written about the "Japanese miracle," though some of the sheen has dimmed as Japan's economy, like many others, has struggled to recover from the financial crisis of 2008 and, additionally, the Great East Japan earthquake of 2011. Still, books such as *World Class Manufacturing* by Schonberger (1986); *Kaizen* by Imai (1986); *The Machine that Changed the World* by Womack, Jones, and Roos (1990); and numerous others have had significant influence on the way many global enterprises involve their human ecology and otherwise conduct their business. This is especially so in select sectors such as the automotive industry which have embraced Lean philosophies and methodologies. Increasingly, this is also seen in such sectors as healthcare and banking.

While each of the cited strategies and methods provide value to the enterprises using them, we will focus primarily on hoshin kanri or, as it is commonly referred to in the West, strategy or policy deployment. Strategy deployment is essentially an organizing framework that directs attention enterprise-wide to corporate purpose, aligns priorities with local plans, integrates these into daily management and activities, and facilitates enterprise learning and enculturation through routine review (Witcher and Butterworth, 2000).

## HOSHIN KANRI OR HOSHIN PLANNING?

Roots of hoshin kanri may be traced to *A Book of Five Rings* written in 1645 by Miyamoto Musashi (Harris, 1982). This book, the essence of which is captured by the word *heiho* or strategy, was a resource intended to provide instruction to samurai warriors, including instruction in what is perhaps the quintessential samurai skill—*kendo*, or precision swordsmanship. Relative to kendo, *A Book of Five Rings*, asserts that those thoroughly conversant with strategy will recognize the intentions of their enemies and, through preparation and recognition, will have many opportunities to cultivate and execute strategies capable of thwarting the objectives of their adversaries and positioning themselves to be victorious.

Like heiho, the word hoshin is comprised of two Chinese characters: *ho*, which means method or form, and *shin*, which is often translated as "shiny metal—the glint from the spear that leads the way" (Lee and Dale, 1998) or, in a more contemporary form, an aim. When assembled, the word hoshin can be taken to mean "a methodology for strategic direction setting." The word kanri is commonly interpreted as "management" so that hoshin kanri becomes "management of the strategic direction setting process." Given this interpretation and as previously noted, in the West, hoshin kanri is commonly referred to as either policy deployment or strategy deployment or by the East/West hybrid term that we will henceforth use: hoshin planning.

At upper organizational levels, a given hoshin is mission and vision critical to an enterprise and is stated in terms of a goal or objective (a policy or strategy) that is intended to elevate associated business processes and outcomes to a target performance level. The underlying structure of hoshin planning enables the possibility of its application at essentially any level of the enterprise, ranging from the senior executive level to the day-to-day operational level.

Often, a high-level (senior executive) hoshin is of such foundational importance to the enterprise that failure to attain or fulfill it within an appropriate timeframe will place the organization at risk. As such, a high-level hoshin can be thought of as representing "big (enterprise) vision." Organizations that practice enterprise-level hoshin planning ordinarily have a limited number of hoshins, typically three to five, that must be realized within a specified time span that, in the West, will ordinarily range from one to five years, with specified mileposts and periodic stage gate reviews along the way.

Those residing in the northern hemisphere can relate to a hoshin as an organizational north star or "true north," whereas those living in the southern hemisphere may think of a hoshin in relation to the Southern Cross. Hoshins are intended to aid enterprise navigation and alignment by riveting the collective enterprise focus on their attainment.

At the enterprise level, hoshin planning begins with "big vision" that is progressively unfolded by cascading the various hoshins from one level of the enterprise to the next to the next and so on—beginning with the executive level and ending with the operational level. Thus, from one level to the next to the next to the bottom of the waterfall, an increasingly detailed scheme emerges. In this way, hoshin planning begins with strategy or policy, is progressively transformed into plan, is progressively executed, leading to full strategy/policy implementation. Hoshin planning beginning at the operations level is executed in like manner, but with generally less far-reaching strategic implications and nearer-term fulfillment needs. In its high-level incarnation, hoshin planning is highly strategic and focused on breakthrough improvement (Witcher, 2003) whereas at the operations level it is ordinarily more incremental and focused on continuous improvement (Hutchins, 2008).

The logical conclusion is that a key benefit of hoshin planning is its ability to create consensus (Watson, 2003) and facilitate enterprise alignment through significant workforce participation (Kondo, 1998). This is accomplished through extensive communication that is both lateral and multilevel in nature. Such communication assures that each individual involved in the hoshin planning process is conversant with the "big goals and objectives" or hoshins of those both immediately before them (their direct supervisor) and immediately following them (their direct reports) as well with those of their immediate colleagues. This occurs because their own hoshins and related activities are driven by hoshins received from their direct supervisor and in turn inform the hoshins and related activities of their direct reports so that all involved in the process are familiar with three or more levels.

This communication process is a negotiated dialog that is often referred to as catchball (Tennant and Roberts, 2001) and "connects the planners and the doers" (Sussland, 2002). Successful hoshin planning implementation is associated with complementary and skilled use of effective performance management and measurement approaches such as the balanced scorecard (Kaplan and Norton, 1996; Witcher and Chau, 2007). Together these approaches provide an exceptional means of rationally applying management of objectives as developed by Peter Drucker, the father of modern strategic management (Greenwood, 1981).

The value of hoshin planning, as with most approaches, is bounded by the value and timeliness of the strategy or policy being deployed, not to mention the quality of the "plan" as it unfolds through the organization. Figure 5.2 provides a view of the larger context within which hoshin planning typically occurs. Although hoshin planning may begin at any level of an organization and cascade downward through relevant other levels until sufficient execution is attained, Figure 5.2 provides the high-level view that emerges by beginning at the senior executive level (CEO) of the enterprise.

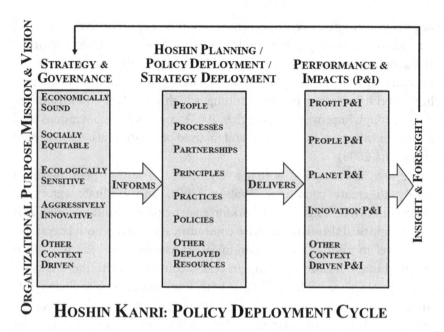

HOSHIN KANRI: POLICY DEPLOYMENT CYCLE

**FIGURE 5.2**
Hoshin planning from an enterprise perspective.

To explain Figure 5.2, we use the increasingly common scenario wherein organizations must produce not only acceptable financial performance and impacts to satisfy key stakeholders, but also socially equitable and environmentally sensitive performance. Impacts are demanded by citizens and regulatory agencies if not by our own consciences. Prior to examining Figure 1, we note that it is naïve to expect such positive "end of the pipe" triple bottom-line performance and impacts (Elkington, 1997) without the formulation of relevant "into the pipe" triple top-line strategy (McDonough and Braungart, 2002a).

Examining Figure 5.2 from left-to-right, we see that most enterprises have a clearly defined purpose, mission, and vision. The function of enterprise strategy and governance is to formulate means of fulfilling purpose, vision, and mission. Contemporary enterprises increasingly strive to be economically sound, socially equitable, and ecologically sensitive and hence formulate their strategy accordingly, with many organizations also needing to incorporate other context-driven strategy elements such as being aggressively innovative in order to better compete or to remain or become relevant in the marketplace. Although a typical organization will have numerous strategies, the Pareto Principle (Juran,

2005) of separating the "vital few" (strategies) from the "trivial many" suggests that a few of these will be primary, that is, will be the hoshins that populate the vital few, while the others will be relatively less important and will constitute the trivial many. Given the growth of triple topline approaches, and the importance of innovation, many organizations may have one or two hoshins that emerge from each of these categories.

Once executive level hoshins are determined, those executives will communicate these "what to" priorities on to the subsequent organizational level. Those responsible at the next level are provided with these hoshins or "whats" with generally little to no guidance regarding "how to" fulfill them: determination of how is up to those at that level, as is the selection of which hoshins are relevant to their span of influence. Those responsible at this next level will then determine the relevant how-to elements and these become the hoshins or whats that are cascaded to the following level.

This process continues, with the hoshins or whats at one level translated into hows at the next level until the plan is fully elaborated, thus transforming in the process from "big vision" to "execution." Relative to Figure 5.2, this process begins with strategy at the executive level seen on the left side of the Figure and is unfolded through various levels—with people doing the unfolding through progressive translation of whats into hows into whats into hows as represented by the center portion of Figure 5.2, ultimately delivering performance and impacts along the way as seen in the rightmost box of Figure 5.2. The mechanisms of the transformation are portrayed in the center portion of Figure 5.2: people, processes, partnerships, principles, practices, policies, and whatever other resources might be deployed/applied.

It is important to note that this is a living or cyclical process in that performance and impacts resulting from hoshin implementation are intended to provide both insight into recent enterprise performance and foresight into future enterprise priorities. It is of course also important for the organization to be externally aware so that future priorities might be influenced by new, pending, or likely legislation; technological changes; economic cycles; emerging megatrends; or other things not herein cited, but yet contextually highly relevant to the enterprise's competitive landscape.

Seen in this context, hoshin planning can be regarded as analogous to the application of Deming's Plan–Do–Study–Act (PDSA) Cycle at the enterprise level or, indeed, at whatever level hoshin planning is practiced (Moen and Norman, 2010).

## ENTERPRISES THAT HAVE SUCCESSFULLY IMPLEMENTED HOSHIN PLANNING

Illuminating examples of hoshin planning used by Western enterprises are abundant and readily available. For that reason, they are mentioned only briefly here and are accompanied by references wherein implementation details can be found. It would be erroneous to presume that hoshin planning is equally well implemented in all areas of a given enterprise, nevertheless, those cited are ones that have made fortuitous use of the method. It is clear in such instances that enterprise-wide transparency has been a critical success factor. When an enterprise's workforce understands the enterprise's mission, vision, and purpose, its members are better able to manage their own priorities and activities and appropriately adjust these as needed to better align them with enterprise goals, especially enterprise-level hoshins (Witcher and Chau, 2007).

Perhaps best known for use of hoshin planning among Western organizations are Xerox Corporation (Witcher and Butterworth, 1999) and Hewlett-Packard (Witcher and Butterworth, 2000). Hoshin planning is used around the globe, with its initial proponents being global enterprises that first experienced positive domestic results. As but a single example among many, we point to Nissan Corporation and their successful use of hoshin planning in their South African plant (Witcher, Chau, and Harding, 2008). Numerous early examples of transfer of hoshin planning and other significant Japanese management innovations can be found in, e.g., Kano (1993) and Lillrank (1995). More general guidance on hoshin planning can be found in Kesterson (2015) and Plenert (2012).

## CLIMBING THE HOSHIN PLANNING LADDER: NUTS AND BOLTS FACILITATION

Figure 5.2 presents a view of hoshin planning's fit in the larger enterprise perspective, but does little to aid implementation, and it is to implementation that we now turn. Although implementation can be and usually is challenging, it can be fruitfully approached through a relatively concrete, almost algorithmic means and focus is here directed by such a step-by-step approach. Figure 5.3 provides one possible depiction of the

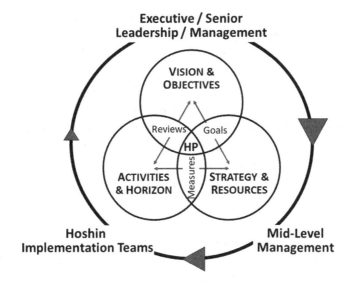

**FIGURE 5.3**
The Hoshin planning process.

hoshin planning process, and the expression of the *Shingo Model* as a complex management systems model is influenced by the formulation of the hoshin planning process as Figure 5.3 reveals.

Figure 5.3 indicates that executive/senior leadership and management is responsible for the formation and communication of "big" vision and objectives to its following management tier, mid-level management, which in turn explicitly translates these into their strategy while also identifying and developing requisite resources that will be needed for deployment. This communication, represented by the two-way arrow connecting vision and objectives to strategy and resources, is a negotiated dialog wherein explicit goals are set. In turn, mid-level management communicates their strategy and distributes resources to hoshin implementation teams that are responsible for determining precisely how and in what time horizon execution will take place. Negotiated dialog or catchball between mid-level management and the implementation teams, represented by the two-way arrow between strategy & resources and activities & horizons, identifies and agrees upon the measures by which success or failure of a hoshin implementation is assessed. Similarly, executive/senior leadership and management review implementation team proposals to determine whether these are sufficiently aligned with vision and objectives and, of course, are sufficiently aggressive to meet strategic/competition critical needs.

As a final note on Figure 5.3, the arrowheads of varying size positioned on the hoshin planning cycle—that is, the outer circle of Figure 5.3—are intended to indicate two things: hoshin planning is in fact cyclical, and the time horizons generally differ. The large arrowhead on the right of Figure 5.3 indicates that executive/senior leadership and management often address longer horizons of three to five years, middle managers address shorter horizons of one to three years, as indicated by the medium arrowhead at the base of Figure 5.3, and implementation teams routinely attend to activities with horizons of one year or less, as signified by the small arrowhead on the left size of Figure 5.3. Figure 5.4 provides one expression of a commonly used hoshin planning tool that is referred to as an X-matrix.

Revealed in Figure 5.4 are executive/senior leadership and management breakthrough objectives (hoshins) at the bottom of the X-matrix, in relation to which are nearer-term objectives on the left side of the graph, with the relative strength of the relationships in the lower right-hand corner of the graph. Near-term objectives are in turn related to executive and senior leadership and management priorities that are reflected

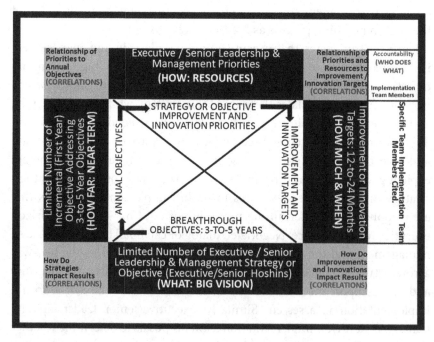

**FIGURE 5.4**
Hoshin planning X-Matrix.

by dedicated resources as revealed at the top of the X-matrix, with the strength of relationships between the two provided in the upper-left corner of the X-matrix. Associated with dedicated resources are specific targeted outcomes that form the right side of the "X" where the relationships between priorities and targeted improvements and innovations are depicted in the upper-right corner of the X-matrix. Finally, we see on the extreme right side of the X-matrix specific efforts associated with specific implementation teams and team members. The relationships (correlations) cited in the four corners of the X-matrix are often symbolized as being strong, moderate, weak, or—in some instances—as an empty cell indicating no relationship between specific elements. Other context-driven elements may be added to the X-matrix as needed.

As another useful aid in hoshin planning implementation, we cite the A3 tool (Chakravorty, 2009) where A3 refers to a commonly used paper size, that is, 11 inches by 17 inches or twice the size of standard U.S. letter format paper. A3 document content is often populated by steps associated with the Plan–Do–Study–Act or PDSA Cycle, an approach that provides the topic of the following chapter.

## A ROSE BY ANY OTHER NAME

Hoshin kanri is known by many names, including policy deployment, strategy deployment, and hoshin planning. Originating in Japan, the primary intention of hoshin planning is to translate strategy into actions that ultimately yield relevant performance and impacts. Seen through the lens processes within a complex systems modeling context, hoshin planning contributes to strategic development and, of course, subsequent deployment thereof, hence the synonym "strategy deployment."

A number of tools and methods are available to support this process, but it is critical not to place undue focus on the tools, numerous variations and adaptations of which can be found. One such tool is the Plan–Do–Study–Act or PDSA Cycle. Relative to our prior taxonomy of enterprise processes within the context of complex systems modeling of operational excellence, PDSA can commonly be positioned as an operative management process that is supportive of process development.

Equally, it is important not to "fall in love" with a given strategy and to recognize that no strategy is perfect—one strategy is only better, worse, more relevant, less relevant, or irrelevant relative to any other strategy. Even if a perfect strategy did exist, its implementation would likely be executed by flawed individuals, however talented those individuals might be, resulting in imperfect implementation.

Hoshin planning has been successfully used in many organizations, among them Bridgestone Tire, where hoshin planning originated; Toyota; Nissan; Hewlett-Packard; and Xerox. Although it is a highly structured strategic planning and deployment process, hoshin planning is also versatile and can be applied beneficially in organizations of any size, in any business sector, in any geography.

# 6

## Bonding the Bricks:
## The Plan–Do–Study–Act Cycle

The Plan–Do–Study–Act (PDSA) Cycle is so commonly used and so versatile that it may be considered to provide the cement that bonds the bricks of our complex management systems operational excellence model. Included among its many uses are such activities as alignment, development, and improvement.

While the most common expression of the PDSA Cycle will be discussed, the recommendation herein is to employ a modified form referred to as FOCUS-PDSA that will also be presented.

### EXPLAINING THE PDSA CYCLE

Due to Walter A. Shewhart and popularized by Dr. W. Edwards Deming, the PDSA Cycle is sometimes referred to as the Deming Wheel or, often, as the PDCA Cycle with the word "check" rather than "study." While still in common use, the term PDCA is "old" language. "Check" was used by Dr. Deming until later in his life when, after much deliberation, he elected to begin using the term "study." He made this choice primarily to avoid the common connotation of "check" with "inspection," whereas "study" is intended to communicate a more thoughtful, more rigorous examination of the results and impacts of any process change that is introduced.

Toyota and many other companies make routine use of the PDSA Cycle relative not only to hoshin planning but as a general use problem-solving tool that at Toyota is commonly used in an A3 format (Shook, 2009). Whether applied and presented within the context of an A3 or other

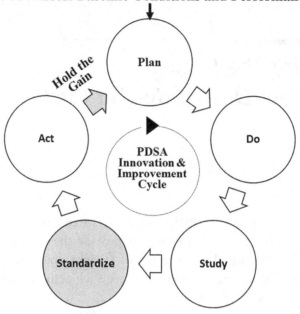

FIGURE 6.1
PDSA Cycle modified to include standardization and gain-holding.

format, it is common to augment the PDSA Cycle in a way that renders it similar in form to Figure 6.1, a description of which follows.

As with any journey on which one embarks, it is prudent to fully understand where the journey originates, that is, to assess the current or baseline conditions, including current performance levels and the root causes of inadequate performance (Doggett, 2005). Use of PDSA implies that there is a gap between current and aspirational performance and that, generally, the decision has been made to pursue an incremental and more gradual approach to improvement, rather than pursuing more rapid breakthrough change. This decision is often informed by such factors as the nature and abundance of resources available to dedicate to change, market factors that may influence how quickly change is needed (market velocity), the size of the change needed, and competition for resources. While assessment of baseline conditions prior to embarking on PDSA can, in brief, be described as an initial study phase, a more thorough initial assessment is recommended. The approach recommended to jumpstart PDSA is represented by the acronym FOCUS and is described in Table 6.1.

**TABLE 6.1**

FOCUS—Beginning the PDSA Journey

| Phase | Description |
|---|---|
| **Find** | Identify specific aspects of the process, system, or product targeted, riveting focus on what needs to be improved. |
| **Organize** | Assemble a team that is sufficiently diverse in competence and with sufficiently specific expertise and experience in relation to the improvement opportunity. |
| **Clarify** | Clarify the improvement opportunity—that is, what improvement entails. |
| **Understand** | Understand the various causes of problems to be solved as well as enablers of improvement. |
| **Start** | Initiate the PDSA Cycle by selecting an initial process, product, or system modification and identifying where change should occur. |

Executive and senior leadership and management hoshins correspond to "big vision." As hoshin planning cascades strategy through the enterprise, strategy at each successive level transforms more and more into tactics, with these increasingly corresponding to incremental change. PDSA Cycles—in whatever format—are useful for anyone, at all levels.

Once the current situation has been assessed, the individual or team preparing the PDSA/A3 will identify *planned* beneficial changes to the process or system under consideration. A common companion to this is determination of the target performance level resulting from those changes as well as quantification or description of the anticipated benefits of the change.

This is followed by *"doing"* (implementing) the planned changes—potentially on a limited or pilot scale since changes may not prove sufficiently beneficial to warrant full-scale implementation.

The status of the changed process or system will then be assessed or *studied* (that is, "checked") to document its new performance capability and whether the gap between prior performance and the goal or targeted performance has been adequately addressed. If the gap has been adequately addressed, the changes will then be *standardized* and fully documented with the purpose of making the solution, resulting from the changes, a more portable one that manifests similarly wherever the change is enacted.

Subsequent to standardization, the identified solution will be *acted* upon, often by fully implementing changes. *Control* over the process is then established with the aim of ensuring that the benefits of the changes are maintained—an ongoing effort that is often referred to as "holding the gain."

Those familiar with the DMADV (define–measure–analyze–design-verify) and DMAIC (define–measure–analyze–improve-control) design and innovation approaches that are applied in Six Sigma projects, the sequence of steps typically applied in statistical hypothesis testing, or the ordinary progression used in the statistical design and analysis of formal experiments, will recognize many parallels with PDSA. Each of these common problem-solving or opportunity-leveraging approaches employs the scientific method to advance or discover knowledge (Ketokivi and Choi, 2014; Van Dijck, 2014). Due to their use of the scientific method, each is highly logical, sequential, versatile, and has stood the test of time.

In noting that PDSA is generally referred to as a continuous improvement cycle, the team or individual responsible for the specific process in question will likely engage in another round of planning, *ad infinitum* until the performance of the process or system in question is sufficient. By sufficient we intend that in many cases the team or individual will turn their focus toward other processes or systems, despite not reaching the true target. There are of course many possible reasons for this, among which are that the resources needed to further advance process or system performance may yield better, or more critical, fruit if invested elsewhere or that further progress will first require some other breakthrough, such as development of a new technology.

It can be further noted that while PDSA ordinarily pursues a series of incremental improvements that collectively yield large-scale improvement, use of PDSA does not preclude attainment of breakthrough improvement on any given iteration.

# 7

## *Brick-by-Brick: Enterprise Processes*

A process can be defined as a series of activities performed in a predetermined order, intended to bring about a specific result. Most processes of interest are not one-off but are instead performed repeatedly. Detailed description of a process requires examination of its activity chain, activities, a supporting information system, process control mechanisms, and process development. These are briefly described as:

- Activity chain is a sequential portrayal of the most important process tasks. A macro-level view of an activity chain is essentially a map of major steps, whereas a micro-level view is a highly elaborated one that provides clear instructions for performing each activity in the chain.
- Activities are tasks carried out by people or technology that require certain inputs from suppliers to the process in question, and for which there is an intended outcome that is then directed to a customer, whether internal or external. This is analogous to the familiar SIPOC model wherein suppliers provide inputs that are then transformed by a process/activity into outputs that are then delivered to a customer (Edgeman, 2011).
- Information systems support completion of activities.
- Process control addresses ongoing monitoring of process performance so that emerged or emerging need for triage can be identified, resources dedicated, and—over time—the process can be improved.
- Process development, that is, evolution and improvement, can be accomplished via application of, e.g., the Plan–Do–Study–Act approach wherein once the process is demonstrated to behave in a stable manner, a change intended to simplify the process or improve

its performance can be planned, then done. Often this is done on a pilot study scale, followed by a study of results of changes made. Subsequently, the change can be acted upon, which will often translate to full-scale implementation of the change if it has proved to be sufficiently beneficial (Moen and Norman, 2010). Numerous formal alternatives to PDSA that are common elements of the Lean, Six Sigma, and quality management batteries of methodologies are available, among which are failure modes and effects (FMEA) analysis (Gilchrist, 1993), but many of these are more detailed in nature and often require greater and more specific expertise if they are to be fruitfully applied.

Once changed, the process is fundamentally different and control over the "new" process must be established.

Every enterprise can be understood in the context of a system of processes or process architecture (Browning, 2009). Multiple sorts of processes are found in any enterprise with management processes, business processes, support processes, and innovation processes together with critical subprocesses of each forming an enterprise's process architecture:

- Management processes govern the operation of a system so that all tasks related to the design, guidance, and development of a purpose-oriented social-technical system must be addressed (Boland et al., 2008). Familiar management processes include strategic management, corporate governance, and corporate social responsibility. Important management subprocesses include:
  - Normative orientation processes that relate to the ethical legitimacy of the enterprise's business activities (Hannah et al., 2011);
  - Strategic development processes that address securing the long-term competitive success of the enterprise and that include the development of new business models, initiation of strategic collaborations, or mergers and acquisitions (Earley et al., 1989); and
  - Operative management processes that refer to the resolution of day-to-day business issues with an emphasis on efficient resource use (Rüegg-Stürm, 2005). Quality management processes provide one example of such processes.
- Business processes constitute the core business of the enterprise and are associated with its main value streams. Examples include

repair services at automotive repair businesses and manufacturing processes. Key subprocesses include:

- Customer processes,
- Continuous improvement processes,
- Six Sigma processes,
- Supply chain management processes, and
- Product, process, and service innovation processes (Rüegg-Stürm, 2005).

- Support processes support the enterprise's core processes through internal services and infrastructure that are essential to efficient and effective accomplishment of business processes. Critical subprocesses include:
  - Human resource management/personnel,
  - Education and training,
  - Infrastructure maintenance,
  - Information technology support,
  - Health and safety,
  - Communication,
  - Risk management, and
  - Legal affairs (Rüegg-Stürm, 2005).

Although innovation appears explicitly only among business processes above, its role is so critical to the survival and growth of many contemporary enterprises that innovation also merits its own main bullet point among the process architecture of the enterprise. Additionally, innovation will be addressed in many forms and contexts throughout this text as it is possible to identify elements within each of the process architecture categories that may be innovative in nature. Equally, innovation will also be seen to provide a key means of advancing or developing the enterprise.

The importance to an enterprise of process efficiency and effectiveness has been greatly magnified in recent years. Driving this shift is that most enterprises have been significantly impacted by changes in the biophysical (ecological), societal, and technological areas of the BEST environmental domains. In at least some instances these changes have birthed landscape-shaping megatrends.

As but a single example, degradation of the natural environment and consequent legislation, together with the collective impact of enterprises on the natural environment, has come to permeate societal consciousness. This in turn impacts how society regards not just the offerings of an enterprise, but also the context in which those offerings are developed and provided. In total, changes in the biophysical, societal, and technological areas of the BEST environmental domains tend to affect the process structures of an organization—how processes are designed and how they operate—far more than they affect the structure of the organization itself. Driving this trend toward increased process focus has been rapid growth in time-based competition wherein competitive advantages often go to the swifter, so that quicker becomes part of the definition of "better." A critical enabling factor in this is the spectacular and rapid advancement of information and communication technology (Dewan and Mendelson, 1998) that feed enhanced analytical capability.

Enterprise focus on processes is often associated with their simplification, elimination of anything that is non-value added, and removal of as many defect sources as possible through use of continuous and breakthrough improvement approaches (Bhuiyan and Baghel, 2005; Imai, 2012; Womack and Jones, 2010). Among dominant approaches aimed at continuous and breakthrough improvement are structured approaches to innovation, Six Sigma, and Lean enterprise methods such as value stream mapping (Hammer, 2002; Hines and Rich, 1997; Koenigsaecker, 2012). Regardless of the motivation for adopting a process view, the effectiveness of doing so is strongly related to the development and use of an appropriate set of key performance indicators or KPIs (Parmenter, 2007).

A reasonable starting point in our examination of enterprise processes then is to concentrate on customer-focused value creating processes rather than on functions. This view facilitates systematic value chain examination in a way that both begins and ends with the customer or, more generally, with stakeholder groups the enterprise chooses to emphasize—a perspective that spotlights the importance of synchronizing the timing in which tasks are completed.

It is advisable when adopting a value chain perspective to differentiate between value chains and value creation chains. The value chain of an enterprise includes *all* task areas and activities that form the specific focus of value added by the enterprise. This is in contrast to the value creation chain necessary to deliver a specific product or service. Value creation chains may span a vast range of activities and a large number of levels of added value that cut across a broad swath of the enterprise.

Before moving on to the modes of enterprise development, it is of value to remind ourselves that enterprise alignment and processes interact strongly. As an example, consider that strategy is a key alignment element while strategy development is an equally key process. As we will see when we examine the *Shingo Model,* such relationships lead to growth, renewal, or improvement cycles in the sense that what happens in one cycle informs the following cycle and hence what happens today shapes tomorrow, and so it goes on into the future.

The preceding discussion is captured in Figure 7.1.

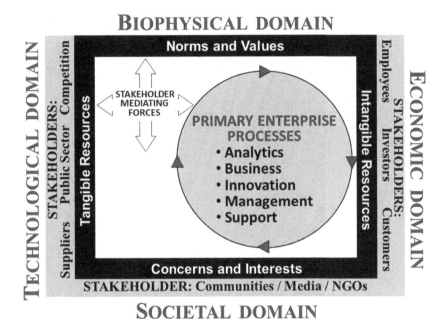

**FIGURE 7.1**
Primary enterprise processes in relation to key stakeholders, mediating forces, and the BEST environmental domains.

# 8

## *Brick-by-Brick: Enterprise Risk Management*

Driven by significant failures due to reasons that range from deep ethical breaches to natural disasters, risk management has grown significantly in importance since the 1990s. Some of these failures were so impactful that national governments enacted legislation aimed at increasing corporate transparency, especially with respect to risk exposure for their investors and other stakeholders.

Perhaps the most high-profile example of such legislation came in the United States with the 2002 passing of the Sarbanes–Oxley Act that requires chief executives and financial directors to provide specific statements addressing risk in their annual reports (Ribstein, 2002). Enterprises are especially required to disclose all significant risks to the well-being of the enterprise, including risks that were previously considered to be outside their span of responsibilities.

Though risk management might have been addressed during our examination of enterprise processes, its importance has been greatly elevated in recent years and hence it demands separate consideration, even if only briefly so herein. Risk management is composed of at least three significant systems (Waters, 2007):

- Identifying significant risks,
- Considering the likelihood that those risks materialize, and
- Assessing consequences if risks materialize.

The exercise of due diligence across these systems can be facilitated by failure modes and effects analysis or FMEA, of which many variations

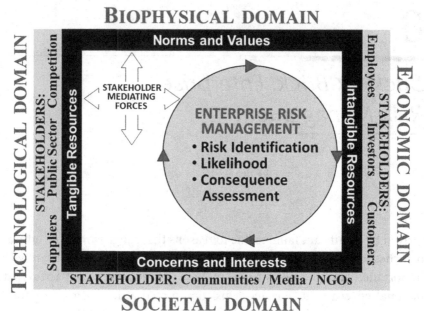

**FIGURE 8.1**
Enterprise risk management in relation to key stakeholders, mediating forces, and the BEST environmental domains.

and applications can be found (Carbone and Tippett, 2004; Shahin, 2004; Stamatis, 2003).

These enterprise risk management elements are portrayed in Figure 8.1 as interior to the enterprise portion of our complex management systems operational excellence model.

## FMEA: FAILURE MODES AND EFFECTS ANALYSIS

The most common form of FMEA requires determination of various potential modes or ways by which a product, process, project, or service might fail together with the various causes of each failure mode. Once these have been identified, three assessments must be made for each failure mode: the severity or consequences of failure to the stakeholder under consideration (S); how likely it is that the failure occurs (O); and the ability we have to detect the failure if it occurs (D).

Most commonly each of S, O, and D are evaluated on a scale that ranges from 1 to 10 with the levels descriptively differentiated. Relative to severity, a scale value of 10 represents the greatest severity level or harm to the stakeholder and is often associated with catastrophic failure leading to fatalities. On the likelihood or probability of occurrence scale, 10 corresponds to almost certain failure. On the probability of detection should the failure occur, increasing scale values correspond to lesser and lesser ability to detect the failure.

Once these numerical assessments have been made, a risk priority number (RPN) is calculated for each failure mode as the product of S, O, and D, that is:

$$RPN = SxOxD$$

One reasonable FMEA progression is provided by Figure 8.2.

The larger the RPN for a given failure mode then, generally, the higher the priority dedicated by the team to identify and implement a mitigating course of action, along with after action controls to ensure that the

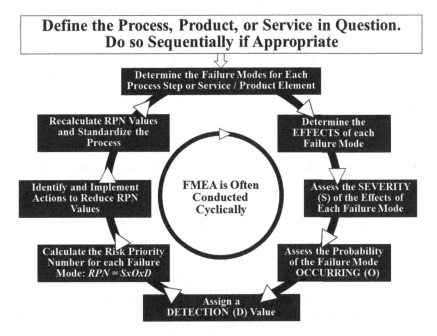

**FIGURE 8.2**
FMEA progression.

**TABLE 8.1**

Example FMEA Severity (S) Rating Scale

| Severity of Effect | Rating | Description |
|---|---|---|
| Extreme | 10 | May endanger equipment or operator and is hazardous *without* warning. |
|  | 9 | May endanger equipment or operator but is hazardous *with* warning. |
| High | 8 | Major disruptions to production line or service. There is loss of primary function with 100% scrap and major loss of takt time. |
|  | 7 | Reduced primary function performance. Product, process, or service requires significant attention or repair, and there is a noticeable loss of takt time. |
| Moderate | 6 | There is moderate disruption of production or service with possible scrap. There is secondary function performance loss that requires repair or attention with noticeable loss of takt time. |
|  | 5 | There is minor disruption of production or in service and repair or attention is needed. There is reduced secondary function performance. |
|  | 4 | There are minor defects in product or minor inadequacies in service. If a product is involved, then it may be repaired with a "use as is" disposition. |
| Low | 3 | The product has a minor defect that may be reprocessed on-line. If it is a process or service in question, then it may continue with limited real-time attention. |
|  | 2 | There is a minor nonconformance that may be reprocessed on-line. If it is a process or service, the effect is small enough that many customers or users may not notice. |
| None | 1 | There is no effect. |

mitigations remain effective. Strategies for mitigation are generally aimed at lowering S, O, or D scale values.

It is reasonable to state that two failure modes with equal RPNs do not necessarily receive equal attention since the routes to the RPN value will often be regarded differently. For example, three failure modes each with RPN equal to 400, but arrived at as $8 \times 5 \times 10$, $10 \times 10 \times 4$, and $5 \times 10 \times 8$, may reasonably be differentiated among by using a secondary consideration—perhaps using severity or consequences of failure modes to rank these and falling to frequency of occurrence as a next level differentiator. In such cases, a clear mandate evolves for lowering, first, severity ratings followed by occurrence ratings.

**TABLE 8.2**

Example FMEA Occurrence (O) Rating Scale

| Likelihood of Occurrence (O) | Failure Rate | Rating | Description |
|---|---|---|---|
| Very High | 1 in 2 | 10 | Failure is essentially inevitable. |
| | 1 in 3 | 9 | |
| High | 1 in 8 | 8 | Process is not in a state of statistical |
| | 1 in 20 | 7 | control. Similar processes commonly experience problems. |
| Moderate | 1 in 80 | 6 | Process is in statistical control but |
| | 1 in 400 | 5 | experiences isolated failures. Similar |
| | 1 in 2,000 | 4 | processes have experienced occasional failures and out-of-control conditions. |
| Low | 1 in 15,000 | 3 | Process is in statistical control. |
| | 1 in 150,000 | 2 | Process is in statistical control. Highly similar processes experience rare, isolated failures. |
| Remote | 1 in 1.5 million | 1 | Failure is highly unlikely with no known failures associated with almost identical processes. |

**TABLE 8.3**

Example FMEA Detection (D) Rating Scale

| Detection (D) Likelihood | Rating | Description |
|---|---|---|
| Very Low | 10 | No known controls are available to detect presence of the failure. |
| Low | 9 | Controls that are in place have only a remote chance of |
| | 8 | detecting the failure. |
| Moderate | 7 | Controls may detect the existence of the failure. |
| | 6 | |
| | 5 | |
| High | 4 | Controls have a good chance of detecting the existence of the |
| | 3 | failure. |
| Very High | 2 | Controls will almost certainly detect the existence of a failure. |
| | 1 | Controls automatically detect failure. |

## EXAMPLE SEVERITY, OCCURRENCE, AND DETECTION RATING SCALES

Example S, O, and D rating scales and an FMEA example are provided in Tables 8.1 through 8.3. While these scales are relatively generic and broadly useful, it is not uncommon to develop scales highly specific to a given product, process, or service. Doing so typically involves significant expertise.

# 9

## *Brick-by-Brick: Enterprise Advancement Means*

Enterprise advancement or development commonly involves a paradox: that both stability and change are required (Farjoun, 2010); though, in the case of micro-changes, flexibility often proves a more apt term. As a part of this paradox, the enterprise constantly experiences changing mixtures of certainty and uncertainty, of tradition and innovation (Leonard-Barton, 1992). Enterprises that routinely and successfully navigate such flux are nowadays referred to as ambidextrous (Tushman and O'Reilly, 1996).

Here emphasized are three means of enterprise advancement—innovation, optimization, and renewal. Of these, optimization and renewal are not always easily distinguished from one another. Further, in any given enterprise, it is likely that both modes will coexist, though not always harmoniously so. Which advancement means is most relevant or prevalent is to a large degree governed by the scale, scope, and velocity of change. Figure 9.1 positions these enterprise advancement means in relation to our developing complex management systems model.

In this context, scope refers to the breadth of change and is associated with issues such as how many people, processes, and areas of responsibility and activity—so-called levers of change—either impact or are impacted by a given change (Simons, 1994). Scale is associated with the depth of change, that is, how shallow or how thorough changes will be in terms of enterprise routines, culture, regular business activities, and enterprise structural compositions. Velocity refers both to how regularly and how rapidly change occurs. Combined, these factors guide the consequences of change and hence deal with where change will be on a spectrum that ranges from passive to disruptive.

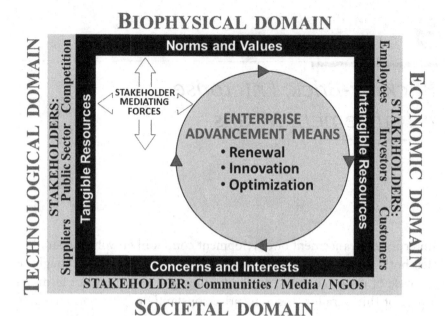

**FIGURE 9.1**
Enterprise advancement means in relation to key stakeholders, mediating forces, and the BEST environmental domains.

When dealing with change we must think multi-dimensionally, as change will usually involve both analytical-technical and cultural-relational dimensions (Rüegg-Stürm, 2005). The analytical-technical dimension addresses changes in enterprise routines that address the contents and functions of enterprise business activities, often as partially facilitated by technology. Cultural-relational changes are less tangible and may involve sweeping changes relative to collaboration, teamwork, leadership of and with other people or entities. When such changes occur, they are observable in such areas as altered behaviors and attitudes, values and sense of identity, sense of belonging, and habits that are regarded as normal.

Most enterprises oscillate amongst periods of relative calmness during which change is more gradual or evolutionary in nature and periods during which change is rapid and revolutionary. Optimization takes place during periods of relative calm whereas *renewal* is most commonly associated with more turbulent periods.

As such, optimization can be likened to continuous improvement activities within the enterprise that ordinarily involve only incremental innovation (Anand et al., 2009; Bessant et al., 2001; Imai, 2012) whereas renewal is associated with revolutionary change that often calls for radical or disruptive innovation (Boer and Gertsen, 2003; Dewar and Dutton, 1986). This characterization is captured by the enterprise advancement means map in Figure 9.2.

Renewal often reveals itself via the development or acquisition of new capabilities, competencies, and enterprise routines as well as new ways in which the enterprise interacts with its stakeholders and its environment. Innovation is integrally related to enterprise capacity to self-renew over time by adapting its responses to internal changes, changes in the BEST environmental domains, and in mediating forces (Contu, 2002).

Given that most enterprises will continuously require a mixture of varied levels of innovation that may range from incremental to breakthrough, it is fruitful for the enterprise to nurture a culture that embraces "sustainable innovation." As opposed to "innovation for sustainability," which may be thought of as innovation that targets social or ecological progress, sustainable innovation is intended to communicate that innovation occurs routinely, is pursued in a rigorous fashion, is systemic throughout the enterprise, and is approached systematically.

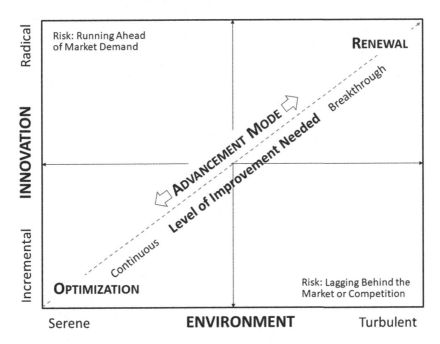

**FIGURE 9.2**
Enterprise advancement means map.

The marriage of sustainable innovation and innovation for sustainability is often referred to as eco-innovation, green innovation, or social-ecological innovation (Desmarchelier, Djellal, and Gallouj, 2013; Chen, Lai, and Wen, 2006; Edgeman and Eskildsen, 2014a). Enterprise attention to such innovation has been rapidly increasing in recent years in response to the demands of diverse stakeholders (Nidumolu et al., 2009). A straightforward way to think of this is that social-ecological innovation is found in new ideas, products, services, institutions, and relationships that offer fresh and innovative approaches to overcoming critical societal and environmental challenges (George, 2003; George et al., 2012; Seyfang and Smith, 2007; Vidaver-Cohen and Altman, 2000).

# 10

---

## *Brick-on-Brick: An Assembled Complex Systems Management Model*

We have now identified the primary components of our complex systems management model. One possible configuration of these components is provided in Figure 10.1, an explanation for which follows. Upon examining Figure 10.1, we see that enterprises are subject to forces that are in large beyond their control that are represented in the outermost reaches or perimeter of Figure 10.1 by the BEST environmental domains.

Enterprises interact with varied stakeholders that impact or are impacted by the enterprise. Stakeholders that (mostly) impact the enterprise are portrayed on the left side of Figure 10.1 whereas stakeholders that are (mostly) impacted by the enterprise appear on the right side of Figure 10.1. Stakeholders identified at the bottom of Figure 10.1 tend to interact with the enterprise, but in ways that are often less tangible.

Mediating forces essentially represent the nature and manner of interactions between the enterprise and its stakeholders. Mediating forces can in many ways be thought of as relevant rules of engagement.

The enterprise itself is represented in Figure 10.1 by a circle that captures means of enterprise alignment, selected primary processes, risk management strategies and activities, and modes of advancing the enterprise. The arrowheads on the perimeter of the enterprise circle are intended to portray the constant evolution of the enterprise through time, as well as ongoing enterprise refinement that is associated with time-based, market-driven organizational learning (Hurley and Hult, 1998). Such learning includes learning that may derive from collaborations in which the enterprise is involved, such as strategic alliances (Larsson et al., 1998) or co-creative innovation efforts undertaken in concert with users (Edgeman and Eskildsen, 2012; Hoffman, 2012).

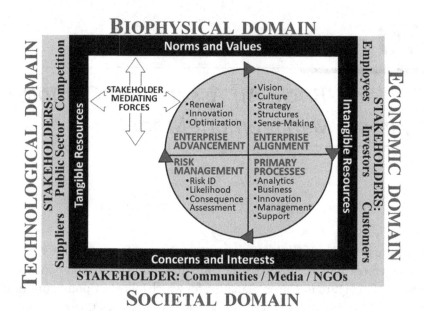

**FIGURE 10.1**

A complex management systems operational excellence model.

Key components of this model will be elaborated in subsequent chapters and in some instances supporting tools will be introduced. As examples, customers are the quintessential stakeholder for many enterprises so that tools and techniques aimed at gathering, interpreting, and activating the voice of the customer will be considered. Similarly, enterprise longevity or sustainability is often driven by the ability of the enterprise to innovate in ways meaningful to its primary stakeholders so that tools supportive of innovation are introduced, including ones important to ideation, product and service concept generation and selection, and deployment of selected concepts.

Finally, once this model and some of its constituent parts are elaborated, the *Shingo Model* will be introduced and dissected, then related to the complex systems management model. The aim of this latter activity is to contextually position the *Shingo Model* within the framework of the complex systems management model, thereby grounding the *Shingo Model* in both theory and practice.

Such grounding is important, in contrast to use of the simplistic argument that the *Shingo Model*—or other models with similar goals— "works." It is important to understand why and how the model works, or else it becomes like the piece of equipment employed by a naïve or unskilled user that, once broken, cannot be fixed.

# Part II

# Elaboration of Key Components of the Complex Management Systems Model

# 11

## Stakeholder Elaboration: The Primacy of Customers and Other Observations

Excellence models generally have a distinct focus on results, where results may be regarded as a composition of performance and impacts. Performance is generally associated with consequences that are directly strategy-driven and consciously anticipated, although the specific performance level attained may not be at the desired levels. Impacts may or may not be central to enterprise strategy and may be only at the periphery of enterprise consciousness. Further, impacts may be either positive or negative, intended or unintentional.

Performance is tangible and measurable. Measurement of performance may be done on either quantitative or qualitative scales. Qualitatively measured performance often employs maturity scales, doing so as a means to "make soft things harder" or more concrete (Jap and Anderson, 2007; Maier, A.M. et al., 2012). Maturity scales are typically descriptive in nature, with each successive step on a scale describing increasing levels of accomplishment relative to specific criteria. Maturity scales are commonly used in enterprise excellence models to measure enterprise progress toward excellence, with excellence being a multidimensional construct. Dimensions of excellence include those cited earlier: sustainment, resilience, robustness, and other more commonly used ones such as supply chain performance, human capital, leadership, and more.

Although impacts may be tangible, they are just as likely to be intangible. As an example of an intangible or at least less tangible impact, an enterprise's reward and recognition system may be intended to stimulate human capital performance in ways that are reflected in enterprise financial performance, but as ancillary results—impacts—may promote increased self-esteem among employees and increased social perception.

As a second example, an engine manufacturer may design an engine that is intended to be more fuel efficient and less polluting over a standard distance driven, but as impacts may serve to encourage more driving due to economic savings from increased fuel efficiency and, with more driving, may generate more total pollution than was generated prior to introduction of the new engine design. These later impacts are tangible and measurable. In situations such as the one provided by this example, it is possible that government intervention may occur, in this case in the form of increased fuel taxes that are intended to mitigate pollution while simultaneously generating increased tax revenues that may then be dedicated to social development purposes. The intervention of government may be thought of as a second-order impact while subsequent contribution to social development may be regarded as a third-order or tertiary impact.

It is important to recognize that performance and impacts are "end of the pipe." More generally, enterprises have guiding principles that provide a sort of framework within which the enterprise formulates its strategy that is subsequently deployed via, e.g., processes, policies, partnerships and alliances, and other means in order to produce performance and impacts. This cycle is scrutinized via an enterprise assessment that generates insight into the enterprise's current state, and foresight that supports enterprise optimization or renewal. This flow is portrayed in Figure 11.1 for a mock enterprise that employs triple top-line strategy (McDonough and Braungart, 2002a) aimed at producing triple bottom-line performance and impacts (Elkington, 1997). Note that Figure 11.1 is essentially identical to Figure 5.2 that was associated with the hoshin planning process and is principally modified only to reflect contributions to enterprise alignment.

Triple top-line strategy refers to strategy that is financially sound, socially equitable, and ecologically sensitive. Similarly, the triple-bottom-line is used to represent social, environmental, and financial performance and impacts that are often referred to as the 3P or people, planet, and profit domains (Sosik and Jung, 2011). Results in each of these domains are commonly reported in annual Communications on Progress by companies subscribing to the United Nations Global Compact or that employ the guidelines of the Global Reporting Initiative (Adams and Petrella, 2010; Voegtlin and Pless, 2014).

While Figure 11.1 provides a mock management for operational excellence model, it also reflects the changing reality that enterprises are more and more overtly serving multiple stakeholders that include society

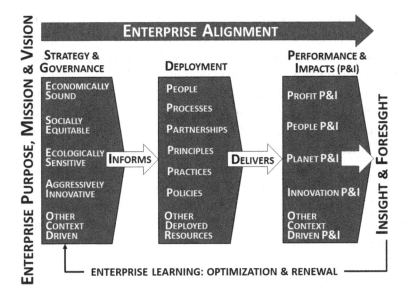

**FIGURE 11.1**
Generic enterprise excellence model format.

and, by proxy, the natural environment. This reality is a key driver of a transition from traditional management systems to enterprise excellence ones emphasizing corporate social responsibility and hence aimed not just at viable financial performance, but also social equity and ecological sensitivity (Zwetsloot, 2003).

Among well-known enterprise excellence models are those supporting America's Malcolm Baldrige National Quality Award (Ford et al., 2014; Karimi et al., 2014), the EFQM Excellence Award (Brown, 2014), the Shingo Prize (Fullerton et al., 2014), and the Balanced Scorecard (Kaplan and Norton, 2015).

## CONVERSATIONS: CONNECTING STAKEHOLDER AND PROCESS VOICES VIA MEASURES

Stakeholder value creation is a complicated process. Many enterprises begin this process "with the end in mind" (Covey, 1992; Haimes and Schneiter, 1996), that is, with careful acquisition and assessment of stakeholder voices. Acquiring and assessing stakeholder voices is only the beginning, however, as ultimately the enterprise must determine which aspects of those voices to pursue, and then how to do so.

Stakeholder voices tangibly impact the shape, form, and functionality of physical, digital, and hybrid services and products. The phrase used to capture the notion of shape, form, and functionality is "dimensions of quality," and these have been divided into product and service quality dimensions. Quality dimensions for a given product or service can also be categorized relative to stakeholder needs and wants.

In considering product and service quality, we do well to remember that product and service quality always come at a price, but that price in itself has little meaning apart from the quality delivered for that price. It is equally important to consciously and continuously bear in mind that the relative importance of the various product or service dimensions will vary from product-to-product, service-to-service, and customer-to-customer.

## Product Quality Dimensions

We will first examine product quality dimensions. Harvard University Business School Professor David Garvin examined customer or, more broadly stated, stakeholder perceptions, ultimately identifying eight product quality dimensions (Garvin, 1987) termed in brief as: performance, features, reliability, conformance, durability, serviceability, aesthetics, and perceived quality. As a product illustrating these dimensions, we will use the smartphone. Though perhaps not applicable in the case of a smartphone, it is often important to consider the intersection of quality dimensions with the product use environment.

Performance ordinarily refers to measurable traits that represent a product's most important operating characteristics. Relative to a smartphone, these include such elements as how long its battery will hold a charge or its screen resolution. Given a trend toward use of mobile phone image, video, and audio capture rather than a more traditional stand-alone device, image resolution may—at least for many customers—provide an additional example of a performance-based quality characteristic.

Features are objective, measurable traits that supplement the basic function of a product. Relative to smartphone examples could include the number and variety of applications such as a clock or calculator, along with screen size, or whether the phone makes use of an android or iPhone operating system. Conformance refers to how closely aligned a product is—a smartphone in this example—with specified product standards and, typically, whether a given element lies within a specific performance or physical range with a chosen target level representing the ideal for that element. Examples of smartphone conformance could include whether its battery will hold a charge within 30 minutes of a targeted eight hours or whether the length of the phone is within 0.01 inch of its specified length of six inches.

Serviceability refers to how easily a product can be attended to when updating or repair is required. Examples of serviceability for a smartphone are how easily its battery or SIM card can be changed. Durability could be the length of time needed before the phone battery must be replaced or the crack or fracture resistance of the phone screen.

Aesthetics are generally subjective in nature and vary from stakeholder to stakeholder. The subjective nature of aesthetic quality is that it is sensual in nature, referring to the visual or tactile pleasure a customer derives from a product or may in some instances from auditory, olfactory, or taste experiences or preferences. Relative to smartphones, customers may prefer white ones to red ones, may prefer one ring tone over another, or may prefer to control volume via holding a button rather than by using a sliding or swiping motion.

Perceived quality is often reputation-based with reputation built up over an extended period of years or large number of experiences, or sometimes represents market buzz or hype. Apple® and Samsung® provide interesting examples. Apple long held a reputational advantage over Samsung, until Samsung achieved parity in 2012. Apple has released several generations of its iPhone® mobile devices and has generated significant loyalty among its customers, with each new generation of iPhone generating high levels of market anticipation. Conversely, Samsung has had multiple generations of highly regarded smartphones. In 2016 however, Samsung suffered substantial reputational and market damage as a result of exploding batteries in one of its most respected and popular smartphones. In the short run at least, this led to a generally higher level of perceived quality of Apple iPhones relative to Samsung smartphones. Whether Samsung can again gain reputational parity with Apple in the smartphone market is a matter of speculation at the time of this writing.

## Service Quality Dimensions

Prior to identifying dimensions of service quality, it is useful to define its meaning, and for this we appeal to the following, due to Lewis and Booms (1983), "Service quality is a measure of how well the service level delivered matches customer expectations. Delivering quality service means conforming to customer expectations on a consistent basis."

Proceeding from this definition, Parasuraman, Zeithaml, and Berry (1985) developed their landmark SERVQUAL model in which service quality is derived as a function of 10 determinants or dimensions. Described in the following, the identified dimensions of service quality are reliability, responsiveness, competence, access, courtesy, communication, credibility, security, understanding or knowing the customer, and tangibles.

Reliability implies that the service is provided correctly and in a consistent and dependable manner. Further, reliable service delivery demands that all promises associated with the service are honored, whether those promises are implicit or explicit.

Responsive service delivery anticipates that service is rendered willingly, fully, and in appropriate timing. To accomplish this consistently requires service provider competence where competence combines requisite knowledge and skill in all relevant members of the enterprise's human ecology, sufficient linkage among those members, and the necessary organizational capacity to meet the demand for the service. Responsiveness additionally implies satisfactory and timely redress of customer complaints.

Closely associated with responsiveness is ready customer access to the service being provided, clear requirements which include simple and convenient contact with appropriate enterprise personnel via multiple means and, if applicable, in convenient locations. Courtesy, obviously enough, suggests that service is provided politely, professionally, respectfully, and with consideration for the customer and the environment in which the service is provided.

Effective service provision requires communication that facilitates responsiveness, access, and courtesy of service delivery. Such communication must be clear and in an easily understood language that may in some instances need to be tailored to varying customer segments or individual customers. Further, communication must be two-way, implying that the enterprise must listen to customers both carefully and respectfully, and not merely impart knowledge. This suggests that listening should be both empathetic and analytical, feeling the customer's pain, diagnosing its causes, and identifying and deploying appropriate remedies.

Security has assumed added significance in light of recent high-profile data breaches at individual, enterprise, and national levels. More holistically, security refers to service provision in a manner and environment that mitigates doubt, ideally providing complete freedom from risk of harm to any and all assets, including physical harm, emotional distress, financial loss, property damage, and—to the first point—unwanted exposure of personal or sensitive information.

Comparable to the product quality dimension of perceived quality is the service quality dimension of credibility. Credibility suggests that the customer trusts the enterprise to be honest and honorable in all dealings related to the service, providing the service in a manner consistent with the best interests of the customer. Such credibility is often built on either personal experience with the enterprise or on broad and positive public perception.

Knowing and understanding the customer is fundamental to the success of learning organizations and requires that the enterprise actively, carefully, and strategically listen to its former, current, and prospective customers. There is a good deal of information available indicating that, depending on the industry in which the enterprise is engaged, the cost of acquiring a new customer ranges from 5 to 25 times more than the cost of retaining an existing customer (Gallo, 2014).

Provision of most services is associated with so-called tangibles, that is, physical or digital evidence of the service. Such evidence could include, for example, physical facilities and associated accoutrements in which the service is provided, personnel appearance, physical presence of other customers, a physical or digital bill, and so forth.

More recently the dimensionality of SERVQUAL has been reduced to five, with those dimensions as reliability, responsiveness, tangibles, assurance, and empathy (Zeithaml, Parasuraman, and Berry, 1990). In this formulation, responsiveness is a combination of responsiveness and access as previously described. Similarly, assurance combines the previously cited elements of competence, credibility, security, and courtesy whereas empathy combines the previously defined elements of communication with understanding and knowing the customer.

Tomáš Baťa, the renowned early 20th century Czech management theorist and entrepreneur and founder of the Bata Shoes company, summarized the importance of service quality in the following way:

> Do not pursue money. He who pursues money will never achieve it. Serve! If you serve as best you can, you will not be able to escape money

**Rybka, 2013**

## THE CUSTOMER CHURN RATE: WHAT IT IS AND HOW TO USE IT

This makes clear the importance of learning from former customers the reasons behind their departure. To track and better understand this phenomenon, many enterprises employ the concept of CCR or customer churn rate (Jahromi, Stakhovych, and Ewing, 2014). CCR is a metric that tracks the percentage of customers choosing to end their relationship with the enterprise over a particular period of time. While the default time period is annual, any enterprise that supplies and prices its products or services on a monthly, quarterly, or other regular schedule is likely to track CCR according to that schedule. Similarly, if an enterprise is plagued by high CCR, it is likely to track and address it more regularly.

Many enterprises elect to address the issue in a more positive light so that, rather than aiming to reduce CCR, those enterprises will aim to track and increase the customer retention rate (CRR). The customer retention rate and customer churn rate represent essentially opposite sides of a coin so that they add to 100%, hence CRR = 100 – CCR. Similarly, many enterprises evaluate customer churn or retention rates across various customer segmentations in order to better understand what motivates or demotivates their customers. As one additional note, investors commonly use CCR or CRR to assess the underlying health of an enterprise.

It is important to know what our current customers want, what they require, and what will enable the enterprise to retain them, as well as factors that could lead to their defection. Research indicates that most enterprises are much more focused on increasing customer life-time value, cross and up-sell revenue, and customer retention than they are on new customer acquisition. Finally, knowledge of the needs and wants of prospective customers contributes to market share expansion or establishment of new markets.

Of course, "knowing and doing" are different, so that in coming to better know and understand customers, the enterprise will focus on the acquisition of actionable intelligence. In that sense, the CCR and CRR are lagging indicators or, more to the point, lagging behavioral indicators— meaning that they can be useful in communicating what has already happened, but in themselves do not indicate what strategy should be formulated and what actions should be taken to improve upon them. This suggests the CCR and CRR can be used to inform the sort of actionable intelligence that is needed, and that once such intelligence has been acquired and understood, that only then should the enterprise formulate and implement appropriate strategy. Moreover, given the nature of lagging indicators and hence lagged action, it may be several months or more before improvement in the CCR or CRR is detectable.

Overall, we seek to acquire, assess, and activate the voice of the customer (VOC)—including those aspects of the VOC that we may not find particularly encouraging. In other words, an enterprise should not accept the CCR or CRR as givens but should instead determine the factors that influence customers to leave, explore alternatives, or to remain with the enterprise—factors that "lead" or "predict" the CCR and CRR, with particular emphasis on identifying internally controllable factors.

Properly understood, identifying such internally controllable factors provides the enterprise with the means to optimize the customer churn/customer retention blend. Choice of the word optimize, rather than minimize customer churn and maximize customer retention, is intentional; there is no single numeric target since what is acceptable varies dramatically by business sector or business model, by how quickly and efficiently an enterprise is able to acquire new customers, and how profitable customers are both in the short and long term (Gallo, 2014).

Whichever side the enterprise chooses to emphasize in its dialogs—customer churn or customer retention—it is important to note that these are fundamentally related to enterprise customer relationship management (CRM) and new customer acquisition strategy and actions. Irrespective of how well or how poorly the enterprise manages its customer relationships, most enterprises willingly acknowledge that their CRM efforts can be improved and are aware of potential changes that may lead to improvement. Similarly, strategies many enterprises use to attract customers are suboptimal in that they attract the wrong customers—often by focusing too much on price competitiveness that may attract one-time customers who come, acquire what they want at a low price, and then move on to the next enterprise offering a price advantage.

In other words, it is important for the enterprise to discern whether its challenges lie primarily in the customer acquisition domain, or in the customer retention domain. As Jill Avery, a senior lecturer at Harvard Business School, stated, "Think about the customers you want to serve up front and focus on acquiring the right customers. The goal is to bring in and keep customers who you can provide value to and who are valuable to you" (Gallo, 2014).

## THE KANO CUSTOMER NEEDS MODEL

In addition to dimensions of product or service quality, it is also of value to be able to characterize specific customer needs, one useful model for which is the Kano customer needs model (Wang and Ji, 2010). The Kano model divides customer needs into three primary categories: attractive needs that are also referred to as exciters or delighters, one-dimensional needs that are commonly referred to as satisfiers, and must-have needs or requirements that are often referred to as dissatisfiers. These can be seen in Figure 11.2.

Must-be needs or dissatisfiers are basic product or service criteria representing customer needs and expectations that are obvious or self-evident in nature and hence that do not, or should not, need to be expressed. If adequate means of meeting these needs are not provided, the customer will be dissatisfied. It must be noted that fulfilling must-be needs does not increase customer satisfaction; they are instead, prerequisites to satisfaction.

One-dimensional needs or satisfiers can be explicitly articulated as needs that can be reasonably expected to be met by the provider. The

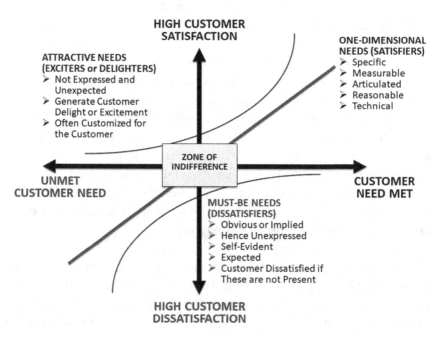

**FIGURE 11.2**
The Kano customer needs model.

degree to which such needs are met can be measured, and the degree of satisfaction experienced by the customer is directly proportional to the level to which the need is met.

Exciters or delighters, sometimes referred to as attractive requirements, are means of fulfilling needs the customer may not be able to identify and hence are unable to express. When a product or service element or combination of elements is presented that positively surprises, excites, or delights a customer, that element or combination of elements may be regarded as an exciter or delighter. David Kearns, the former CEO of Xerox, unintentionally summarized these ideas in an interview he provided shortly after Xerox Business Products and Systems Division won the Malcolm Baldrige National Quality Award in 1989 when he said (paraphrased): "Sometimes you have to lead the customer, you have to say, 'If we could do these things, what sorts of uses might you have?'" (Caudron, 1991). Kearns' statement points to a very important issue—that no enterprise should expect its customers to be fully aware of its capabilities and expertise. Indeed, even the enterprise is not likely to be fully cognizant of its own capabilities and expertise and how to best exercise either.

Not evident in Figure 11.2 is the nature of evolving customer needs and expectations through time. For this reason, some representations of the Kano customer needs model will include a diagonal line that falls from the upper left-hand corner to the lower right-hand corner to represent the time dimension. In some instances, a given customer need will grow in emphasis; in others, a need will be relatively constant, and in still other cases a customer need may disappear altogether. Similarly, though a customer need may not fundamentally change, new concepts or new technologies may dramatically alter the way in which a provider addresses that need. Two simple examples illustrate some of these ideas.

Consider the early years of global positioning systems (GPS) in motor vehicles. Such navigation systems were expensive options that customers found exciting. This in large is no longer true since most mobile phones now have GPS capability and a majority of drivers choose to use the built-in capability of their phone rather than pay for an expensive GPS option on their motor vehicle. Relative to the Kano customer needs model, embedded motor vehicle navigation systems have migrated from the category of being an exciter or delighter to being "off the map" in the sense that the majority of drivers needing navigation capability need not fulfill this need via vehicle capability, but rather may do so via a portable GPS device that may well be a stand-alone device or an application on their mobile telephone.

A second example is provided by vision correction surgery. Lasik is a low-cost procedure used to correct myopia, hyperopia, and astigmatism. It makes highly precise use of lasers to reshape the cornea, takes only a few minutes as an out-patient surgery with minimal patient discomfort, quick healing, and presents minimal risk to the patient. Prior to the advent and refinement of Lasik surgery, the primary surgical alternative to use of contact lenses or glasses was radial keratotomy (RK). Although RK remains the preferred surgical approach in some instances, it has in large been replaced by Lasik. RK essentially requires incredibly precise use of micro-razors to repeatedly cut and reshape the cornea, is painful, expensive, has a longer healing period during which the eye is covered so that usually only one eye is corrected at a time, and presents more risks to the patient than Lasik. RK did, however, generally produce vision results that satisfied patients undergoing the procedure and was in that sense an exciter or delighter. Due to the combination of pain, time to heal, risk, cost associated with RK, and advances in Lasik technology, RK has passed from the category of an exciter or delighter into a procedure that many consider to be barbaric.

## SELECTED METHODS FOR ACQUIRING THE VOICE OF THE CUSTOMER

Most contemporary enterprises have active voice of the customer (VOC) or, more generally, voice of the stakeholder solicitation programs, usually employing multiple methods of obtaining such inputs. The use of the word "input" here is highly intentional in that these voices often provide the fuel for product or service offerings, innovations, and designs. It should go without saying that careful and accurate delineation and segmentation of enterprise stakeholders can provide important and varied views of what is expected or desired from the enterprise.

Given the obvious importance of the VOC, it is of value to effectively acquire that voice. Numerous methods that facilitate the acquisition process are available, the most common of which are customer surveys, interviews, use of focus groups, and extraction of critical information from the enterprise's customer complaint system. Perhaps the most effective means of elaborating the voice of the customer is ethnographic research. Each of these methods has relative advantages and disadvantages so that most enterprises tend to use a combination of approaches rather than rely on a single method to acquire the VOC.

Customer surveys provide a relative cost advantage over other methods and tend to provide fast results. Surveys conducted by telephone tend to yield high response rates. Training of personnel needed to effectively execute surveys conducted by mail or email is generally low. While these are desirable characteristics, there are also drawbacks to use of customer surveys that are administered by mail or email, among which are incomplete responses and skipped questions—problems exacerbated by the lack of opportunity to clarify customer understanding of questions. Similarly, mail or email surveys tend to have low response rates. Telephone surveys often experience the difficulty of reaching geographically targeted respondents—an artefact of human mobility and the increased tendency of individuals to maintain their mobile telephone number when they relocate. Telephone surveys have the additional drawback that survey personnel can be influential and lead customers to provide responses that do not accurately reflect customer perspectives.

Customer interviews allow use of visual or other sensory aids and provide a good means of addressing complex questions or a wide range of topics. Equally, customer interviews conducted by appropriately trained personnel provide a good means of obtaining the VOC when customers are reluctant to respond or are likely to respond inaccurately if—as an alternative—customer surveys were administered by telephone, mail, or email. As with other VOC acquisition methods, there are disadvantages associated with conducting face-to-face interviews, among which are the time and expense involved in training of interviewers and a relatively long amount of time required to complete interviews.

Focus groups allow for substantial interaction and for the mutual stimulation that accompanies such interaction. This approach ordinarily allows for freeform or unconstrained forms of responses as well as responses that are more nuanced or in-depth. Equally, focus groups enable more complex, qualitatively oriented issues to be addressed. For all of these positives, focus groups also have negatives, among which are that learnings extracted from a focus group represent the group members so that it is difficult to generalize results. Similarly, the "data" gathered from focus group interaction may be overly anecdotal and is typically qualitative so that skilled facilitation is required as is expertise in extracting key learnings.

Customer complaints review can provide significant information not usually provided by surveys, interviews, or focus groups, unless, that is, customers surveyed, interviewed, or composing the focus group have been specifically selected on the basis of having formally complained to the enterprise. In particular, customer complaints review typically provides information about customer dissatisfaction and how that dissatisfaction could have been better resolved (Zairi, 2000). Use of this approach will usually provide very specific feedback and provides opportunities to respond appropriately to dissatisfied customers and has the potential to convert the dissatisfied customer, who is ready to abandon the enterprise for an alternative source of the product or service in question, into a loyal customer (Goodman, 2006; Homburg and Fürst, 2005). Understanding and addressing customer dissatisfaction is regarded as so important that the criteria of some enterprise excellence models formally assess the adequacy of such systems and whether they are reactive or proactive. A key challenge is that of not "over-responding" to customer complaints by allowing a very small number of possibly non-representative data points to unduly influence changes in enterprise policy, practices, products, or services.

Ethnographic research may be used when either a "big win" or a "big loss" is at stake. This approach is ordinarily time-consuming, expensive, and requires keen observation of product users or service recipients in the actual use environment. A clear advantage of ethnographic research is that it enables nuanced learning from real, rather than contrived, situations. Among common VOC methods, ethnographic research is generally regarded as providing the most complete understanding (Cooper and Dreher, 2010). Despite its high level of effectiveness, ethnographic research is such a resource-intensive VOC approach that its use is ordinarily relegated to high stakes situations where success can deliver big gains or failure can yield exorbitant losses.

## CUSTOMER SATISFACTION, LOYALTY OR ADVOCACY?

Understanding the voice of the customer is essential to cultivating customer satisfaction and, historically, enterprises have focused on satisfying their customers, but in many instances, satisfaction is not sufficient. This applies particularly in the case of low-cost environments and environments in which customers have an array of similarly preferable alternatives from which to select.

As a simple example of these ideas, consider a product such as breakfast cereal. Consumers often experience similar satisfaction levels for each of a large selection of similarly priced products. For that reason, brand switching is both common and frequent at the individual consumer level so that, in such instances, enterprises tend to focus on maintaining or growing market share.

Beyond satisfying customers, a common enterprise goal is cultivation of customer loyalty, a result of which is reduction of brand switching. Clearly, this is preferable to simply satisfying the customer.

Stronger still, however, is the customer whose satisfaction and loyalty levels generate such high levels of enthusiasm that the customer becomes the walking, talking, posting, blogging advocate for a product or service. Such customers become product or service marketers whose only compensation is their product or service experience.

Every enterprise has customers and the very existence of the enterprise is contingent on its relationships with those customers so that these relationships must be consciously and continuously attended to. While enterprises commonly dream of highly satisfied customers, highly dissatisfied customers can be the stuff of enterprise nightmares— potentially walking, talking, posting, blogging nightmares. Just as a delighted customer can help to attract additional consumers to the enterprise, dissatisfied, disappointed, or disgruntled customers can drive existing or potential customers away.

For these and other reasons, it is important for enterprises to discover not only what is attractive to customers, but also what drives customers away. This means that the varied customer segments should be examined and that each category of customer need or requirement—must-be, satisfiers, and exciters or delighters—should be fully elaborated and subsequently addressed.

## WHO IS THE CUSTOMER? A BROAD CONTEMPORARY PERSPECTIVE

The concept of customer satisfaction has evolved toward addition of customer loyalty, and even advocacy of the customer on behalf of the enterprise. Similarly, the contemporary view of the customer has evolved.

Although the traditional view of the customers as end users, or as a chain of immediate recipients of a product or service en route toward an end user may be appropriate in some contexts, this view is often too narrow.

In the context of the *Shingo Model*, the concept of customers may be expanded to include multiple relevant stakeholders that may span the supply and value chains and beyond. This view will address the needs, wants, and sensitivities of producers or providers; users, consumers, or recipients of products and services; and those directly or indirectly impacted by the manufacture, distribution, use, or provision of a product or service including individuals, civil society, policy makers, and the natural environment. This view requires a balancing of stakeholder considerations and is consistent with increasing expectations that enterprises should be both socially and environmentally responsible. When the profit motivation to which enterprises are obligated is added, we now see the familiar triple bottom-line to which more and more businesses subscribe and that more and more consumers and investors are rewarding (Ahmed, 2014; Kreander et al., 2005; Yan, Shaukat, and Tharyan, 2016).

To better understand this perspective, one need only consider the highly influential global role of business, with approximately half of the world's 100 largest economies and one-third of the world's 25 largest economies as businesses, rather than nations (Kiss, Danis, and Cavusgil, 2012). Enterprises, especially large ones, often lack the resources or, sometimes, the resolve to exercise significant oversight in their supply chains. Similarly, the activities of many enterprises adversely impact the natural environment, with some of those impacts being of a nature that will quite literally persist for thousands of years.

Related to these issues are issues such as corruption, global slavery, natural resource depletion, and environmental degradation. Consider, for example, that as of 2016 there were an estimated 45.8 million slaves in the world (http://www.globalslaveryindex.org/). Slavery most commonly assumes the form of forced or child labor, though other forms exist. Of these 45 million slaves, many are working in various supply chains and some are in generally unexpected places. Consider, for example, that Europe is home to an estimated 1.2 million slaves, 18.3 million slaves are in India—home to significant global outsourcing activities for numerous influential enterprises—and an estimated 1 in 20 people in the North Korean workforce are slaves (http://www.telegraph.co.uk/news/2016/05/31/the-world-has-over-45-million-slaves---including-12-million-in-e/).

Viewing customers from an integrated stakeholder perspective is essential to positioning enterprises as partial solutions to such problems by serving the best interests of their customers/stakeholders. In proceeding from this perspective, it is legitimate to note by balancing various stakeholder considerations that the enterprise is essentially pursuing a constrained optimum result—a balance—rather than proving the best possible result for any single stakeholder segment (Voegtlin, Patzer, and Scherer, 2012; Welford, 2013).

# 12

## Enterprise Advancement Means: The Future of Renewal, Optimization, and Innovation

There are numerous trends to which it is likely the *Shingo Model* and others such as the Baldrige Model and EFQM Excellence Model will likely adapt, whether that adaptation is soon or more gradual. It is clear, for example, that a rapidly increasing number of enterprises are concerned about their social and environmental performance and impacts. Such concerns may be driven by conscience, regulatory demands, or market pressures, but whatever the driving force behind such concerns, business strategy, practice, and performance emphases are shifting. We see that significant components of enterprise strategy are concerned not only with being financially prudent but with social equity and environmental sensitivity—the three components of triple top-line strategy (McDonough and Braungart, 2002a). It is not only enterprise policies and practices that must be aligned with these, but processes, systems, and partnerships.

It is through these mechanisms that performance and impacts result. Most if not all enterprises seek to deliver performance and impacts that are relevant to their stakeholders and, at the same time, socially and ecologically responsible.

Further, given the now well-known criticality of needs, it appears obvious that innovation is needed which is associated less with continuous improvement than with breakthrough advances in areas that, among others, are socially or environmentally relevant, timely, and impactful.

When these observations are combined, it is reasonable to assume that a critical subset of the sorts of performance and impacts that will need to be considered will be ones in the so-called triple bottom-line areas of people, planet, and profit (Elkington, 1997), as well as innovation. Performance is driven partially by processes and systems, however, so that processes and systems supporting innovation will be of increasing concern.

This suggests that shifts will occur in the sorts of performance and impacts that will be accessed, and how those are gotten to: it isn't just *what* that is of importance—it is also *how*: relevance and responsibility. That having been said, critical or more desperate needs tend to place far more value on pragmatism than on ideals.

There are other enterprise consequences of the sort of social volatility that are increasingly common, as well as the strains seen in the natural environment. As such, it is likely that enterprises will pursue sustainability by simultaneously pursuing a strategically determined blend of excellence, resilience, and robustness where an enterprise is (Edgeman and Williams, 2014):

- Sustainable to the extent that it is able to create and maintain economics, ecological, and social value for itself, its stakeholders, society at large, and policy makers;
- Resilient to the extent that it possesses the capacity to self-renew through innovation by adapting its responses to negative shocks and challenges over time;
- Robust to the degree that the enterprise is highly resistant or immune to a critical subset of such shocks and challenges; and
- Excellent when its leadership and strategy, as deployed through people, processes, partnerships, and policies, deliver superior performance and impacts in specified areas.

The "specified areas" in which enterprises must deliver superior performance may change over time. A current and future list of areas might include, for example, the following domains: enterprise human capital, innovation, financial, environmental, social, data analytics and intelligence, marketplace, supply chain, operations, increased leisure time, improved physical and emotional health, and various more context-specific ones.

In acknowledging the validity of interaction between the enterprise and the societal, ecological (e.g., biophysical), and technological domains of BEST as both relevant to and the responsibility of the enterprise, we have a somewhat reimagined representation of what it means for the enterprise to be sustainable. Formal incorporation of continuous and breakthrough improvement as manifestations of enterprise innovation further contributes

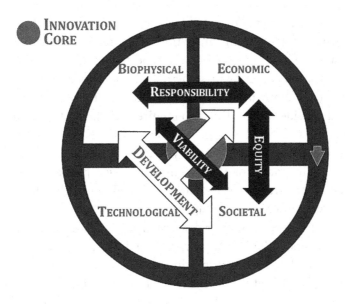

**FIGURE 12.1**
Sustainability and the BEST sustainable enterprise.

to a reimagining of sustainability and the sustainable enterprise through what we here refer to as the "quad" or BEST Bottom Line.

These ideas are presented in Figure 12.1. This perspective regards innovation as core to enterprise consciousness, and hence strategy and practice that in turn produce results in the form of both direct and indirect performance and impacts. All two-way interactions among the four BEST environmental domains are represented so that, for example, key considerations regarding an enterprise's value creation activities are that these activities should:

- produce ecologically (biophysically) responsible and
- societally equitable performance and impacts that should be viable and
- sustainable in nature.

The primary role of technology then becomes to positively contribute to enterprise economic performance while at the same time enabling social and ecological development/advancement.

Benefits of this approach include better and more conscious alignment of enterprise strategy and activities with the external BEST environment and its stakeholders through a highly intentional BEST strategy. This requires a high level of employee engagement; something that is generally true when innovation in the form of both incremental and breakthrough improvements is expected to become routine and when innovation targets will sometimes be less tangibly connected to enterprise (economic) performance and more clearly related to social and ecological considerations. This also requires significant trust, exceptional coordination and collaboration, a strong sense of shared purpose, and highly directed organizational unity that manifests in performance and impacts. While many of these comments refer primarily to cultural elements, others are strongly strategy-oriented, and still others are very much process- and activity-oriented.

This essentially positions our discussion at the center of "creating value for stakeholders"—the CV appearing later in this text at the center of Figures 23.1 and 23.2, so that in principle the whole of Figure 12.1 can be substituted for "CV" at the core of each of these figures.

There are no fundamental reasons that enterprises cannot begin to integrate such an approach immediately as, indeed, many enterprises are

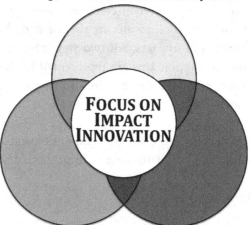

**SOCIALLY POSITIVE:**
Inventions & innovations must solve important social challenges and address critical community needs.

**FOCUS ON IMPACT INNOVATION**

**ECOLOGICALLY SOUND:**
Inventors, designers, and manufacturers must make sound decisions relative to materials, production processes, suppliers, and distribution in order to minimize environmental footprints.

**ECONOMICALLY SELF-SUSTAINING:**
Inventions & innovations that are scalable, market-tested, and economically viable, generate long-term impacts, revenue and employment.

**FIGURE 12.2**

Innovation culture in sustainable, excellent, resilient, and robust enterprises.

already triple bottom-line oriented and use technology to facilitate their efforts. Similarly, innovation is prominently featured at many enterprises.

The keys to the kingdom, in this case, may be to prioritize and synthesize these elements, embed them in enterprise culture, align them with enterprise strategy, and deploy them appropriately. As such, our vision for innovation is captured by Figure 12.2, where three primary desirable innovation criteria are that innovation should be socially positive, ecologically sound, and economically self-sustaining. Ideal innovation practice would require that all innovation is economically self-sustaining and that, at the least, is entirely socially and ecologically neutral to positive, meaning it does not produce any negative social or ecological consequences.

In all, the "new" innovation expectation is that enterprises should create invention and innovation ecosystems that confront challenges worth solving, and not only those that can be solved. Seen through a product, system, and service creation lens, this goal can be supported by well-thought-out and executed concept ideation, generation, selection, and deployment processes—topics discussed in some detail in Chapters 13 through 17.

# 13

## *Running with Cheetahs: Market Velocity, Need for Speed, and Outside-the-Box Thinking*

An enterprise is rarely better than its portfolio of product and service offerings and enterprises face the near-universal challenge of matching their performance and portfolio of product and service offerings with market velocity that is driven by ever more technologically sophisticated, more informed, and more demanding customers. At the same time, regulatory restrictions mandate transparency and areas of compliance, whereas social and ecological pressures constrain the limits of what is permitted in some instances and acceptable in others.

Some enterprises face challenges of other sorts as, for example, technology manufacturers faced with rapidly diminishing (known) global levels of key natural resources that are driving increases in both the cost of and competition for those resources. In such cases, a key pressure to innovate at the design and materials levels arises.

Still other enterprises are subject to various supply chain threats that may include modern forms of slavery, regional conflicts, or other issues that may be unobvious or beyond their control.

In all cases, agility and creativity can aid the enterprise in derivation of full or partial solutions to its challenges or development of strategies by which it might leverage its opportunity.

Much of the data or intelligence that enterprises work with is qualitative in nature and can often be characterized as "ideas." Among the sorts of ideas that may be generated are ones related to strategy development, new product or service development, problem mitigation, or process improvement.

As a cautionary word, no method is failsafe—methods generally work no better than the diligence devoted by the team or individual using the method. In addition, —and perhaps more than with quantitative information—value derived from use of methods that follow is influenced by a team's knowledge and experience repositories, the way the team uses these as they draw insight and foresight from their work, their ability to interpret findings, and, ultimately, to translate these into value-adding improvements, innovations, and designs.

Although numerous alternative approaches can be cited, a limited set of approaches aimed at sequentially generating ideas, organizing ideas, identification of relationships among ideas, prioritization of ideas, and deployment of ideas are described next. In many ways this progression is akin to the use of PDSA and, indeed, the methods presented can be successfully applied in a PDSA context to yield a sort of "PDSA on steroids." Each of the methods that will be cited is highly flexible with applicability that is limited more by the imagination and experience of the team or individual involved than by limitations inherent to the approach itself. Further, each approach described can be used in isolation or, as indicated herein, chained together to form a cohesive and more extensive problem-solving or opportunity-leveraging set. Ultimately tools and techniques introduced in this chapter contribute to the larger process, product or service development, and deployment methodology as cited in Figure 13.1.

Relative to Figure 13.1, identification of stakeholder needs and specifications in general and customer needs in particular have been previously addressed. If competitive products or services are on the market, they can be analyzed by numerous means, among them benchmarking. Although coverage of benchmarking is beyond the scope of this work, there are numerous widely available and useful resources on the subject (Bendell, Boulter, and Kelly, 1993; Camp and Camp, 1989; Sarkis, 2001; Shetty, 1993; Watson, 2003). Content in the present and the following few chapters address the remainder of Figure 13.1, namely concept generation, concept selection, and deployment of the selected concept via quality function deployment.

Creativity is central to concept generation and often requires thinking that is outside the norm. A few illustrations of outside-the-box thinking are provided in the following section. Afterward, focus will move toward formal concept generation methods.

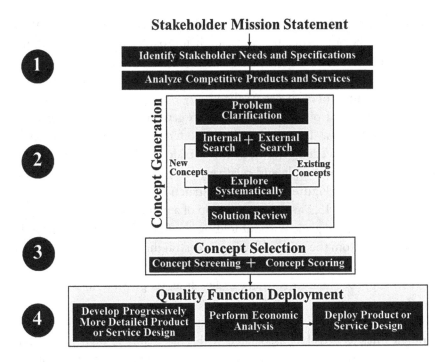

**FIGURE 13.1**
Concept generation, selection, and deployment methodology.

## IDEATION AND OUTSIDE-THE-BOX THINKING

The creative process of generating, developing, relating, and communicating new ideas is referred to as ideation. There are of course many ways by which ideas might be generated, developed, related to one another, and communicated—best practices for which are identified in Cooper and Edgett (2008). Among idea generation approaches are patent searches, scouring of industry publications, use of ethnographic methods to observe the use of environment in which there is an opportunity or need to develop a new product or service offering, and many more not cited herein. Equally, it is possible to apply a portfolio of approaches in the idea generation process, rather than use simply one.

One means of generating ideas for which there are many variations is brainstorming. Brainstorming may be practiced by individuals or teams and the extent to which brainstorming is successful is influenced by numerous factors that include the skill of any facilitator of the process, the breadth and depth of knowledge and creativity of the individual or team doing the brainstorming, the overall approach used, and the stimuli employed. Careful identification and definition of the issue or challenge that provides the focus for the brainstorming activity can also limit or enhance the amount of success realized.

Naturally, a goal of brainstorming is to generate better ideas leading to better solutions. To accomplish this often means that outside-the-box-thinking is needed. The need for outside-the-box thinking can be illustrated by a few simple and relatively familiar examples. As our first example, consider Figure 13.2 and an instruction set that follows:

Instructions for 13.2 are to place the tip of a pen or pencil on any of the black points on the grid. Without folding the figure, without lifting your pen or pencil from the grid, and using only straight lines, connect the grid points.

Next, suppose the aim is to use as few lines as possible to connect all points.

Unless a person trying to fulfill the instructions and objective (as few straight lines as possible) associated with Figure 13.2 is highly unusual, or has seen this or a similar exercise previously, the likelihood is that the solution delivered will be similar to the one in Figure 13.3.

In Figure 13.3 the numbers 1 through 5 merely indicate a sequence of lines. The instructions have been fulfilled perfectly, beginning at one point, not lifting the writing implement, and using only straight lines.

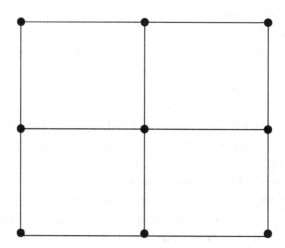

**FIGURE 13.2**
A simple 3-by-3 grid.

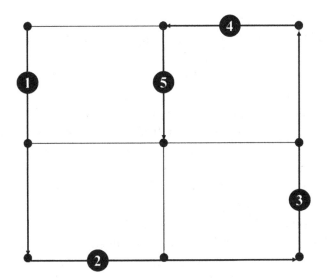

**FIGURE 13.3**
A common solution that perfectly fulfills the Instructions.

The solution, however, is suboptimal, in that it required five straight lines when the stated aim of the exercise was to fulfill the instructions, doing so using the fewest straight lines possible.

Figure 13.4 provides another possible solution to the exercise that fulfills all instructions, yet does so using only four straight lines, where

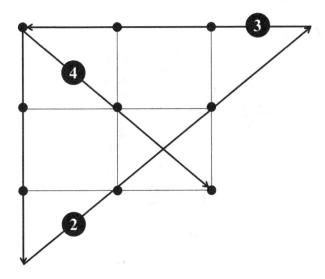

**FIGURE 13.4**
Using outside-the-box thinking to deliver a better (optimal) solution.

the numbers 1 through 4 in Figure 13.4 indicate the specific sequence of lines used. Application of graph theory indicates that this latter solution is in fact an optimal one (Deo, 2017).

One lesson to be learned from this exercise is that derivation of the solution portrayed in Figure 13.4 required—quite literally in this instance—outside-the-box thinking or "thinking outside the norm," where the "box" for most people confronted by this exercise was defined by the perimeter of the points forming the grid. Such boxes are especially effective in constraining our solution sets because we are the ones who have built the boxes, and they perform the function of boxes quite well— of keeping things in the box.

Multiple other sequences or patterns that also perfectly fulfill the provided instructions, and do so with only four straight lines, are possible. This yields a second lesson, namely that multiple approaches might lead to equally good (or poor) solutions so that multiple individuals or teams given the same objective and resources would likely derive different yet equally good solutions.

To reiterate the value of unconventional or outside-the-box thinking, briefly consider a second example, to be completed by two people working together—one who is "sighted" together with one who is "blind." The assigned task is for the sighted person or guide to lead the blind person (or neophyte) from the origin of the maze portrayed in Figure 13.5 to the destination. This maze—if that is all it happens to be—is an intentionally

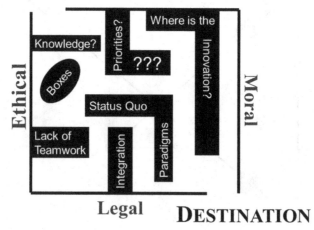

**FIGURE 13.5**
A "simple" enterprise maze.

simple one with many alternative solutions. In many regards, it is not unlike what "mazes" enterprises routinely confront. Such mazes are commonly situations in need of resolution in the face of multiple perceived barriers and constraints that range from enterprise culture or tradition; to resource limitations; to legal, ethical, moral; or other boundaries. Selected common enterprise challenges are represented as barriers in the interior of the maze.

A large majority of sighted guide/blind companions will use an approach similar to the one below:

- The sighted guide will help to position a pen or perhaps the finger of the blind companion on the "origin."
- This will be followed by the sighted guide providing a series of instructions, aimed at the blind companion navigating their way through the maze by moving the pen or their finger appropriately, commonly bumping into barriers: "down, down, down, right, right, right, down . . . right, right, down . . . great!"
- At this point, the pair will exchange roles and repeat the exercise, feeling a great sense of accomplishment when they have completed the task.

Certaintly, the companions completed the task as assigned. But was the task completed as successfully as possible?

Imagine that there are other solutions. As one example, imagine the approach some organizations have taken to navigate their "competitive mazes"—skirting ethical, legal, or moral boundaries—effectively "going around" the maze to their own peril or the peril of others.

As another possible approach, some sighted guides may take hold of their blind companion's finger or pen and use their sight to simply "push/pull" the companion through the maze, producing no learning in their blind companion apart possibly from the learning that comes with muscle memory.

A third approach that is opposite to the adage dating back to 1625 from Sir Francis Bacon, "If mountain will not come to Muhammad, then Muhammad must go to the mountain" (Bacon and Montagu, 1854) is to treat the finger or pen of the blind companion as fixed, and to move the maze itself. This is indeed a very common industrial solution, used often in robotic operations.

Still another approach to this challenge would be to test the permeability of the various barriers as the maze is negotiated. It is rare that all barriers are equally rigid and indeed some barriers are perceived ones only, existing because "we have always done it that way!" By challenging barriers, the maze becomes reconfigured in a way better suited to the enterprise's current culture and competitive landscape.

It can be debated as to which of these solutions is best since "best" may be circumstantial. Still, the maze exercise illustrates yet again the value of outside-the-box thinking in derivation of alternative or novel solutions to challenges.

As an example of where such thinking proved especially helpful can be found at IBM. In back-to-back years in the 1990s, "Big Blue" lost approximately $12 billion. Losses of such magnitude tend to focus one's attention and that was certainly the case for IBM. In examining the failures that most contributed to these losses, IBM found—and here the situation will be stated somewhat in hyperbole—that its human ecology "looked alike, dressed alike, were trained alike, and thought alike" so that its vast talent pool was in fact too homogenous to resolve challenges that were unlike ones previously faced. Part of IBM's solution to this dilemma was to intentionally diversify its human ecology, thereby creating a more heterogeneous and richer talent pool that was better able to navigate unfamiliar territory. Stated briefly, IBM's talent pool had become one that was too stale relative to its competitive landscape. Remember: "the same old way delivers the same old results!"

One way to become intentionally more creative and stave off stagnancy is to routinize and practice creative problem-solving approaches. The process will be initiated by examining idea generation—commonly referred to as brainstorming. A few commonly used approaches are discussed next, with the initial cautionary note that brainstorming rarely delivers a final solution, rather, it is often just a first step in a problem-solving progression.

# 14

## *Customer-Driven Improvement and Innovation Processes: Tapping and Organizing the Enterprise and Customer Minds*

It is important here to provide some immediate clarification. Chapters 14 through 17 begin with the phrase "customer-driven improvement and innovation processes." Essentially all tools and methods presented in these chapters can be applied in ways and for reasons limited only by the expertise and imaginations of their users. Certainly, the tools and methods presented in these chapters might be applied purely internally and hence invisibly to the customer, for reasons that are intended only to produce process or system improvements or innovations.

This begs the question: why refer to the methods of these chapters as being customer-driven? The answer is a simple one: that whether the (external) customer provides the conscious or visible impetus for an improvement or innovation, the customer will almost always be the beneficiary of these—whether intentionally or unintentionally, directly or indirectly. Consider that an improvement or innovation will virtually always produce one or more of the following, non-exhaustive list of benefits:

- An efficiency boost that yields a cost reduction for the enterprise and in turn either the ability to maintain or reduce prices for the customer;
- An improvement in effectiveness that improves the power or potency of that provided to the customer;
- Access to a desirable product, process, service, or outcome;

- A social benefit in which the customer participates as a member of that society;
- A (natural) environment impact or benefit that improves physical state of world in which the customer lives, whether that improvement is nearby or distant.

Note that no claim is made that a given improvement or innovation is uniformly positive: its impact may differentially impact various customers or stakeholder segments. Equally, a given improvement or innovation may deliver a mixture of impacts that are on the whole positive, but with some of those impacts being desirable, some neutral, and some negative.

It is with the above qualifying comments in mind that this chapter, together with the following three chapters, have titles that begin with the words "customer-driven."

## GETTING STARTED: SEEDING THE BRAINSTORMING PROCESS

Brainstorming is used to generate ideas, often in large numbers, with the goal of one or more of those ideas being of high value in solving a specific problem or leveraging a given opportunity. In enterprise contexts, those problems or opportunities will commonly demand derivation and implementation of product, process, or service improvements, or innovations. Brainstorming will often produce ideas that are either directly or in adapted form of value in solving challenges other than the one giving rise to the idea initially. This is a value-added aspect of brainstorming.

Brainstorming can be practiced either individually or as a group with the focus here being on group brainstorming. Several methods of group brainstorming that vary in their level of formality will be described. In describing each approach, it is assumed that time has been devoted to clearly stating and agreeing upon the issue, problem, opportunity, or challenge with respect to which brainstorming is to be conducted.

It is often helpful to "jumpstart" the brainstorming process by "seeding" it (Gallupe and Cooper, 1993). The idea is similar in intent to cloud seeding as practiced in arid regions with little precipitation. In cloud seeding, clouds are chemically seeded as a means of stimulating rain.

Rather than chemically seeding brainstorming, sensual seeds are used. Given that seeds are sensual, and given that different group members are likely to differ from one another relative to how they are stimulated, it is common to use some combination of seeds. Brainstormers—being fully informed concerning that which they will brainstorm—are exposed to the "seeds" and given a moment to "contemplate" or consider the seeds, usually in relation to the brainstorming topic.

Brainstorming facilitators often have a catalog of images or statements they use with groups. These may or may not have any clear connection to that about which the brainstorming is centered. Depending on the facilitator, seeds may be intended to lead brainstormers in a specific direction, or may be simply intended to stimulate initial thinking, with no specific direction intended. Example seed stimulants include the following:

- An image: the image may range from serene to provocative, from bright to dull, from some thing or event that is well known, to some thing or event that is fictional or obscure. Similar in concept to a seed image would be use of a seed video clip.
- Music or sound: this could range from a few notes to a full song and may or may not include lyrics. Similarly, style may vary from classical, to blues, to rock-n-roll, or other. As a precaution, it is generally unwise to use a piece that is too familiar since this is more likely to stimulate old and familiar ideas, rather than new ones.
- Something to eat or taste: there is the possibility that if this method is used that brainstormers may be asked to close their eyes and, possibly, may not be allowed to touch that which is being tasted or eaten. The purpose behind denying brainstormers the ability to see and/ or touch the "taste seed" is to make it otherwise as "unfamiliar" as possible. The taste seed can of course range from something pleasant to something disgusting with the natural precautionary note of learning in advance whether any of those involved in brainstorming have food or other allergies related to taste.
- Something to touch: with texture that may range from smooth to rough to sharp, regular to highly nuanced, small to large, that may be soft or squeezable or hard, that may be bright or dull, that may be familiar or unfamiliar, and that may be pleasing or repulsive.

- A statement, word, passage, or paragraph: this may be highly targeted or may simply be thought-provoking. Experienced facilitators will often have a catalog of quotes from famous people, or favorite paragraphs from books, etc., from which they draw.

As an example of just one stimulus, consider the following seed passage, drawn from a work of historical fiction by Morgan Llywelyn (1992), *Strongbow: the Story of Richard and Aoife*:

*Aoife:* Our Irish warriors are as good as any of yours.
*Richard:* Perhaps. But we have knights on horseback and skilled archers, and our men fight in one unit, following one order. The Irish fight man-by-man, each according to his own desire. They cannot overcome one hundred men all following the same order.

This fictional dialog is between Aoife (Eve), the daughter of an Irish chieftain and her husband, Richard de Clare. De Clare, better known as Strongbow, was the knight who led the 12th century Norman conquest of Ireland. Different readers of this passage will no doubt have differing thoughts considering its content so that what is next written is only one possible collection of thoughts that a brainstormer might draw from this dialog:

Aoife raised this as a "quality of people" issue, asserting that, from a human resource perspective, Irish warriors were as good as their Norman foes. Strongbow did not dispute this when he responded "perhaps." Instead, he altered the course of the argument, shifting it from one about people to a comparison and contrast of the ways and means in and with which the two groups of combatants engaged in conflict. Namely, Strongbow examined differences in equipment or technology (horseback), training (skilled archers), organization (as one unit vs. man-by-man), and purpose and direction (following one order vs. according to their own desire).

Given that one goal of brainstorming is to generate a lot of ideas—some of which will almost certainly be irrelevant, while others are likely to be highly germane—the hope is that the various individuals engaged in the brainstorming effort will in fact see different things in a seed passage such as that above. Equally, given that people respond differently—or don't—to different sorts of stimuli, it is common to use multiple (forms of) seeds in a single brainstorming exercise, thus increasing the likelihood of generating more and better ideas.

Brainstorming seeds are meant to take root and grow quickly, rather than requiring deep contemplation and hence a longer time to germinate and bear fruit. In part this is because most brainstorming is meant to be fast and furious—a sort of feeding frenzy—where each member of the group or team engaged in brainstorming feeds off the energy and ideas of others in the group.

Regardless of the brainstorming approach used, it is important to generate not only many ideas, but to generate relevant ones that can be effectively developed and implemented to solve the problem or leverage the opportunity that gave rise to the brainstorming effort.

## 6–3–5 BRAINWRITING

The numbers in this brainstorming approach are guidelines, rather than hard-and-fast requirements, with six (6) as the number of members of the team or group involved in the brainwriting (brainstorming) effort (Gausemeier, Fink, and Schlake, 1998). Each of the group members is instructed to write down three (3) ideas in five (5) minutes that they believe may solve or partially address the target problem.

At the end of five minutes, each member of the group will discuss one of their ideas briefly—about one minute—then go through a second rotation—followed by a third, until all ideas are discussed. In most cases, this process will stimulate new ideas in a second round of brainstorming or will lead to refinement of ideas presented in the first round of brainstorming.

This process can be repeated as many times as is deemed useful. Often brainstorming will have an initial goal—for example, "generate at least 100 ideas"—in which case six rounds of brainstorming would be needed.

## CHANGE THE CONTEXT OR KEEP IT? WHAT WOULD YOU DO IF YOU COULD ...

Remember that a goal of brainstorming or ideation is to generate a lot of ideas, with some or many of those ideas being outside-the-box in nature. Still another approach is to carefully analyze the box itself. One potentially helpful means of stimulating outside-the-box thinking is to

**TABLE 14.1**

Context Changing and Box Analysis Approaches

| Context Change | Description |
| --- | --- |
| Culture and Demography | What would you do if the issue arose in a different cultural context? What are the effects of changing the gender/age/ethnicity/intellect/ etc., and how might these change things? |
| Exaggeration | Enlarge the goal, shrink it, multiply it. What would this lead you to do in these or similar situations? |
| Iconic Persons | What would you do if you were an iconic person such as Jesus or Martin Luther King, Jr.; or Mahatma Gandhi; or Mother Teresa? A hero? A villain? |
| Ideal Final Result | Imagine what the "ideal final result" might be. For example, one view of an ideal laptop computer might be that it is invisible except when in use, weighs nothing, has infinite memory and unlimited processing speed, interacts with your mind in a way that makes data/keyboard entry unnecessary, perfectly and automatically corrects spelling and grammar, connects to the internet effortlessly, etc. |
| Mercy | What is the most merciful solution? |
| Resources | What would you do if you didn't have any resource constraints (time, people, money, etc.)? |
| Reversal | What if you did the opposite of what would usually be done? |
| Rolestorming | What would you do in a different role or within a different stakeholder category? |
| Superpowers | What would you do if you had unlimited superpowers and could do as you pleased? |
| Teleportation | What would you do if you were in a different place? |
| Time Travel | What would you do if you were in a different time period? This enables boundary change via envisioning the future or invoking the past. |

| Box Analysis | Description |
| --- | --- |
| Aggregate and Disaggregate | What factors can be considered independent of the others and what factors must be aggregated? |
| Challenge | Challenge every assumption believed to be relevant to the situation. |
| Escape Artist | Flip each assumption and review the situation from a new perspective to escape the status quo. Loosely translated, status quo is Latin for "the mess we're in." |
| Force Field Analysis | Consider enabling and disabling forces. How can you magnify the drivers or enablers and how can you reduce or eliminate barriers? |
| Synergy Analysis | What synergies can we identify and exploit that will magnify or ease the solution? |
| SWOT Analysis | This is an assessment of internal strengths and weaknesses together with external opportunities and threats. |

first attack the box, thus changing the context. Contextual considerations typically fall into four main areas: how (the application context), where (the environment context), who (the customer context), and the market. Table 14.1 cites just a few examples of context changing approaches and box analysis approaches often found to prove useful.

## ORGANIZING AND IDENTIFYING RELATIONSHIPS AMONG IDEAS

Brainstorming, as previously noted, is commonly a fast-paced process with no conscious organization of the ideas and principles generated during the process. As such, any commonalities, distinctions, or relationships between and among ideas will typically need to be determined afterwards. Two tools useful in this later effort are the affinity diagram and the interrelationship digraph (Brassard, 1989).

## AFFINITY DIAGRAMS: REVEALING RELATIONS AMONG IDEAS

Affinity can be taken to mean that two or more things share something in common. In a social context, the fan club for a band or singer or actor would provide an example of an affinity group. Similarly, those engaging in costume play (cosplay) that share the practice of dressing up as a character from a book, cartoon, comic book, movie, or video game can form an affinity group. In our context, affinity groups are groups of ideas that share something in common. Often, there is only a vague initial sense of what that commonality is, so the commonality may not be described until later in the process of constructing an affinity diagram. This is typically done by consensus.

An affinity grouping may be further subdivided into one or more subgroupings in the same way that transportation could be broken into modes (e.g., air travel, marine travel, motor vehicle, train, etc.), each mode could be subdivided (e.g., motor vehicle travel into automobiles, SUVs, trucks, buses), automobiles subdivided again (e.g., Fords into Mustangs, Fusion, Taurus, etc.), and so on. In this example, the various groupings are generally well defined, with little debate as to where any given element belongs. When dealing with more qualitatively oriented elements, such as ideas or principles, groupings are often of the "in the eye of the beholder" sort so that labeling of groupings (clusters of ideas) will most commonly result from discussion.

A step-by-step process of constructing an affinity diagram can be described as follows, where the assumption is that a team effort is applicable:

- Clearly state the subject around which brainstorming will take place.
- Whether via brainstorming or another approach, generate the ideas that are to be sorted into affinity groupings. In "fast-and-furious" brainstorming, the usual advice is to express ideas in three to seven words each so a reasonable balance is struck between clarity and spontaneity.
- Record each idea in a movable form such as a 3" by 5" index card or a sufficiently sized sticky note. The issue of sufficient size here is one where each card or note can be read from a distance of approximately six to ten feet (two to three meters).
- In random order, lay each card or post each sticky note on a flat surface.
- As a group and in silence, sort these into "affinity" groups. This is done by each person, whenever they are inclined to do so, moving a card or sticky note near to another card/sticky note or group of cards/sticky notes with which they feel there is something shared in common—whether that commonality can be clearly expressed at the time, or merely sensed. During this stage of the process, any given card or sticky note may be moved multiple times by multiple people. If this continues to occur, it may be helpful to construct duplicate cards or sticky notes to be (preliminarily) placed in multiple affinity groupings. This sorting process will typically begin slowly, gain momentum, and slow to a point where there is no more movement.
- Once the sorting process has stopped, the group should discuss what the "red thread" or commonality is that describes each grouping. Often that red thread is captured by one of the cards or sticky notes in the group, but if not, a new card or sticky note that describes the red thread can be constructed. The card or sticky note representing the red thread for a given group is referred to as a "header card" and is used to label or describe the affinity grouping. If useful, a given

affinity group may be further subdivided into two or more affinity subgroupings.

- Gather the results in a more professionally formatted affinity diagram and submit it to the project champion for feedback and finalization.

---

## BRAINSTORMING AND AFFINITY DIAGRAMS: AN EXTENDED POP CULTURE EXAMPLE

As a simple illustration, consider societal leisure and entertainment trends and enterprises that have developed around these, with one segment of such enterprises being the area of conferences and conventions. One type of convention or conference that has gained a rapid and rabid global following is focused around fandom. These conventions or conferences attract large groups of fans or enthusiasts—often numbering 50,000 or more—of characters of specific genres of movies, books, comic books, cartoons, and electronic games. Imagine that a company formed in a given city is capable of hosting such an onslaught of people, many of whom will travel to attend the conference and convention.

There will be a number of issues the company will need to address. A few among many such issues will be funding, venue and availability, security, parking, accommodation, handicap accessibility, attracting recognizable "stars" that attendees will want to see and meet, categories of those stars for which a critical mass will be able to attract thus allowing convention themes, and attraction of vendors and sponsors. As one of many steps in this effort, the company may want to brainstorm as related to these issues and subsequently form an affinity diagram.

Unsurprisingly, many of those involved in company leadership have participated in many such conferences held elsewhere. Conference viability is driven foremost by fan attendance and fan attendance is driven by several factors such as appearances with photoshoot and autograph opportunities by specific celebrities and celebrities from specific movies or television programs; specific cosplay opportunities; and appearances of specific authors or comic book artists. Sponsor recruitment, vendor attraction, and cosplay opportunities are important to conference success and are driven in large by the same factors. After consulting with leadership of similar conferences, conference leadership elected to brainstorm around authors, actors, and artists associated with adventure, fantasy, and science fiction movies. Brainstorming results are portrayed in Figure 14.1.

Conference organizers subsequently engage in the process of organizing these ideas into affinity groupings, with Figure 14.2 providing the product of this effort.

Proceeding from the top right corner of Figure 14.2, we can see that a large group of the ideas are associated with works by former Oxford University Professor J.R.R. Tolkien (1892–1973), *The Hobbit* and *The Lord of the Rings Trilogy*. Similarly, in the lower right corner of the affinity diagram, a large number of ideas were generated that are associated with the seven books in *The Chronicles of Narnia* series by Tolkien's friend and colleague, C.S. Lewis (1898–1963). Highly successful movies associated with these enduringly popular works of both Tolkien and Lewis are relatively recent as are television series or movies associated with many of the other works/ authors identified during the brainstorming process, namely various movies and television series based on comic book characters from both the *DC Universe*™ and *Marvel Constellation*™ of superheroes, the *Game of Thrones* book series by George R.R. Martin, the *Indiana Jones* movies

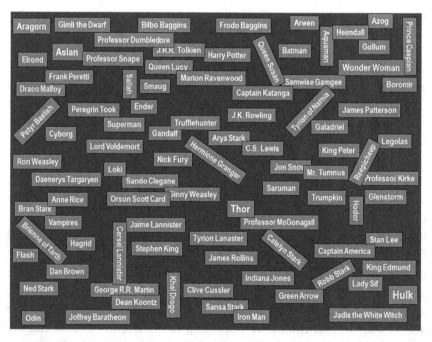

**FIGURE 14.1**
Brainstormed adventure, fantasy, and science fiction convention ideas.

**FIGURE 14.2**
Affinity diagram for brainstormed ideas.

and books, the highly popular *Harry Potter* series of books and movies by J.K. Rowling, and books—some with associated movies—by various popular authors.

Note that to this juncture, numerous ideas have been generated via brainstorming, and these ideas have been organized into logical groupings using an affinity diagram approach. No formal priorities among these ideas or groupings of ideas have been determined however, nor have formal courses of action been decided. These will be examined next.

## INTERRELATIONSHIP DIGRAPHS: CAUSE-AND-EFFECT RELATIONSHIPS

Consider again the case of the conference cited in the prior section, with the issue to be examined as "factors critical to holding a successful conference" of the sort described. A few of the factors examined, with the aim of identifying cause-and-effect or cause-and-consequence

**TABLE 14.2**

Factors Thought to be Critical to Conference Success

| Factor | Description |
|---|---|
| A | Costume play (cosplay) themes, opportunities, and events. |
| B | Movies and characters emphasized. |
| C | Television series and characters emphasized. |
| D | Book/series and characters emphasized. |
| E | Comic books and characters emphasized. |
| F | Authors and genres represented in attendance. |
| G | Actors/actresses and characters portrayed who will be in attendance. |
| H | Merchandise available for purchase. |
| I | Autograph and photo opportunities available to participants. |
| J | Number of registrants, registration levels (e.g., VIP, Gold, Silver, Participant), limits per registration level, and privileges by level. |

relationships among them, are identified in Table 14.2 and will be used to illustrate construction and interpretation of an interrelationship digraph (ID). The resulting ID is presented in Figure 14.3.

IDs are intended to identify cause-and-effect relationships among qualitative elements or issues. There are two primary forms of IDs, with the form illustrated in Figure 14.3 providing a matrix representation. IDs are constructed such that the various issues to be examined form both the rows and columns of the matrix.

| Conference Success Factors | A | B | C | D | E | F | G | H | I | J | IN | OUT | TOTAL |
|---|---|---|---|---|---|---|---|---|---|---|---|---|---|
| A |  | ⇐ | ⇐ | ⇐ | ⇐ |  | ⇐ | ⇑ | ⇑ | ⇑ | 5 | 3 | 8 |
| B | ⇑ |  |  | ⇐ | ⇐ | ⇑ | ⇑ | ⇑ | ⇑ | ⇑ | 2 | 6 | 8 |
| C | ⇑ |  |  | ⇐ | ⇐ | ⇑ | ⇑ | ⇑ | ⇑ | ⇑ | 2 | 6 | 8 |
| D | ⇑ | ⇑ | ⇑ |  |  | ⇑ | ⇑ | ⇑ | ⇑ | ⇑ | 0 | 8 | 8 |
| E | ⇑ | ⇑ | ⇑ |  |  | ⇑ | ⇑ | ⇑ | ⇑ | ⇑ | 0 | 8 | 8 |
| F |  | ⇐ | ⇐ | ⇐ | ⇐ |  | ⇑ | ⇑ | ⇑ | ⇑ | 4 | 4 | 8 |
| G | ⇑ | ⇐ | ⇐ | ⇐ | ⇐ | ⇐ |  | ⇑ | ⇑ | ⇑ | 5 | 4 | 9 |
| H | ⇐ | ⇐ | ⇐ | ⇐ | ⇐ | ⇐ | ⇐ |  | ⇐ |  | 8 | 0 | 8 |
| I | ⇐ | ⇐ | ⇐ | ⇐ | ⇐ | ⇐ | ⇐ | ⇑ |  | ⇑ | 7 | 2 | 9 |
| J | ⇐ | ⇐ | ⇐ | ⇐ | ⇐ | ⇐ | ⇐ |  | ⇐ |  | 8 | 0 | 8 |

(Columns A–J labeled under **FACTORS**; IN, OUT, TOTAL labeled under **ARROWS**; rows labeled under **FACTORS**.)

**FIGURE 14.3**

Interrelationship digraph for conference success factors.

Constructing an ID matrix consists of following a sequence used to populate the matrix. This sequence is described as follows:

- Proceeding across the columns of each row of the matrix, one-by-one, and asking a simple question: "Does the row factor cause/enable the corresponding column factor?"
- If the answer to the question is "yes," a causal (upward pointing) arrow (⇧) is entered in the cell. If the answer to the question is "no," the cell is left empty.
- This process continues row-by-row until this question has been addressed for each cell in the matrix.
- Once the table has been fully swept through in a row-by-row manner, it is completed by recording an "is caused/enabled by" (inward pointing) arrow (⇐) in the mirror image cells.

As an illustration of completing a mirror image cell, consider the question "Does A cause G?" That is, "Do cosplay opportunities, themes, and events cause conference participation by actors and/or actresses?" The answer to this question was "no," and hence—initially—the row A, column G cell in Figure 14.3 was left empty. However, when the G row was completed and the question, "Does G cause A?" or "Does the actor/actress participation in the conference create cosplay opportunities, themes, and events?" resulted in a "yes" answer, then an "out" or causal arrow (⇧) was entered in the cell at the intersection of row G and column A. Once this arrow was entered, the companion "caused/enabled by" arrow (⇐) was entered in the cell at the intersection of the A row and G column.

As the row and column elements are qualitative in nature, it is not uncommon to form arguments such as "B and E cause one another." When this occurs, the individual or team constructing the interrelationship digraph must resolve "which of these is the stronger cause."

As an aid to interpreting the interrelationship digraph, it is common to add three columns to the table—one each for the number of caused by (⇐) arrows, number of causal arrows (⇧), and total number of arrows that are associated with the row factor. A factor with which a large number of causal arrows (⇧) are associated commonly functions as a key enabler of other factors; a factor with a large number of "in" or caused by arrows (⇐) will ordinarily indicate a potential bottleneck or obstacle; and a factor with a large but mixed total number of arrows tends to simply indicate a key factor that is in some instances an enabler and in other instances an enabler or obstacle.

Relative to our example, conference revenue is driven largely by the number of conference registrants and, as a factual statement, merchandise sold, and services provided—including photo opportunities and autographed photos, and other autographed items. Such conferences are primarily attended by enthusiasts of specific movies, television series, comic books, and books. Thus, authors and artists of these works, together with actors portraying characters in these works, provide the main means of attracting fans and selling merchandise and services to those fans. These are key enablers of conference success. Knowing which books, comic books, movies, and television series to emphasize will inform decisions concerning the talent pool of authors, actors, and artists from which conference organizers should recruit.

## NOMINAL GROUP TECHNIQUE: A METHOD FOR ARRIVING AT GROUP CONSENSUS

Although ultimate responsibility for a decision and its consequences may reside with a single individual, decisions are often made by groups or teams. Decisions often require selection of one option or course of action from among several alternatives. The specific decision made and the quality of that decision is commonly guided by how knowledgeable and informed the decision maker or decision-making body is, the amount of risk and uncertainty involved, the reward or consequences of the decision, ease of implementation, and various additional factors.

When a group (team) is either responsible for selection or recommendation of an alternative from among several possibilities, it is natural that some differences of opinion or perspective among team members will arise so that harmonization of those perspectives is required. Harmonization, more commonly referred to as consensus, usually results from a combination of conversation or debate, collaboration, and making concessions in some areas to secure support in other areas. There are many possible approaches to group and individual decision making that vary greatly relative to their complexity, reliability, and amount of transparency involved.

One simple procedure that may be used when there are a relatively large number of alternatives from which to choose is to simply list pros and cons for each decision or action and choose from among alternatives based on these. Still another simple group decision-making tool is multi-voting (Bens, 2012; Kessler, 1995), wherein each member of the group or team is assigned a specific number of "votes"—e.g., five—that they may distribute in any way they choose across the various alternatives, with the winning (or top few) alternatives being the one(s) receiving the most votes. The "votes" are often represented physically as "sticky dots." A team member could, to illustrate, have five votes to distribute across several alternatives and could assign three of those votes to one alternative, one vote each to two other alternatives, and no votes to the remaining alternatives. Once all members have voted, the vote tally for each alternative would be determined and the one or few alternatives emphasized thereafter would be the ones receiving the most votes. For example, in our conference example, each member of the organizing committee might be given five votes to distribute across Factors A through G and I cited in Table 14.2 with the few factors receiving the most total votes obtaining the most subsequent attention. This could lead, e.g., to an emphasis on attracting actors from specific movies and television series, with lesser emphasis or perhaps even no emphasis given to (some of the) other factors.

Multi-voting and use of pros and cons lists are simple group decision-making approaches and may be used to reach a "final" decision or may be used simply to screen a larger number of alternatives with the aim of narrowing these to a lesser number of alternatives. This reduced set of alternatives might then be more carefully scrutinized by the team or group using some other, more detailed method to assess and select from alternatives.

Two, often used group decision-making approaches that can be used to facilitate the harmonization process and that are more detailed are the analytic hierarchy process or AHP (Saaty, 2008) and the nominal group technique or NGT (Claxton, Ritchie, and Zaichkowsky, 1980). Because it employs a very transparent group decision-making process, is straightforward to use, and is easily adapted to other uses, the nominal group technique will be discussed and illustrated. Although it is described here as a group decision-making approach, it is often described as a prioritization approach or tool since it is commonly used not to arrive at a single decision or alternative, but rather to prioritize (rank order) the considered alternatives. Steps in the NGT process are listed in Table 14.3.

To illustrate the use of NGT, the conference example cited previously will be revisited. Suppose that the committee is composed of four individuals:

**TABLE 14.3**

Nominal Group Technique (NGT) Group Decision-Making Steps

| NGT Step | Description or purpose |
|---|---|
| 1 | Generate the list of alternatives that will be considered by the group. |
| 2 | Clarify the meaning of each alternative. |
| 3 | If there are any alternatives that essentially duplicate other alternatives, determine which duplicate to retain and which to eliminate. |
| 4 | Assign letters A, B, C … to the alternatives and record both the alternatives and their corresponding letters in a location that is clearly visible to group members. |
| 5 | If, or as appropriate, state and clarify any criteria against which the alternatives will be assessed. |
| 6 | Each member should then individually and without influence from other group members prioritize the alternatives by ranking them from 1 to $n$, where $n$ is the number of alternatives prioritized. In using this approach, $n$ is the most highly prioritized alternative (bigger ranks indicate higher priority) and 1 is the lowest priority alternative. There are no ties allowed, only the numbers 1 through $n$. Represent the total for any specific alternative by $T$. |
| 7 | Add the priority ratings received by each alternative across all group members. Record these totals for each alternative. Represent the number of group members by $k$. As such, the smallest total possible for any alternative will be $k$ and the largest possible total will be $nk$. |
| 8 | The total of the priority ratings for each group member should be $n(n+1)/2$ so that—with $k$ group members—the total sum of ratings across all alternatives and all group member is $S = kn(n+1)/2$.<br>For each alternative, divide and record the proportion of total priority ratings received, that is $P = T/S$. If desired, multiply $P$ by 100 to yield the percentage received by each alternative. |
| 9 | Some NGT users find it useful to allocate some fixed number of points across the alternatives, e.g., 10 or 20 or perhaps 50 or 100. The choice is up to the group and is typically related to the number of alternatives prioritized, so that this value may be 10 for 6 or fewer alternatives, 20 for 7–14 alternatives, and 50 or 100 for more than 14 alternatives, again, this number is more a preference of the group rather than backed by any scientific criteria. To determine how many points are allocated to a given alternative, $Z$, simply multiply $P$ by $A$, that is, $Z = AP$. |
| 10 | It is likely that the $Z$ values determined in step 9 will not be whole numbers. If whole numbers are more appealing to the group, then the $Z$ values may be rounded to the nearest whole number, $R$. That is: $R = round(Z)$. |
| 11 | The relative priority of the various alternatives is represented by any of $T$, $P$, $Z$, or $R$ with the choice of which of these to use left to the group or perhaps guided by software or tradition. |

**TABLE 14.4**

Nominal Group Technique Prioritization of Conference Success Factors

| Alternative (Factor) | Group Member and Priority Rankings | | | | Total | Percent Priority | Weighted Priority | Rounded Priority |
|---|---|---|---|---|---|---|---|---|
| | Karin | Rahim | Søren | Camilla | T | P × 100 | Z | R |
| A | 2 | 3 | 2 | 3 | 10 | 6.9% | 1.38 | 1 |
| B | 8 | 7 | 8 | 8 | 31 | 21.5% | 4.30 | 4 |
| C | 7 | 8 | 7 | 7 | 29 | 20.1% | 4.02 | 4 |
| D | 4 | 5 | 5 | 5 | 19 | 13.2% | 2.64 | 3 |
| E | 5 | 4 | 6 | 4 | 19 | 13.2% | 2.64 | 3 |
| F | 1 | 1 | 3 | 2 | 7 | 4.9% | 0.98 | 1 |
| G | 6 | 6 | 4 | 6 | 22 | 15.3% | 3.06 | 3 |
| I | 3 | 2 | 1 | 1 | 7 | 4.9% | 0.98 | 1 |
| **Totals** | **36** | **36** | **36** | **36** | **144** | **100% \*** | **20** | **20** |

Karin, Rahim, Søren, and Camilla. It is the first such conference the city will host, and it is important to choose wisely what to emphasize from among alternatives A through G and I as recorded in Table 14.2. The committee will use NGT to prioritize among these alternatives. The results of the NGT are reported in Table 14.4. In creating the rightmost four columns of Table 14.4, it is useful to first identify $k = 4$ group members, $n = 8$ alternatives to prioritize, and $S = kn(n+1)/2 = 4(8)(9)/2 = 144$. Given that there are nine alternatives to prioritize, the value $A = 20$ will be used while noting again that this value is not rooted in a scientific principle, but rather in experience.

A quick perusal of the priority rankings of the four organizing committee members reveals generally strong agreement. Recalling what the various Factors A through G and I represent, it appears that the organizing committee will dedicate careful attention to determination of which movies and television series and which characters in these should be emphasized (Factors B and C). Having made these determinations, NGT results indicate that attention should then be turned to recruitment of actors and actresses who portray key or popular characters in those movies and television series (Factor G). Afterwards and of similar importance will be the identification of books, book series, and comic books and characters therein to be emphasized (Factors D and E).

Significant disagreement among group members is most often indicated by very different priority rankings across members. Before assuming significant disagreement, it is wise to first determine where all members have approached the priority ranking activity in the same way since it is relatively common for one or more members to "reverse" the scale: remember $n$ is the highest priority alternative and 1 the lowest priority alternative, but many people are accustomed to precisely the opposite approach. As such, this is a first point to check when it *appears* there may be significant disagreement. True disagreement will ordinarily require substantial dialog.

# 15

## Customer-Driven Improvement and Innovation Processes: Concept Generation, Selection, and Deployment

In the preceding two chapters, the value of outside-the-box thinking with the aims of generating, organizing, and prioritizing ideas was addressed. Generic, highly flexible processes and tools able to advance these aims were introduced and examples of their use provided. Given their flexibility, these processes and tools can be used for many purposes, either in isolation or in consort, and quality management literature as well as other literature is replete with cases illustrating their application and value.

The power of these tools and processes is magnified when one feeds on the results of another, and in the present chapter it is assumed that results from their application will energize generation of multiple product or service concepts. Once concepts have been generated, it is important to select one or more from these to deploy. As such, this chapter addresses generation of multiple process, product, or service concepts. Subsequent chapters address selection from among multiple concepts of one or more concepts that will be deployed, as well as a common means of concept deployment that is referred to as quality function deployment or QFD (Griffin and Hauser, 1993; Matzler and Hinterhuber, 1998) and its primary tool, the house of quality or HOQ (Hauser and Clausing, 1988; Vairaktarakis, 1999).

### BRING YOUR TOYS: JUMPSTARTING CONCEPT GENERATION

Various situations may motivate pursuit of this sequence. Among these are the need to improve a given process or to introduce significant product, service, or product innovation. Equally, social or technological development on one hand, or stakeholder demands—including customer demands—on another hand, may dictate that the enterprise must design new or alternative products or services. The concept generation process begins with a set of expressed needs and target specifications and is intended to provide enterprises organized means capable of delivering improvements, innovations, and designs to meet the needs supplying that motivation. Traditionally these needs are referred to as customer needs so that the express voice of the customer is critical to successful concept generation; in principle, however, needs representing the voice of society and the ecological voice may also be solicited and included in the concept generation process.

There are many concept generation processes that range from highly methodical to highly creative. Although a comprehensive discourse on concept generation is beyond the scope of this work, presentations of several highly effective, yet complex, concept generation processes can be found in a variety of readily accessible resources (Herstatt and Von Hippel, 1992; Liu et al., 2003; Ulrich and Eppinger, 2015).

Irrespective of the specific concept generation approach used, the inherent nature of concept generation is a creative one that can be advanced by numerous aids—toys, so to speak—that are intended to enable team members to be individually and collectively more creative. Among useful aids are pencils, paper, paper cups, paper plates, markers, sticky notes, paper clips, glue, toothpicks, Lego® bricks, Styrofoam, wood, nails, hammers, tape, string, scissors, clay, and more. Having these or similar resources on hand both enables and encourages inexpensive physical and visual representation of ideas or concepts, especially for physical products, that can be easily manipulated or amended. These might be regarded as basic prototypes.

While the resources cited are useful concept generation aids, ordinarily these will be embedded in a more formal concept generation structure. The concept generation structure presented herein progresses through five stages and is simultaneously useful, straight-forward, and transparent, yet is one that allows product or service development teams to be methodically or structurally creative.

## CONCEPT GENERATION

Five-stage concept generation now discussed is portrayed in Figure 15.1 and is initiated by first clarifying the product, service or process

# (A) POINT COVERING

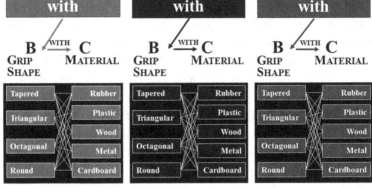

**FIGURE 15.1**
Concept diagram for simplified pen design.

improvement, innovation or design problem/opportunity at hand with the goal of ensuring common understanding. Decomposing the problem into smaller, bite-sized pieces can be helpful at this stage of concept generation, as can riveting focus on solving the most critical components of the problem.

Once clarity is attained, two complementary searches for full or partial solutions to the problem will be undertaken. One of these searches is an external one that seeks to identify full or partial solutions to critical sub-problems that might be available in existing literature or patents, might be found through external benchmarking, or may be found in the knowledge or habits of experts and lead users. The other search is internally oriented and relies to the individual and collective knowledge and creativity of team members. The fourth concept generation stage requires systematic exploration of various ways in which the intelligence gathered in the internal and external search processes might be parsed and combined to generate product, service, or process concepts—with the likely result that many concepts will be eliminated early on and only a relative few will advance to the stage of receiving in-depth consideration. The final concept generation stage requires reflection on the specific concept generation journey undertaken with the purpose of ensuring that all reasonable path alternatives have been comprehensively probed.

## A "Simple" Concept Generation Illustration

To illustrate use of this five-stage process, consider something as apparently mundane as designing a (writing) pen.

Concept generation begins with a set of customer/stakeholder needs and target specifications and ends with a set of product, service, or process concepts from which a final selection will be made. As such, it is possible this task of designing (specifically) a pen has been too narrowly focused, at least initially, since there may be many means of meeting the customer/ stakeholder need ordinarily fulfilled by a pen. If this is the case, the range of potential solutions (concepts) generated is likely to be overly narrow, possibly excluding more creative or attractive alternatives.

To expand the range of initial possibilities, it may be desirable, for example, to position the eventual product/service as one enabling written communication. This expands the range of solutions to ones that may include, at least in theory, electronic possibilities such as voice translation, keyboard entry, optical scanning, visual translation (e.g., of movement), or perhaps even something as unconventional as "telepathic." This latter possibility is intended to illustrate the point of being open to highly novel, full or partial solutions, where partial solutions are often referred to as concept fragments. At the same time, this approach does not preclude more conventional solutions associated with the act of physically writing or drawing (e.g., pen and paper) that which it is desired to communicate or otherwise express.

Concept generation's first stage demands problem clarification. As an example of problem clarification, in moving forward with the example, assume that relevant and sufficient discourse has occurred, leading to the decision to focus on design of a pen (writing implement). Further assume it has been determined that the pen will transfer ink from the pen to whatever surface it is used to write or draw upon. To connect this to the conference setting example used in Chapter 14, suppose that the resulting pen will be distributed to each conference participant to be used, ostensibly, for collecting autographs. Additionally, assume that the resulting pen design is sufficiently flexible so as to enable straight-forward customization for other commercial uses, so that the design will be marketed to the organizers of similar conferences. Conferences of the sort discussed in the prior chapter often attract 50,000 or more participants, many of whom travel great distances, spending money on airline travel, rental cars, hotels, autographs, photo opportunities, merchandise, and more. In other words, the cost of registration for such conferences is often low in comparison with the total amount of money spent: tickets may cost $100 and more, whereas the full cost of participation can easily surpass $1,500 with the full economic impact of the large conferences or conventions of this sort approximating $200,000,000.

A further consideration that is involved in problem clarification is to decompose critical requirements and functions of that which is designed, in this instance, a pen. Relative to a pen, these include a means of covering the point of the pen to prevent ink from drying in its cartridge or container, the shape of the grip by which a user will hold the pen, and material from which the pen will be made. Since the purpose of this discussion is to simply illustrate concept generation, the preceding list of considerations will be sufficient; however, various additional factors would ultimately need to be addressed, such as whether the ink used should be "permanent" or "erasable," color(s) of ink to be used, general quality level of the pen, cost range and sales price ranges, and whether to enable simple product variations.

Once the problem has been clarified, both internal and external searches are likely to be conducted. Although it is possible to engage in patent and literature searches, it is more likely that the external search in this example will be limited to examination of a (potentially large) number of pens already in use in the marketplace. The internal search, however, is likely to be one of many opportunities a team—the conference organizing team in this case—will use to engage in organized ideation, including brainstorming. Together these searches will be used to identify alternative possibilities (partial solutions) for each of the critical design considerations identified:

1. Pen point covering—separate cap, twistable point, clickable (three possibilities);
2. Type of grip: round, octagonal, triangular, tapered (four possibilities);
3. Grip/pen material: rubber, plastic, wood, metal, cardboard (five possibilities).

Note that, even in this highly simplified example, 60 different concepts can be generated, with each of the 3×4×5 distinct combinations of design considerations (A), (B), and (C) representing a unique concept. This can be seen in the concept diagram of Figure 15.1.

It must be noted that in a more comprehensive consideration of pen design that many more design considerations, each with multiple possible alternatives to choose from, would deliver a far larger number of pen concepts from which to select. This dilemma implies that it is particularly useful, when possible, to "trim the tree" represented by the concept diagram. This is done by eliminating one or more possibilities for a given concept aspect as early in the concept generation process as is practical. For example, it may be that the conference organizing committee makes the decision that a capped pen is undesirable, in which case all 20 (yellow) combinations of grip options with material options in Figure 15.1 can be eliminated from consideration. Similar action can be taken multiple times so that the conference organizing committee might further determine that it does not want to provide a plastic pen to participants. This would further enable reducing four grip options connected to plastic for each of the twistable and clickable point covering approaches, hence removing eight more concepts from consideration. In this way, the original 60 possible concepts would be reduced to 32 that might be examined more closely.

Ultimately, the number of process, product, or service concepts must be reduced to a manageable number that can be more carefully considered. This is commonly done in two steps: concept screening followed by concept scoring.

# 16

## Customer-Driven Improvement and Innovation Processes: Concept Selection

If more than (roughly) a dozen concepts must be evaluated more carefully, then it is common practice to quickly winnow the number to a manageable number using the process of multi-voting described in Chapter 15. Once the number of concepts to be considered is no more than—again, approximately—one dozen, a more formal concept screening approach may be used that is likely to be followed by concept scoring.

## CONCEPT SCREENING

To apply concept screening to the remaining concepts, (usually) multiple criteria must be identified that are applicable to each concept and by which each concept can be evaluated. Criteria should be at similar levels of detail, should enable objective assessment, and should be able to discern differences among concepts relative to a standard concept. The standard concept can be an existing comparable product, process, or service and can be selected— including arbitrarily selected—from among the concepts to be compared.

As with criteria, the various concepts should be described at similar levels of detail, though not necessarily in the same manner. Concepts may be detailed in any one or a combination of several forms, including written description, sketches, or physical models.

It is usually the case that both concepts and criteria are provided at a relatively crude level of detail at this early stage and all criteria are treated as though they are of equal or similar importance.

Screening is then carried out by comparing each concept to the standard concept on each of the identified criteria. Relative to each criterion, the concept being compared will be rated (assessed) as better (+1), similar (0), or worse than (–1) the standard concept. These values are then summed across the various criteria for each concept and the sum is recorded. These sums are then used as directional aids for each concept, after which the organizing committee, team, or individual conducting the screening will assess each concept to determine whether it should be dropped from further consideration, refined, combined with one or more other concepts, or advanced directly for further consideration.

The concept screening process is illustrated in Table 16.1 in which it is assumed that eight (8) different pen concepts—A, B, C, D, E, F, G, and H—will be screened, using six different criteria—1, 2, 3, 4, 5, and 6. For example, Concept B could be that the point of the pen is exposed by clicking and has a triangular grip (shape) that is of rubber composition (material). Similarly, Criteria 3 might be related to the durability of a given concept. For discussion purposes, Concept A will be designated as the standard.

Various observations can be extracted from Table 16.1 to aid decisions as to how or whether to continue consideration of the various pen concepts. Among these are that a "+" (–) rating indicates only that a given concept

**TABLE 16.1**

Concept Screening Table for Pen Design

| | | | Concept Screened | | | | | |
|---|---|---|---|---|---|---|---|---|
| Selection Criteria | A Standard | B | C | D | E | F | G | H |
| 1 | 0 | + | + | + | 0 | + | – | + |
| 2 | 0 | + | 0 | + | – | + | + | – |
| 3 | 0 | 0 | 0 | + | 0 | + | – | + |
| 4 | 0 | + | 0 | – | 0 | 0 | – | 0 |
| 5 | 0 | – | 0 | – | + | + | + | + |
| 6 | 0 | 0 | + | + | + | – | 0 | + |
| Sum of +s | 0 | 3 | 2 | 4 | 2 | 4 | 2 | 4 |
| Sum of 0s | 6 | 2 | 4 | 0 | 3 | 1 | 1 | 1 |
| Sum of –s | 0 | 1 | 0 | 2 | 1 | 1 | 3 | 1 |
| Net Score | KB | 1 | 2 | 2 | 1 | 3 | 1 | 3 |
| Rank | 7 | 4 | 4 | 4 | 6 | 1 | 8 | 1 |
| Continue | No | Combine | Refine | Combine | No | Yes | No | Yes |

rates better (worse) than the standard concept relative to the criteria being assessed. In other words, "not all +'s (–'s) are created equally," it merely appears so due to our crude comparison scheme. Similarly, not all concepts with the same net scores may be equally preferred since those scores may arise in many ways. Even if there are identical patterns across the +, 0, and –, subtle or perhaps not so subtle differences will exist among the concepts themselves and hence the reasons behind why +, 0, or – judgments arose. This can be seen for Concepts G and H, the two top-rated concepts, along with Concepts B, C, and D, each of which had a net score of 2 that were derived in very different ways. Beyond these comments, it is unlikely that all criteria are of equal importance—another factor that might help to differentiate among concepts. Such concerns are better addressed by the more refined methods used in concept scoring.

Given preceding comments, decisions concerning each of the concepts can be explained as follows. Concept A, the standard, need not be retained as—collectively considered—the remaining concepts are superior to A on each criterion; a comment implying that there will be ways to leverage or combine the best aspects of the various concepts to provide one that is uniformly better than A. Concept B is the only concept to score better than each of the others on the fourth criterion—a factor that may or may not be important, depending on the relative weight of the various assessment criteria. In the simple case of concept screening where all criteria are considered equally important, this suggests that Concept B should be carefully evaluated to determine how or whether its advantage relative to the fourth criterion can be used to improve any of the remaining concepts.

Concept C is the lone concept having no negative assessments relative to Concept A, the standard. That alone does not assure that Concept C will receive further consideration, although the final row of Table 16.1 indicates that Concept C will be refined and further considered. Subject to some level of exploration, it might as easily be argued that other concepts can be combined in one or more ways that match or dominate Concept C relative to each criterion since—relative to the six criteria—at least one of Concepts B, D, E, F, G, and H score positively—an indication that it may be possible to create a concept that will yield only positive comparisons against standard Concept A, whereas Concept C scores neutrally relative to four of the criteria and positively relative to the two remaining criteria.

These sorts of arguments should be made on a concept-by-concept basis. Stated differently, decisions concerning any given concept as to whether to refine, combine with one or more other concepts, drop from further consideration, or to continue to consider should not be based solely on counts of −, 0, or + assessments. It is such argumentation that ultimately delivers the concept-by-concept decisions recorded in the bottom row of Table 16.1.

## CONCEPT SCORING

On relatively rare occasions, screening alone may yield the one concept that will be developed. More commonly, concept screening is used to reduce a larger number of concepts to a smaller number of concepts, a relative handful, that will then be described in greater detail, using criteria that are both more refined and weighted according to relative importance and assessed using a more refined scale. This more careful assessment is referred to as concept scoring.

The more refined assessment scale that is commonly applied with respect to each criterion is described in Table 16.2.

Multiple approaches are available that can be used to weight the various criteria. As but one example, once the criteria to be applied have been identified and suitably refined and described, design team members could use a nominal group technique (NGT) to distribute an agreed upon number of points, say $P$, across the criteria. The number of criteria used is typically small so that $P$ is likely to be 10 if only a handful of criteria are used, but could be some arbitrarily larger number, such as 25, 50, or 100 for progressively larger numbers of criteria. If $k$ criteria are used for concept scoring purposes, then the NGT points assigned to each criterion will be $P_1, P_2, \ldots, P_k$, where each of these is greater than zero and in total sum up to $P$.

### TABLE 16.2

Rating Scale Commonly Used in Concept Scoring

| Rating | Value and Description |
|---|---|
| 1 | Much worse on the assessed criterion than the standard concept. |
| 2 | Worse on the assessed criterion than the standard concept. |
| 3 | Same or similar on the assessed criterion than the standard concept. |
| 4 | Better on the assessed criterion than the standard concept. |
| 5 | Much better on the assessed criterion than the standard concept. |

Based on design team preferences, these points may or may not be rounded to whole numbers. Regardless of whether rounding is or is not used, concept scoring will transform (normalize) these point values into weights that are proportions of the total points allotted and that can be represented as decimal values. These will of course each be greater than zero and will collectively add to one. If these weights for the k criteria are symbolized by $W_1, W_2, \ldots, W_k$, then the weight for the *i*th criteria, $W_i$ where i = 1, 2, ..., k is simply the decimal representation of $W_i = P_i/P$.

If there are C concepts, $C_1, C_2, \ldots, C_C$, then the *score*, $S_j$, for the *j*th concept where j = 1, 2, ... C is determined by first comparing $C_j$ to the standard concept on each criterion using the scale provided in Table 16.2 to determine the comparative ratings for each criterion, $R_i$ where i = 1, 2, ..., k. The ratings are then multiplied by the corresponding weights, $W_1$ through $W_k$, after which results are added to obtain $S_j$. This yields the following expression for the score of the ith concept:

$$S_j = \sum_{i=1}^{k} R_i W_i$$

To illustrate concept scoring in the pen design example, the following is assumed:

- Concepts A, E, and G have been dropped from further consideration.
- Concepts B and D have been combined to yield a new concept that is designated as BD.
- We have designated new concept BD as the standard to which others are compared.
- Concept C has been refined with resulting designation of C+.
- Concepts F and H have been refined to yield F+ and H+ and have been advanced for deeper consideration.
- The original six criteria, together with other concept (product) considerations, have led to a new, refined, and more explicit set of five criteria recorded as 1', 2', 3', 4', and 5'. While these criteria are related to the ones used in concept screening, they need not be in specific correspondence either numerically or materially to those prior criteria.
- The product design team has used nominal group technique or perhaps an alternative approach to weight the criteria. These weights are positive and add to one.

**TABLE 16.3**

Concept Scoring Table for Pen Design

| Criterion | Weight | Concept Scored | | | | | | | |
| --- | --- | --- | --- | --- | --- | --- | --- | --- | --- |
| | | BD (Reference) | | C+ | | F+ | | H+ | |
| | | Rating | Weighted Score | Rating | Weighted Score | Rating | Weighted Score | Rating | Weighted Score |
| 1' | 0.35 | 3 | 1.05 | 3 | 1.05 | 5 | 1.75 | 4 | 1.40 |
| 2' | 0.20 | 3 | 0.60 | 4 | 0.80 | 5 | 1.00 | 3 | 0.60 |
| 3' | 0.25 | 3 | 0.75 | 3 | 0.75 | 4 | 1.00 | 5 | 1.25 |
| 4' | 0.15 | 3 | 0.45 | 2 | 0.30 | 2 | 0.30 | 2 | 0.30 |
| 5' | 0.05 | 3 | 0.15 | 5 | 0.25 | 2 | 0.10 | 4 | 0.20 |
| Total Score | | 3.00 | | 3.15 | | 4.15 | | 3.75 | |
| Rating | | 4 | | 3 | | 1 | | 2 | |
| Action | | Leverage Criterion Four Advantage | | Leverage Criterion Five Advantage | | Best Design Combine if Possible | | Leverage Criterion Three Advantage | |

- The rating scale used to compare each concept to the standard concept on a criterion-by-criterion basis is 1 = much worse than the standard, 2 = worse than the standard, 3 = comparable to the standard, 4 = better than the standard, and 5 = much better than the standard.

Concept scoring results for the pen design example are reported in Table 16.3 and can be interpreted in the following way:

- The reference concept, Concept BD, is the lowest rated of the four designs by a relatively large margin; however, it is the most highly ranked design with respect to criterion 4'. The weight assigned to criterion 4' is lower than that of all but criterion 5'. While Concept BD will not be pursued further, it is worthwhile to determine whether there is a reasonable way to incorporate whatever element or elements of the concept that led to its higher performance on criterion 4' into one or more of the other concepts.
- A similar comment can be made with respect to Concept C+ which, while rated as only marginally better than Concept BD, was more highly rated than all other concepts on Criterion 5'. If possible then, it would be desirable to identify and incorporate into Concept F+ or Concept H+ that which led to the superior rating of Concept C+ with respect to Criterion 5'.
- While Concept F+ is the most highly rated of the four pen concepts overall, and especially so with respect to Criteria 1' and 2', it may still be possible to improve upon F+ by identifying and adapting those elements of the other three concepts that led to Concept H+ outperforming F+ on Criterion 3', Concept BD outperforming Concept F+ on Criterion 4', and Concept C+ outperforming Concept F+ on Criterion 5'. For future reference purposes, we will symbolize the final concept at F++. This is the likely strategy the design team would pursue moving forward.

# 17

## Customer-Driven Improvement and Innovation Processes: The House of Quality and Quality Function Deployment

Once a specific concept with which to move forward has been selected, the specifics of the design that will be produced must be determined. There are alternative means by which this can be accomplished, with quality function deployment (QFD) as a commonly used approach (Akao and Mazur, 2003). Residing at the heart of QFD is the house of quality (HOQ), its principle tool (Hauser, 1993). QFD discussion herein is limited to a basic level, and the interested reader seeking a more nuanced discussion is referred to the outstanding work by Xie, Goh, and Tan (2003).

The historic intention of QFD is to carry the voice of the customer from concept to customer. A more forward-thinking-and-acting approach is to eschew this traditional cradle-to-grave product design mentality that, essentially, stops with the "death" of the product at the end of its lifecycle and, instead, embraces and employs a circular economy (CE) or cradle-to-cradle (C2C) approach (McDonough and Braungart, 2002b; Murray, Skene, and Haynes, 2017).

Cradle-to-cradle and circular economy concepts are for practical purposes identical, with the idea that the inputs or "raw materials" of a given product can be divided into two primary sorts: technological nutrients and biological nutrients. Each of these has finite supply so that conservation of resources is important to C2C and CE approaches. The goal of CE and C2C product development is to design products so that at the end of their useful lives, full recyclability, reusability, or repurposing of those nutrients should occur. The closer a product and its subsequent progeny come to this goal, the better the product design from CE and C2C perspectives.

Implicit to C2C and CE product design is that such products and their progeny should be produced and used in socially and environmentally responsible ways, using as little material as is responsibly possible. In many ways, C2C and CE can be thought of as representing the ultimate form of Lean production and manufacturing.

Redirecting this discussion to QFD then results in a mindset and approach that could be characterized as "socially and environmentally responsible QFD" or "C2C QFD" or, perhaps more to the point, "QFD for sustainability." This point will be reinforced in the ensuing discussion.

## THE HOUSE OF QUALITY

To move forward, it is important to identify the "whats and hows." These can be regarded as rooms R1 and R2 respectively in the HOQ.

"Whats" are those things the product (or service) must, to varying degrees, fulfill. Traditionally these have been described as customer needs and wants or customer requirements. It is here that other requirements such as social or ecological concerns can be directly incorporated.

Given that these requirements are unlikely to be of equal importance, it is critical to involve the customer and those representing the voice of society and voice of the environment in two ways—not only to identify the whats or requirements, but also to determine the relative importance of these requirements. This is commonly practiced using a rating scale of 1 to 5, where 5 = highly important, 4 = important, 3 = moderately important, 2 = less important, and 1 = least important. Other scales can of course be used, but regardless of the employed scale, the results are referred to as importance ratings and represent room R3 in the HOQ.

Having identified the whats, it is imperative for the enterprise to identify those internally controllable actions and processes that correlate with the whats, and hence that can be used to fulfill the whats. These internally controllable actions and processes referred to as the "hows" are design elements that represent engineering or technical requirements. It is generally desirable for these to be quantitative, and hence quantifiable. The issue is one of how much of each of these should be in a final mixture that is true to the product concept, while also fulfilling the various whats.

The issue of "how much" of a given design element should be included in the final mixture typically gravitates toward one of three solutions: a target value, or a minimum or maximum value within a specified range. Rather than one-by-one determination of design element values, better or best designs result from simultaneous or concurrent optimization of the various design elements. This suggests that, in organizations that possess better analytic capabilities, optimization of the final product design should be pursued by first using QFD to obtain a close approximation to the best design, then fine-tuning this approximation using an optimization method such as response surface analysis (Box and Draper, 1987) or evolutionary operations (Box and Draper, 1998). Non-quantifiable or qualitative design elements are generally features that represent elements of the product concept itself. The list of "how much" values can be thought of as room R4 in the HOQ with these generally represented by a specific numeric value or target (T), with ⇑ when a maximum value within specified limits is desirable, and a ⇓ when a minimum value within specified limits is desirable.

The whats and hows are listed in a table, with the whats representing the rows of the table and the hows recorded in its columns. The first column, either to the right or left of the corresponding whats, is used as a place to record the importance rating for each what. Initially, symbols will be recorded in the body of the table, with the symbol at the intersection of each row and column—that is, the intersection of each what with each how—representing the strength of the relation between the what and how. While another classification system may be used, the strength of a given what-how relationship is typically classified as $S$ = strong, $M$ = moderate, $W$ = weak, or $N$ = none or negligible. While we have used $S$, $M$, $W$, and $N$, the set of symbols used is arbitrary and may be determined by the design team or software, if HOQ/QFD software is used. The portion of the table expressing these relationships is room R5 in the HOQ.

Symbols are used initially so that the design team will focus on what-how relationship strengths. Later numerical values will be substituted for the symbols for strong, moderate, weak, and no and negligible relationships replaced by 9, 3, 1, and 0, respectively. For more mathematically inclined readers, these are $9 = 3^2$, $3 = 3^1$, $1 = 3^0$, and 0. This is merely a customary substitution and other values could be used to represent relationships of various strengths. That said, the intention of using a set of values to replace symbols is to create a reasonable degree of separation in subsequent QFD development, with such separation better enabling the design team to make important decisions.

These values may then be added across each row—that is, across the hows or design elements—to determine the raw ability of the enterprise to adequately fulfill the corresponding expressed customer, social, and ecological needs through the identified design elements. These are referred to as completeness values. Larger completeness values indicate greater enterprise ability to meet a given customer, social, or ecological need, whereas low values indicate that the enterprise may need to identify additional design elements (hows), or may need to modify its objective relative to a given need. A column in the table that reports these values in room R6 in the HOQ. As a supplement to these values, it is common practice to multiply each of the totals by the weight of the corresponding expressed customer, social, and ecological needs and record these in a companion column as room R7 in the HOQ.

Similarly, if these values are added across whats recorded in the rows of the table—that is, across the expressed customer, social, and environmental needs—resulting column totals will indicate the raw technical importance or ability of a given design element or *how* relative to collective fulfillment of those needs. A row with these values can be added to the table to form room R8 in the HOQ. The higher a given total is, the more important the corresponding design element. Design elements associated with low totals are less important to fulfill needs and represent candidates for exclusion or, alternatively, as elements whose values may be conveniently set. A companion row representing room R9 in the HOQ is commonly added to the table that is intended to reveal the weighted technical importance of each design element. The values populating room R9 are calculated column by column (design element by design element) by multiplying one by one the importance ratings for each expressed customer, social, and environmental need by its corresponding numeric strength of the relationship with the design element, then adding these values with higher values representing greater (weighted) technical importance for that design element.

Lastly—relative to expressed customer, social, and ecological needs—design elements are sometimes unrelated to one another, are at other times synergistic, and in some cases conflict with one another. When design elements are unrelated to one another, their values can be separately optimized. When design elements are synergistic or positively correlated, their effects on expressed customer, social, and ecological needs will be multiplicative. These two situations are desirable. The case where design elements are in conflict, and are hence inversely or negatively correlated, is a more troublesome one wherein the design team must identify compromises to make in terms of which needs will be emphasized. These (co-)relationships are not expressed in the highly refined ways associated with statistical correlation coefficients, but rather using a simple three- or five-level symbolic scheme. A five-point scheme could be strong positive relationship (++), positive relationship (+), no relationship (0), negative relationship (–), and strong negative relationship (––). Similarly, a three-point symbolic scheme could be strong relationship (+), no relationship (0), and negative relationship (–). While standard QFD practice will record these as the so-called roof in the HOQ or room R10, it is also possible to record these relationships in the top (or bottom) half of a separate table formed by using the design elements as both the rows and columns of the table.

As examples of these sorts of relationships, consider an automotive manufacturer seeking to design a car subject to varied expressed customer, social, and ecological needs. Among these needs are rapid acceleration; exceptional braking ability; excellent maneuverability; quiet inside when windows and doors are closed; safety in cases of collision; achieves high fuel efficiency; produces low emissions; easy serviceability; durability; quietness while in operation so that noise pollution is minimal; and made for maximum recyclability, reusability, and repurposing. Design elements that deliver rapid acceleration are likely to conflict with those design elements that deliver higher fuel efficiency, lower emissions, and quietness inside when windows and doors are closed, and are hence likely to be negatively correlated. Similarly, design elements rendering a car safer in case of a collision are likely to add weight to the car, thereby negatively impacting its ability to accelerate. Material design elements delivering a car with higher recyclability, reusability, and repurposing levels are likely to be consistent with design elements that deliver lower emissions and greater fuel efficiency so that these design elements are likely to be mutually positively correlated. As an example of design elements that may be weakly related or unrelated are design elements that yield a car that is quiet when the car is in operation, and design elements that yield exceptional braking ability.

## BUILDING THE HOUSE OF QUALITY

An empty mock HOQ displaying rooms R1 through R9, using five customer/social/ecological needs (whats) and four identified design elements (hows), is portrayed in Table 17.1. This table is included herein primarily to indicate the relative positioning of the rooms.

**TABLE 17.1**

House of Quality (HOQ) Denoting Relative Positions of Its Rooms

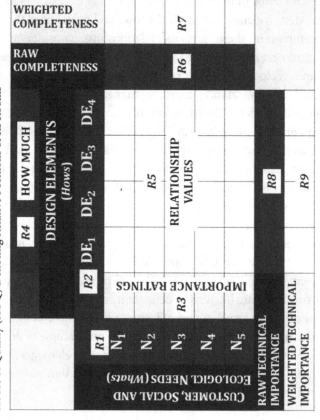

Table 17.2 represents the HOQ with mock importance ratings (R3), design element "how much" values (R4), and relationship values (R5)—rooms that must be completed before numerical values can be substituted for the symbolic relationship values (R5). Once rooms R1 through R5 have been completed and numerical relationship values have been substituted for symbolic ones, the associated raw and weighted completeness and technical importance values of rooms R6 through R9 can be determined. Table 17.3 represents the HOQ with rooms R1 through R9 completed. Finally, the roof of the HOQ or room R10 is portrayed in Table 17.4.

All values and relationships portrayed in Tables 17.2 through 17.4 are contrived and have been used only to illustrate HOQ completion since the HOQ is foundational to QFD. In completing these tables, the simple schemes discussed earlier in this chapter have been used to represent the nature of relationships and their strengths, as well as for the importance ratings for customer, social, and ecological needs.

In examining the content of Table 17.2, it is first noted that within a limited range it is desirable to maximize design element $DE_1$, minimize $DE_4$, and seek specific target levels for each of $DE_2$ and $DE_3$. This information can be found in the "how much" room of the HOQ, room R4.

Further, it may be seen that, for example, there is only a weak relationship between design element $DE_1$ and expressed need $N_2$, implying that the first design element is of relatively little value relative to meeting the second expressed need. Given that the second expressed need is rated as the most important of the whats, it is critical to fulfill this need so that, thankfully, the fourth design element, $DE_4$, is strongly related to this need. Similarly, there is a strong relationship between the fourth design element, $DE_4$, and the fifth expressed need, $N_5$, so that $DE_4$ will be highly useful in fulfilling $N_5$.

As a general statement, fulfilling a given need will generally require that there is at least one strongly related design element or, alternatively, that there are at the least several design elements that are moderately related to the need. The importance of this observation is magnified for more highly rated needs.

The content of Table 17.3 enables determination of how well met a given need or what is and, also, the overall contribution or importance of a given design element. Note first that numerical values have been substituted for corresponding symbolic strength ratings in the white cells at the core of Table 17.3.

Focusing on the fifth expressed need, $N_5$, and adding the numerical strength values across the design elements yields the value of 16 that is

**TABLE 17.2**

House of Quality Including Importance Ratings and Relationship Strengths

| Customer, Social and Ecological Needs (*Whats*) | | Importance Ratings | Design Elements (*Hows*) | | | | Raw Completeness | Weighted Completeness |
|---|---|---|---|---|---|---|---|---|
| | | | $DE_1$ | $DE_2$ | $DE_3$ | $DE_4$ | | |
| $N_1$ | | 4 | N | W | W | S | | |
| $N_2$ | | 5 | W | W | M | S | | |
| $N_3$ | | 2 | M | S | M | N | | |
| $N_4$ | | 1 | N | W | S | W | | |
| $N_5$ | | 3 | M | W | M | S | | |
| Raw Technical Importance | | | | | | | | |
| Weighted Technical Importance | | | | | | | | |

Relationships:
N=None
W=Weak
M=Moderate
S=Strong

**TABLE 17.3**

Completed House of Quality Including Raw and Weighted Completeness and Technical Importance and Completeness Values

| Customer, Social and Ecological Needs (*Whats*) | Importance Ratings | Design Elements (*Hows*) | | | | Raw Completeness | Weighted Completeness |
|---|---|---|---|---|---|---|---|
| | | DE₁ | DE₂ | DE₃ | DE₄ | | |
| $N_1$ | 4 | 0 | 1 | 1 | 9 | 11 | 44 |
| $N_2$ | 5 | 1 | 1 | 3 | 9 | 14 | 70 |
| $N_3$ | 2 | 3 | 9 | 3 | 0 | 15 | 30 |
| $N_4$ | 1 | 0 | 1 | 9 | 1 | 11 | 11 |
| $N_5$ | 3 | 3 | 3 | 3 | 9 | 16 | 48 |
| Raw Technical Importance | | 7 | 13 | 19 | 28 | | |
| Weighted Technical Importance | | 20 | 31 | 43 | 109 | | |

Relationships:
0=None
1=Weak
3=Moderate
9=Strong

**TABLE 17.4**

Roof of the House of Quality Showing Correlations Among Design Elements

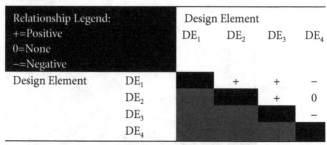

| Relationship Legend:<br>+=Positive<br>0=None<br>−=Negative | | Design Element | | | |
| | | $DE_1$ | $DE_2$ | $DE_3$ | $DE_4$ |
| Design Element | $DE_1$ | | + | + | − |
| | $DE_2$ | | | | + | 0 |
| | $DE_3$ | | | | | − |
| | $DE_4$ | | | | |

recorded in the leftmost green cell in the table, with this value representing the raw overall ability of the enterprise to meet $N_5$ via deployment of the four identified design elements.

Although the design team is perhaps best able to determine "how much is enough" in terms of a given expressed need, it can be noted that the raw completeness value for $N_5$ is the largest such value among the five expressed needs or whats. As such, $N_5$ is the need that can be best met through the identified design elements, although its importance rating is only the middle of the five expressed needs.

Conversely, needs $N_1$ and $N_4$ have the lowest raw completeness values at 11 each, and are hence the needs that the identified design elements have the poorest ability to fulfill. Given that $N_4$ has the lowest importance rating of the expressed needs, this may not be critical and perhaps 11 may be sufficient for the design elements to adequately fulfill this need. This issue is more critical for need $N_1$ as it has the second highest importance rating, and hence the design team must carefully consider whether $N_1$ can be adequately addressed via the identified design elements.

The position taken herein is that raw completeness values are more informative than weighted completeness values. For the HOQ/QFD user preferring weighted completeness values, the rightmost green cell of Table 17.3 is used to illustrate how such values are determined. Computation of weighted completeness values is straightforward and requires only the multiplication of raw completeness values by the importance ratings for the corresponding expressed needs (whats). As an example, the weighted completeness value for the fifth need, $N_5$, is simply WC = 16×3 = 48, as recorded in the rightmost green cell in the table.

Discourse concerning raw and weighted technical importance values is analogous to that concerning completeness. This discussion is advanced by considering the two yellow cells in Table 17.3, with the topmost of these cells representing the raw technical importance of the second design element, $DE_2$, and the lower of these cells representing the weighted technical importance of $DE_2$.

Raw technical importance of $DE_2$ is determined simply by adding the strength ratings of DE2 across the five expressed needs, that is $1 + 1 + 9 + 1 + 1 = 13$ as recorded in the topmost yellow cell in Table 17.3. This value is approximately twice the raw technical importance of design element $DE_1$, two-thirds the raw technical importance of design element $DE_3$, and only one-half the raw technical importance of design element $DE_4$.

These observations indicate that $DE_2$ contributes strongly to fulfilling need $N_3$, but relatively little to fulfilling any of the remaining expressed needs. $DE_4$ is especially valuable to fulfilling expressed needs $N_1$, $N_2$, and $N_5$ but completely unrelated to $N_3$ and only weakly related to $N_4$. With the second greatest raw technical importance rating, $DE_3$ appears to possess good overall ability to address expressed needs. Finally, $DE_1$ is at most moderately related to two expressed needs, weakly related to another, and unrelated to the remaining two needs so that, overall, $DE_1$ is a relatively inert design factor. While this does not of necessity imply that $DE_1$ can be completely ignored, it is a relatively solid indicator that it can be set to a level that is economically, socially, environmentally, or otherwise advantageous to the producer.

As with completeness values, the perspective herein is that raw technical importance values are more informative than weighted technical importance values. Nevertheless, some experienced HOQ and QFD users prefer weighted technical importance values. To compute the weighted technical importance values for a given design element, one must multiply the importance rating for each need by the corresponding relationship strength values of the design element, then add these results.

As an example, the weighted technical importance of design element $DE_2$ is recorded in the lower yellow cell in the table as 31 and is computed as $(4\times1) + (5\times1) + (2\times9) + (1\times1) + (3\times1)$. The remaining weighted technical importance values can be similarly computed.

Considered independently, $DE_4$ is the most important design element to fulfilling the express set of needs, with $DE_3$ the second most important design element, and $DE_1$ the third most important design element. As is common in design settings, potential obstacles are revealed in the roof of the HOQ where it is seen that both $DE_1$ and $DE_3$ are negatively correlated with $DE_4$. *Negative correlation among two design elements implies that pursuit of one design element without regard for the other will produce detrimental effects.*

In the presence of negatively correlated design elements, the design team must arrive at a compromise solution that seeks the best mixture of the negatively correlated design elements. If such compromise is not pursued, the resulting design will be suboptimal. Formal design optimization in the presence of conflicting design element relationships, that is, in the presence of negative correlation, is beyond the scope of the present work so that interested readers are referred to the iconic product design and development text by Karl Ulrich and Steven Eppinger (2015).

Despite this present limitation, some useful observations can be made. It may be seen in the roof of the HOQ of Table 17.4 that design elements $DE_1$, $DE_2$, and $DE_3$ are mutually synergistic as revealed by the positive correlations among these design elements. It can also be seen that there is no relation between design elements $DE_2$ and $DE_4$.

In determining what to do in the face of negative correlations, it is axiomatic that "not all needs are equally important" and that, as a corollary, "not all 9s are equally valuable." With this axiom and corollary in mind, we note that design element $DE_4$ is strongly related to the three most important expressed needs, that $DE_3$ is only strongly related to the least important need, $N_4$, and that $DE_2$ is only strongly related to the second least important need, $N_3$. As previously noted, $DE_1$ is almost inert relative to the expressed needs.

At first glance, the mutually synergistic relationship among $DE_1$, $DE_2$, and $DE_3$ appears to marginally overshadow the impact of $DE_4$ when $DE_4$ is independently considered. However, in view of prior observations, a likely path forward is that of emphasizing design element $DE_4$, and hence—via a single design element—focusing on the three most important expressed needs, $N_2$, $N_1$, and $N_5$. Although this would neglect $N_4$ and $N_3$, it is of value to note that these represent the two least important expressed needs.

Further, $DE_2$ is uncorrelated with $DE_4$ so that $DE_2$ may also be deployed. Given that $DE_2$ is strongly related to $N_3$, this need can also be met. Design elements $DE_1$ and $DE_3$ are unlikely to be pursued and, as a result, expressed need $N_4$—the least important need—will be only partially met at best since our selected design needs, $DE_4$ and $DE_2$, are only weakly related to this need.

## QUALITY FUNCTION DEPLOYMENT AND FLOWDOWN

QFD practice is executed via sequentially cascading multiple HOQs wherein the hows in one HOQ become the whats in the subsequent HOQ. The cascading HOQs is referred to as QFD flowdown or requirements flowdown (Zhang et al., 2015). The number of successive HOQs used in developing and deploying a given product, service, or system will depend in part on enterprise culture, as well as the level of detail desired.

In manufacturing (product development) applications of QFD, Japanese enterprises have historically tended to use four successive HOQs, whereas enterprises in the West have more commonly used only the first two or three HOQs. This may be due in part to the historic development of QFD in Japan by planning specialist Yoji Akao, who described QFD as a "method to transform qualitative user demands into quantitative parameters, to deploy the functions forming quality, and to deploy methods for achieving the design quality into subsystems and component parts, and ultimately to specific elements of the manufacturing process" (Akao, 1994).

Flowdown will manifest differently in varying development environments. The cascading nature of QFD is revealed for three development environments—manufacturing, software, and service—in Table 17.5.

Though it is not standard QFD practice in the design and manufacture of tangible, physical produces, it is possible to further adapt or expand QFD to be more sensitive to circular economy considerations. This "macro QFD" approach may require out-of-the-box thinking to develop additional HOQs to cascade in a given flowdown or may be addressed by addition of social and environmental needs at each stage throughout the QFD process (Edgeman and Hensler, 2005).

To an extent, this can be addressed in the concept generation and selection stages, as well as in the initial HOQ where social and environmental concerns can be included among the set of whats. Indeed, such considerations can be further addressed throughout the QFD process by incorporating such issues as refurbishment, reuse, recyclability, decomposability, repurposing of the product in whole or in part, biodegradability, ability of the product to generate its own energy, work environment health and safety, material sourcing, shipping and delivery mechanisms.

Finally, just as it is imperative to identify and incorporate critical needs—must-haves and exciters or delighters in the parlance of the Kano

**TABLE 17.5**

QFD Flowdown for Manufacturing, Software, and Service Development Environments

| HOQ | | Environment | | |
|---|---|---|---|---|
| | | **Manufacturing** | **Software** | **Service** |
| HOQ 1 | WHAT | Customer/ Society/ Ecological Needs | Customer/ Society/ Ecological Needs | Customer/ Society/ Ecological Needs |
| | HOW | Design Elements | Product Functionality | Service Requirements |
| HOQ 2 | WHAT | Design Elements | Product Functionality | Service Requirements |
| | HOW | Part Characteristics | System Requirements | Service Processes |
| HOQ 3 | WHAT | Part Characteristics | System Requirements | Service Processes |
| | HOW | Manufacturing Process | Design Alternatives | Process Controls |
| HOQ 4 | WHAT | Manufacturing Process | QFD uses up to four cascading HOQs in manufacturing environments and up to three cascading HOQs in software development and service environments | |
| | HOW | Production Requirements | | |

customer needs model—throughout the ideation, concept generation, concept selection, and deployment process, it is also imperative to know what must be avoided. As such, in concluding coverage of customer-driven improvement and innovation processes, the Kano model should serve to remind product, service, and system designers—whether teams or individuals—that it is not only the must-haves and exciters/delighters that must be identified and addressed throughout the design process, but also the so-called dissatisfiers. Though the Kano model is a customer needs model, it is highly adaptable and can readily accommodate and incorporate social and environmental components that might be otherwise ignored.

# Part III

# The Shingo Model

# 18

## Stakeholder Mediating Factors: Underlying Principles and Insights of the Shingo Model

*The more deeply leaders, managers, and associates understand the principles of operational excellence and the more perfectly systems are aligned to reinforce ideal behavior, the greater the probability of creating a sustainable culture of excellence where achieving ideal results is the norm rather than the aspiration.*

**Shingo Institute Enterprise Excellence Insight #3**

We next turn our focus to the *Shingo Model* and criteria, against which enterprises applying for the Shingo Prize are assessed. The Shingo Prize is administered by the Shingo Institute, a program in the Jon M. Huntsman School of Business at Utah State University in Logan, Utah, USA.

The formal purpose of the Shingo Institute, based on timeless principles, is to shape enterprise cultures that drive operational excellence. Similarly, the mission of the Shingo Institute is aligned to fulfill this purpose by conducting cutting-edge research, providing relevant education, performing insightful enterprise assessment, and recognizing organizations that are committed to achieving sustainable world-class results.

While the Shingo Prize, Shingo Silver Medallion, and Shingo Bronze Medallion awards are integral to the priorities and activities of the Shingo Institute, the scope of the Institute has expanded in recent times. Among the various thrusts of the Shingo Institute are a focus on leading-edge research, networking with like-minded organizations, multiple educational offerings, a large and growing international network of Shingo Licensed Affiliates—companies that provide training in areas relevant to the *Shingo Model* and *Shingo Guiding Principles*, and various regional and international conferences.

The Shingo Institute also acknowledges relevant and impactful research and practitioner publications through its Shingo Research Award and Shingo Publication Award initiatives. Among other criteria, recipients of these awards must document significant impact of their work on relevant theory or practice.

The Shingo Prize was established with the endorsement of late Japanese Lean manufacturing and quality guru, Dr. Shigeo Shingo (1909–1990). The Shingo Prize was created in 1988, the same year the Malcolm Baldrige National Quality Award was first awarded, and pre-dating by a few years the establishment of the EFQM Excellence Award—first known as the European Quality Award—in 1991. Though not a prize or award system or program, the balanced scorecard provides a relatively like-minded approach to management, development, and advancement of the enterprise that has been prominent since the 1990s and that—like the Shingo Prize, Baldrige Award, and EFQM Excellence Award—has much deeper historical roots.

Dr. Shingo was instrumental in the development of contemporary quality philosophy and practice. Among the many developments for which he was responsible are such familiar approaches as single minutes exchange of die (SMED), poka-yoke or error-proofing, and—together with Taiichi Ohno—the famed Toyota Production System that today is equally well known as just-in-time (JIT) manufacturing that is at the heart of Lean manufacturing and Lean enterprise approaches (Ohno, 1982, 1988; Shingo, 1981, 1985, 1986, 2007; Shingo and Dillon, 1989).

> We hold these <u>truths</u> to be self-evident, that all men are created equal, that they are endowed by their Creator with certain unalienable Rights, that among these are Life, Liberty, and the pursuit of Happiness. Thomas Jefferson, author of America's *Declaration of Independence* (July 2, 1776). (Wills, 2002)

The *Shingo Model* is founded upon ten guiding principles that are regarded as both universal and timeless, with these principles giving rise to three insights of enterprise excellence (Shingo Institute, 2017). Although additional principles may be identified that are more context-specific, those regarded by the *Shingo Model* as *Shingo Guiding Principles* are divided into four interrelated categories or dimensions: Cultural

Enablers, Continuous (and breakthrough) Improvement, Enterprise Alignment, and Results, where results may be regarded as a combination of performance and impacts.

## THREE INSIGHTS OF ENTERPRISE EXCELLENCE™

The *Three Insights of Enterprise Excellence* are discussed below, whereas the *Shingo Guiding Principles* are provided in Table 18.1 and discussed extensively in subsequent chapters.

- Insight #1: *Ideal results require ideal behavior.* Performance and impacts are the aim of every enterprise, with these varying from enterprise to enterprise, as do the means by which these may be attained—some of which are more suitable and some of which are less so. Ideal results should not be interpreted as optimal, but rather as positive outcomes that are sustainable over the long-term. Simply learning or acquiring new tools or systems does not lead to ideal results, though of course these may be supportive of ideal results. Consistent achievement of ideal results requires leaders and managers to create an environment or culture where ideal behaviors

**TABLE 18.1**

Shingo Guiding Principles

| Dimensions | Current Principles |
|---|---|
| **Cultural Enablers** | Respect every individual |
| | Lead with humility |
| **Continuous (and Breakthrough) Improvement** | Seek perfection (Pursue excellence) |
| | Embrace scientific thinking (Embrace scientific and critical thinking) |
| | Focus on process |
| | Assure quality at the source |
| | Flow and pull value |
| **Enterprise Alignment** | Think systemically (Think and act systemically) |
| | Create constancy of purpose (Create unity of purpose) |
| **Results (Performance and Impacts)** | Create value for the customer (Create value for stakeholders) |

are practiced by each enterprise associate. Exceptional leaders understand that a cause-and-effect relationship exists between results and behavior, with behavior serving as causes or catalysts and results as effects or consequences. This implies that it is important not only to identify and use an appropriate set of key performance indicators (KPIs)—something that most enterprises are accustomed to—but also an accompanying array of key behavioral indicators (KBIs)—something unfamiliar to most enterprises, despite that all enterprises are familiar with behaviors themselves. In the context of the *Shingo Model*, ideal results are any results that are both excellent and sustainable. This definition of course means that it is incumbent on the enterprise to determine precisely what "excellent" means within their competitive context.

- Insight #2: *Purpose and systems drive behavior.* The beliefs that we hold collectively and as individuals profoundly impact our behavior. Commonly overlooked is the substantial effect that systems have on behavior. The work of people within enterprises is largely governed by systems that have been designed to create specific business results. Often this occurs without dedicating due attention to behaviors generated by the system—meaning that there is a lack of adequate alignment between systems, behaviors, and results. Many enterprises have *de facto* systems that have evolved due to specific needs for specific results at specific times—times that have often passed. As such, leaders and managers are confronted by the necessary and often massive challenge of creating or realigning management and work systems that drive the ideal behaviors that are essential to producing business results that are ideal in their nature and timeliness. Relative to the *Shingo Model*, ideal behaviors are any behaviors that lead to results that are both excellent and sustainable. In the same way that it is up to the enterprise or, more appropriately, its key stakeholders, to determine what constitutes excellent results. Given that ideal behaviors are informed by principles, it is of central importance to the enterprise to form systems that promote ideal behaviors. Equally, it is important to identify or develop actionable key behavioral indicators that communicate the degree to which actions are or are not ideal, the direction in which actions (behaviors) vary from ideal, and that suggest corrective steps that can be taken when actions vary too greatly from ideal ones. The value of building such systems lies in making the practice of ideal behaviors (actions) simple and straight-forward while simultaneously making it difficult to not practice such behaviors—that is, a sort of "behavioral error-proofing." In such cultures, achievement of ideal performance and impacts becomes normative, rather than aspirational. As such, it is incumbent on enterprise leadership to engender a culture where ideal behaviors are both expected and routinely practiced among the human ecology of the enterprise.

- Insight #3: *Principles inform ideal behavior.* Principles are foundational rules that help to reveal both positive and negative consequences of our behaviors. Such rules inform our decisions, especially decisions concerning behaviors, noting that behaviors equate to actions. When decisions and subsequent actions align with principles the result is cognitive consonance, whereas decisions and actions contrary to principles are likely to generate cognitive dissonance and, in turn, moral or ethical dilemmas. The more deeply leaders, managers, and associates understand the principles of enterprise excellence and the more perfectly that systems are aligned to reinforce ideal behaviors, the greater the likelihood is that a sustainable culture of enterprise excellence will be established. Given that ideal behaviors are informed by principles, it is of central importance to the enterprise to form systems that promote ideal behaviors. Equally, it is important to identify or develop actionable key behavioral indicators that communicate the degree to which actions are or are not ideal, the direction in which actions (behaviors) vary from ideal, and that suggest corrective steps that can be taken when actions vary too greatly from ideal ones.

Relative to selected entries in the right-hand column of Table 18.1, it is here noted that, like enterprises themselves as well as other enterprise excellence models, the *Shingo Model* is in constant development so that—for example—as principles become more clearly and pervasively understood, the ways in which they are stated and explained also evolve.

Relative to specific *Shingo Model* vocabulary, principles are said to be universal and timeless. This implies that principles are ontologically invariant, that is, constant across cultures and eras, although they may manifest differently in different cultures and different eras (Reiss, 2004). Principles are sometimes held to be self-evident and, in that sense, akin to the truths stated in America's *Declaration of Independence*. Self-evident is not intended to be a synonym for obvious, but rather that practice of a principle will reinforce its truth. There are a couple of other appropriate clarifying points that should be noted at this point. The first is that cultural enablers are not the only dimension in which culture resides; behaviors, and therefore culture, are in every dimension. Second, the same is true for results. There are results and relevant measures in all dimensions, although KPIs reside mainly in the results dimension, leading indicators and KBIs are evident in all dimensions.

*Shingo Guiding Principles* are reported in Table 18.1 and will be elaborated more fully over the course of the following four chapters, on a dimension-by-dimension basis.

# 19

## Shingo Model: Cultural Enablers Principles

*All truth passes through three stages. First, it is ridiculed. Second, it is violently opposed. Third, it is accepted as being self-evident.*

**Arthur Schopenhauer (Schroeder et al., 2008)**

The principles or truths identified in the Cultural Enablers dimension of the *Shingo Model* speak to the issue that knowledge, insight, and foresight are found in abundance and are pervasive across individuals in essentially any organization. As such, enterprise leaders demonstrate both humility and wisdom when they acknowledge and actively pursue such knowledge and wisdom.

## THE A7 APPROACH

While there are in most instances multiple paths to truth, its pursuit can be advanced through practice of what may be referred to as an A7 Approach, with the elements of this approach described as follows:

- *Anticipate* and believe this truth, that is, that knowledge and wisdom which can be leveraged for the good of the enterprise resides in every member of the enterprises' human ecology.
- *Actively* pursue this truth by actively and positively querying the human ecology, being careful to listen attentively. Include team and individual knowledge generation measures in the enterprise performance management and measurement system, being sure to

include both key performance indicators (KPIs) and key behavioral indicators (KBIs).

- *Acknowledge* openly the validity of any truth wherever, whenever, and by whomever it is found.
- *Attribute* found knowledge—especially that which contributes to fulfillment of enterprise purpose and vision—to the person or groups of people that are its source.
- *Appropriately* reward those sources of knowledge, recognizing that some individuals are better compensated by tangible rewards, others by intangible rewards, and still others by a combination of tangible and intangible rewards. Build knowledge generation into the enterprise reward and recognition system.
- *Actively avail* the enterprise and its leadership of the rich and diverse expertise resident in enterprise human ecology, carefully determining what relevant portions of that expertise and accompanying knowledge can be implemented and how best to do so.
- *Archive* and advertise the collected intelligence so it is widely known and in readily accessible, user-friendly formats. One purpose of this is to encourage subsequent direct or adapted use of the knowledge contained in this archive.

Finally,
- Call positive *attention* to and frequently access this archive.

## CULTURAL ENABLERS PRINCIPLES

Consistent with the A7 practices, the *Shingo Model* cites two principles within the Cultural Enablers dimension: respect every individual and lead with humility. These are described as follows:

**Respect Every Individual:** Every person in any organization has the right to and expectation of being respected (Edgeman and Scherer, 1998). When people perceive that they are respected and valued, they are more likely to contribute to enterprise purpose, not with their hands only—that is direct labor—but with their minds and hearts also in the forms of ideas, improvements, and their intellectual and emotional commitment. When such respect is uniformly expected and practiced within the enterprise, it provides the sort of nourishment necessary for unity of purpose and a shared vision to flourish in the enterprise. Such respect not only mandates listening to individuals; it requires that each member of the enterprise's human ecology should be adequately trained and resourced, held accountable for their decisions, actions, and results, and forgiven for honest errors, recognizing that the system or process is often the source of fault.

**Lead with Humility**: Enterprise and personal growth is enabled when a leader is less self-focused and thinks more about the health, general welfare, and growth of others—not only out of concern for individuals, but out of concern for the health, welfare, and growth of the enterprise itself, through the individual and collective contributions of its human ecology. Such leaders seek out and value the ideas of others and are willing to change or alter course appropriately when relevant and authenticated new knowledge is obtained, irrespective of the source of that knowledge. It is such respect that opens the ears, eyes, and minds of leaders to knowledge and ideas from others, irrespective of their station inside or outside the enterprise. Respecting every individual is thus considered prerequisite to leading with humility.

Relative to the role of enterprise leadership in advancing these principles, Robert Noyce, co-founder of Intel, provided a reasonable summary: "If ethics are poor at the top, that behavior is copied down through the organization" (Berlin, 2005). By implication, an obvious corollary to Noyce's statement is that superlative ethics at the leadership level are reproduced throughout the enterprise. The contention here is that respect for every individual and leading with humility are central to the ethics Robert Noyce had in mind.

## RESPECTING EVERY INDIVIDUAL, ENTITY, AND STAKEHOLDER SEGMENT

Practicing the principle of respecting every individual extends well beyond the boundaries of the enterprise. It is in fact an omnibus principle wherein "every individual" encompasses—among others—not only the human ecology of the enterprise, but its supply chain members, its customers, and society.

The importance of customers has already been addressed extensively so here it will only be noted that the enterprise exists only through the willingness of its customers to invest in its offerings. This existence is not an enterprise birthright and becomes precarious when an enterprise takes for granted or betrays the trust of its customers—just as extreme honesty on behalf of the enterprise can create a competitive advantage (Peppers and Rogers, 2016).

Similarly, society provides a contextual home within which the enterprise finds its liquid of life, with this in itself presenting a positive argument for corporate social responsibility practices (Carroll, 1991. It must nevertheless be noted that societal interests and those of the enterprise may at times be in conflict, so that respect for society and the legitimate, thoughtful concern for its interests are critical (Schwartz and Carroll, 2008).

Supply chain members are critical to the success of almost any enterprise, and as such it is important that these members of the enterprise's ecology must mutually benefit. Moreover, respect implies there will be active concern that these benefits are equitable, that members each have a stake in the health of all others, although the stake may not extend as far as direct financial investment. This is culturally analogous to the Japanese business practice of *keiretsu*, wherein a collection of enterprises have interlocking business relationships, though in this case the intent is one of having mutual concern for the well-being of other supply chain members, since the health of one has some systemic impact on the health of all others.

That mutual respect should be the rule both in attitude and practice among an enterprise's leadership, management, and associates is often taken as a given. More than a given, there are many positive points in the business case that support the practice of mutual respect that is extended to and received from each individual in the enterprise. These are the collective people upon whom the quest for greatness is thrust. This quest for greatness is equivalent to the *Shingo Guiding Principle* of seeking perfection, or as cast herein as pursuit of excellence, and each member of the enterprise is individually responsible in differing measure for the success of the quest (Darling, Keeffe, and Ross, 2007). Note that while any specific individual can choose to outwardly practice and inwardly possess respect for any or all others in the enterprise, that it is not within the power of any single individual to demand or culturally establish these elements, for these are elements that require a coexistence and symbiosis of central direction and individual autonomy (Grunig, 1992).

Implicit in respect within the enterprise is trust, as these are two key characteristics of a people orientation that pervades the structure, culture, and processes in operationally excellent organizations (Peters and Waterman, 1982). Driving this symbiosis is—in whatever forms are contextually relevant—an array of structural devices, systems, styles, and values, all reinforcing one another so that operationally excellent enterprises are highly proficient at achieving extraordinary results through ordinary people (Peters and Waterman, 1982).

## LEADING WITH HUMILITY AND THE PERIL OF POWER

It is of value to address the proverbial elephant in the room—the peril of power—prior to more extensively addressing the principle of leading with humility. The peril of power—and the clinical evidence of it—is captured by the time-worn adage usually attributed to the late English historian, politician, and writer John Emerich Edward Dalberg-Acton (1834–1902), better known simply as Lord Acton, that "power tends to corrupt, and absolute power (sometimes) corrupts absolutely" (Rogow and Lasswell, 1963).

Recent research indicates that leading with humility may be a more difficult matter than simply making a choice to do so. Leading is commonly associated with leadership and in turn leadership with power. Power comes in many varieties, including positional power, power that is associated with earned respect, and power that is fleeting in which a person rises to the moment with herculean acts of courage or judgment. It is the extended practice of power that has the greatest attached levels of hazard associated with a form of "brain damage" wherein leaders progressively lose the ability to sympathize and empathize with the very people associated with their rise to power, that is, the ability to identify with the common person, so to speak, a process referred to as mirroring (Hogeveen, Inzlicht, and Obhi, 2014; Keltner, 2017; Useem, 2017).

The inherent dangers of these findings are that leaders—thus power-corrupted or "brain damaged"—will surrender the leadership high ground by losing touch with how reality is perceived by the common person and will hence find it difficult to respect those individuals. Given that respect for every individual is the cultural enabler sibling of leading with humility, the paradox of power is the potential challenge the powerful person—in some cases leaders in an enterprise—lose their own sense of humility, and in turn forfeit at least a modicum of respect for those they lead.

It is with the preceding caveat in mind that the principle of leading with humility is now further addressed.

Basic research pointing to the conundrum that an authentic leader without humility can lead to the very type of counterproductive actions that authentic leadership is meant to protect against (Chang and Diddams, 2009, McKenna, 1996) suggests that it is so-called servant leaders and transformational leaders who have the best opportunity to lead with humility, where by servant leadership we intend leadership that subjugates the needs of a leader to those of the enterprise and its people—more broadly—to its varied stakeholders (Reinke, 2004).

By transformational leadership, we intend leadership that transforms the personal values of followers to support the vision and goals of the enterprise by guiding those followers to a place where the synergy of their personal values with the vision and goals of the enterprise is maximized (Gregory-Stone, Russell, and Patterson, 2004). Building on the work of Collins (2005), Morris et al. (2005), and Smith et al. (2004), we conclude that the humble leader is that individual whose ambition is directed toward facilitating the success of the enterprise by prioritizing on the care, guidance, and—ultimately—success of those being led, and not those only, but also those with whom the leader is in peer relationship, those to whom the leader is herself or himself subordinate, those who impacted and those impacted by the activities of the enterprise.

It is perhaps the case that the two cultural enabler principles can be summed up in either of two familiar admonitions, one from late management consultant Steven Covey and a second, much earlier one from the wisdom literature. In the case of Covey, the admonition is captured by one of his famed seven habits of highly effective people, that is, seek first to understand, then to be understood (Covey, 1989). Covey's summary is regarded by many as a restatement of the biblical principle that may be translated as "be quick to listen, slow to speak, and slow to get angry" (Christian Bible: James 1:19). In other words, the humble leader *commits first to being certain to understand the perspectives, assumptions, and opinions of others, and only afterwards to making certain that their own perspectives, assumptions, and opinions are understood by others.*

## COMMUNICATION AND CULTURAL ENABLERS

Although communication can assume multiple forms, often simultaneously, focus relative to respecting every individual and leading with humility is placed particularly on two forms: advocacy and inquiry

(Lencioni, 2012). In advocacy-oriented communication, the communicator will most usually state and advocate for their case. More rarely and—again relative to leading with humility and respecting every individual—more importantly, the communicator is first an inquirer, who seeks clarity about another's statement of advocacy. In the first case, statements tend to begin with phrases such as "I think," "I feel," "I believe," or "I recommend." Whereas in the latter instance the communicator is more likely to inquire, asking questions such as "why do you think that?," "how certain are you?," or "how strongly do you feel about that?," where we again see an effort made to know and understand the perspective of others, prior to making one's own perspectives known and understood.

In many ways the role of cultural enablers—remembering that enterprise culture can be regarded as "the way we do things around here"—is to make the doing of those things more efficient, effective, innovative, and reflexive. Paradoxically, this is accomplished by slowing down to know and understand—to become more reflective—and to add to the wealth of individual and enterprise insight and understanding that in turn fuels the collective innovative imagination.

This comes as a counterbalance to what Lencioni (2012) calls the "fundamental attribution error." At the core of the fundamental attribution error is the tendency of people to attribute negative or frustrating behaviors of colleagues to their intentions and poor attitudes, yet (more positively) attribute their own negative or frustrating behaviors to circumstances beyond their control, or to environmental factors.

These observations lead to a communication strategy that employs both inquiry and advocacy for those seeking to become humble, respectful individuals:

- Actively engage in conversations that create learning opportunities through inquiry. This necessitates asking questions of others, seeking to understand as much as possible about who that person is and why they might be saying or doing the things they are, confirming with others both points of correct interpretation or errors therein. Implied then, is that it is incumbent on the humble and respectful individual to strenuously seek to understand the intellectual, emotional, and contextual cues and nuances of the answers to those questions.
- Do not neglect use of advocacy, but recognize that the original perspective of the humble and respectful individual—the perspective held prior to inquiry—may have been altered by the act and results of inquiry.

- In the same way that it is important to understand the intellectual, emotional, and contextual value in that learned through inquiry, it is important to clearly surrender equal value in perspective advocated by the humble and respectful individual.
- Believe and assume the best in others and do not fall into the sort of bad habit that embraces the fundamental attribution error.

Being humble and respectful enables enterprise culture by creating trust and goodwill that will ultimately deliver swifter and better resolution to challenges faced by the enterprise (Wildman et al., 2012).

For other supporting concepts, systems, and tools relevant to this dimension please refer to the Shingo guidelines mentioned earlier and available to download from http://www.shingo.org/.

# 20

## Shingo Model: Enterprise Alignment Principles

When an automobile is "out of alignment" its tires will wear unevenly, it will persistently wander off its intended path, and it will consume more energy and produce more waste than it will when perfectly aligned. In other words, its parts and processes will work at cross-purposes and its operator will engage in non-value-added activities that prevent them from pursuing ideal ones in ideal ways. Should we then expect that something as inherently more complex as an organization should perform any better when it is misaligned?

## THE S7 STRUCTURE

The idea of enterprise alignment is well captured through an S7 Structure that is described as follows:

- *Sense of self* implies that enterprise leadership is well aware of "who" the enterprise is and its purpose on this earth, the values and beliefs upon which it was founded, its path forward, and that it is confident of not only surviving but of prospering both in and beyond its present circumstances. By confidence, we do not intend a false sense of security, but rather a fact-based, data-driven knowledge of circumstances and means of navigating those circumstances.
- *Solidarity* in an enterprise means that leadership and a critical mass of other enterprise human ecology are sufficiently galvanized as to move forward with unity and a shared sense of purpose.
- *Systematic* communicates that enterprises are complex with many people, processes, and motivations so that less than holistic consideration

will *almost surely* in the mathematical sense and *always* in the practical sense lead to compromised, suboptimal results. This implies that there exist relationships between and among enterprise people, processes, and organizational units that form both singular and interrelated systems and that such systems should not be thought of solely in isolation.

- *Sequential and consequential* suggests that there is a progression in both the order and way that actions are performed and decisions made and that these deliver consequences that are either degraded or enhanced by those antecedent actions and decisions. As such, it behooves the human ecology of the enterprise to think and act from the perspective of "cause and effect," that is, sequence or linkage.
- *Systemic and scientific* implies that the above elements are best practiced throughout the enterprise, possibly with local adaptations influenced by unique local circumstances, but always from the perspective of enterprise integration—consideration of what is best for the organization as a whole. Scientific—the added "S"—is not so much an addition to its predecessors as it is a reminder that people, processes, partnerships, policies, systems, and any legal, moral, ethical, or other dilemmas or boundaries inside which the enterprise functions are fundamentally an integrated whole. We must be aware that the complexity is so great that challenges should be faced with an awareness of the value of scientific rigor that is tempered by the exercise of human wisdom.
- *Synergy* is based on the tenet that universal (holistic) exercise of the preceding beliefs and practices will lead to overall results that are more than simply the accumulation of the results of the individual components.
- *Stand* with one foot on earth and the other in the clouds by being attentive to the current business environment, while searching for likely or potential near-, medium-, and long-term changes. In other words, simultaneously develop and make use of enterprise insight and foresight.

## ENTERPRISE ALIGNMENT PRINCIPLES

The S7 Structure forms a foundation upon which enterprise alignment is more solidly built and from which the following principles of the Enterprise Alignment dimension can be derived:

**Create Constancy of Purpose:** The intention of this principle is to *Create Unity of Purpose and Shared Vision*. When leaders communicate with unwavering clarity why an organization exists, where it is going, how it will get there, and the principles upon which it acts, people become empowered to innovate, adapt, and take risks with greater confidence. This enables the enterprise to advance in unity with a sense of shared purpose and vision.

Relative to the ten guiding principles of the *Shingo Model*, creating unity of purpose is more commonly stated as "create constancy of purpose," a term derived from the (quality) management philosophy of W. Edwards Deming (1985) and reiterated by many others (Choi, 1995; Spencer, 1994). The stark reality however, as previously noted herein, is that Deming was very specific: constancy of purpose is to be interpreted as commitment to a never-ending cycle of improvement of products, services, and systems.

The intent behind "create constancy of purpose" among the *Shingo Guiding Principles* includes Deming's original meaning but is more encompassing as it also intends unity of purpose within the enterprise itself—why and for whom it exists, how it chooses to behave and not behave. Fulfillment of purpose requires more than unity. In mathematical terms, unity of purpose is necessary for fulfillment of enterprise purpose but is not sufficient in and of itself to accomplish this. It must be augmented by a vision shared by a critical mass of enterprise human ecology that possesses the collective will to carry out enterprise purpose and is equipped, empowered, and resourced at sufficient levels to do so. The ability to build shared vision is referred to by famed systems thinker Peter Senge (1990) as the "third discipline of the learning organization" wherein building shared vision is the ability to unearth shared pictures of the future that cultivate genuine commitment to the vision and purpose of the enterprise and not merely compliance.

**Think Systemically:** Solutions to enterprise problems must embrace the connectedness and impact of the one on the many as well as the many on the one. The broader the perspective of any individual or team, the greater their ability to conceive and implement solutions that create a positive outcome for the enterprise. It is not enough simply to think systemically—we must subsequently act systemically where "act" is the outward expression of thinking systemically. As such, this principle could be stated as *think and act systemically*.

Thinking and acting systemically is a fuller statement of the *Shingo Guiding Principle* Think Systemically where "and act" has been added to emphasize that this is an action-oriented principle. It first requires holistic understanding, rather than seeing the activities and processes of the enterprise only in isolation from one another. Holistic understanding contributes to more abundant, more creative, and better solutions to enterprise challenges that range from process level to system level to enterprise level in stature (Jackson, 2003). Equally, systems and systemic thinking have been linked to better ability to manage complexity, improved enterprise performance (Skaržauskienė, 2010), improved enterprise learning (Senge and Sterman, 1992), and improved ethical decision-making (Kunsch, Theys, and Brans, 2007).

Systems thinking is the "fifth discipline of the learning organization" (Senge, 1990) and serves as the integrative chord for the first four disciplines: personal mastery, the ability to form mental models that explain how and why things work, building shared vision, and collaborative or team learning wherein those collaborating are able to suspend judgment and engage in "thinking together." Thinking together is meant to communicate synergistic thinking wherein collaborative logic and results exceed the sum of the logic and results produced by individuals. As such, thinking together delivers thinking and solutions that differ decidedly from those resulting from "group thinking" wherein an unhealthy desire for harmony arises among collaborators that is so great that it leads to irrational or dysfunctional decision-making and subsequent results.

Understanding and holistic thinking alone are insufficient to initiate needed changes. Needed changes can only be implemented through action.

It is reasonable in most enterprises to assume that no consciously malevolent or deceitful act is undertaken with the aim of making a process or system less effective, less efficient, or more challenging to manage. Instead, the intention is to design and implement processes and systems that deliver optimal performance.

Indeed, key arguments in favor of development of Lean operations are their aim and track record of success over time of creating and continuously improving smooth, self-restoring value flows. In point of fact, systems thinking, when coupled with a process focus that is filtered through the lens of shared vision and unity of purpose, is critical to successful enterprise evolution (Hines, Holweg, and Rich, 2004). Fundamentally, these principles inherent in the *Shingo Model* serve as soft enablers of such evolution that must be coupled with hard, thoughtful execution.

For other supporting concepts, systems, and tools relevant to this dimension please refer to the Shingo guidelines mentioned earlier and available to download from http://www.shingo.org/.

# 21

## Shingo Model: Continuous Improvement Principles

Continuous improvement can be regarded as effective and efficient integration of enterprise philosophy, systems, techniques, and structure to achieve sustained improvement in all activities, performance, and impacts on an uninterrupted basis. Improvement does not just happen on its own: left on its own, the nature of almost any process or system is toward entropy or decay. It is thus up to the enterprise to consciously combat entropy, with erstwhile attention to continuous improvement providing one means of engaging in such combat (Jenner, 1998).

### THE R7 REGIMEN

If the principles in the Cultural Enablers dimension can be pursued through an A7 Approach, then the principles in the Continuous Improvement dimension can be advanced by pursuing an R7 Regimen. This regimen may be described as follows:

- *Relentlessly* pursue beneficial change. Such change may range from incremental to breakthrough in magnitude and may hence involve innovation that is incremental, radical, or disruptive. Such pursuit contributes to enterprise optimization and renewal.
- *Regularly* or near constantly do this in the sense that the ongoing search for improvement becomes a clear element of enterprise culture and hence a clear expectation throughout the entirety of the enterprise's extended human ecology. The extended human ecology

of an enterprise is more than its own human capital and is intended to include relationships with its partners or collaborators, as well as—where appropriate—its customers. Customers may become engaged via such vehicles as customer suggestion systems or more extensively through formal customer-enterprise co-creation practices such as crowdsourcing. If the "enterprise" is a governmental entity or NGO, then the related practice of citizen sourcing may be of value. In this way, we see interaction between the enterprise and its stakeholders in a way that can effectively tap into mediating forces.

- *Recognize* that most real improvement is accomplished through process change and innovation. As such, processes should be subject to ongoing review and reexamination, always seeking improvement as far upstream in processes as possible. In short, processes should routinely be placed under the microscope as a means of facilitating organizational learning and advancement (Fang et al., 2010; Santos-Vijande et al., 2012).

- *Reenergize* and *retool* the enterprise's human capital on a continuous basis in the sense of exercising diligence in the currency of their knowledge and skills and the opportunity to practice these. Similarly, be forward-looking in being prepared for both anticipated and unexpected changes that may be on the enterprise's horizon. This contributes in fundamental ways to enterprise development while simultaneously demanding active pursuit and implementation of enterprise foresight.

- *Routinely* engage in these practices. While some approaches may be less organized or less predictable, on the whole there is a systematic or relatively standardized approach used to pursue improvements, whether those improvements are incremental or monumental, and whether they are the result of individual or collaborative efforts.

- *Rigorously* seek improvement on both incremental and breakthrough scales. While some methods used may be appropriately straight-forward or simplistic in nature, do not eschew more rigorous and demanding approaches that could be, for example, highly analytical and hence require thoughtful use of specialized technology or expertise. Similarly, do not forsake incremental gains as you pursue breakthrough ones; often breakthrough improvement is the result from accrual of many hard-won incremental gains.

- *Remember* that one means of pursuing improvement while simultaneously building resilience is to pursue a portfolio approach, distributing efforts across a critical array of enterprise strategies and activities. At the same time, remember that thoughtful risk-taking is to be encouraged and that failures often provide learning opportunities that birth later success. Be sure to share new learnings and standardize processes, with the purpose of standardization to produce more portable solutions.

In sum, these ideas support the widely acknowledged tenet that the pursuit of perfection is likely never-ending as "perfection" is a moving target in a dynamic, rather than static, environment where stakeholder preferences and needs are both changing and increasingly demanding. In such environments variation, if not inevitable, is at least the norm.

## CONTINUOUS IMPROVEMENT PRINCIPLES

In light of these considerations, the principles in the Continuous Improvement dimension are described below, and are recorded in a specific order, intended to communicate one logical flow from one principle to the next.

**Seek Perfection**: Although this principle is stated as "seek perfection," the underlying intention is that of *pursuing excellence*. Perfection is an aspirational goal, fulfillment of which is not likely to be achieved. Having acknowledged this, we nevertheless see that pursuit of perfection creates a mindset toward and culture supportive of both continuous and radical improvement. The realization of what is possible is fundamentally limited by the paradigms through which we see and understand the world, and in adopting a mindset and engendering a culture that strives toward excellence. We form a paradigm that assumes it is always possible to do better than we are doing now and that we can discover a way to do so.

**Embrace Scientific Thinking**: Innovation and improvement are consequences of repeated cycles of experimentation and learning. Experimentation is associated with scientific thinking, whereas learning requires cognition, that is, critical thinking. As such, this principle can be more fully expressed as *embrace scientific and critical thinking*. Embracing scientific thinking requires engaging in activities such as planned change or simulation. Embracing critical thinking requires mental processing and assessment of the result of simulation or change, whether the change was planned or unplanned. In other words, "embracing" requires a blend of thinking and action. The ability to replicate results is important: if similar outcomes cannot be obtained when multiple observations are obtained under essentially constant conditions, then it is fallacious to make changes based on a single or even few "best" or "worst" outcomes. While failure is not to be intentionally pursued, failures that do occur provide opportunities to learn through relentless and systematic exploration of new ideas.

**Focus on Process**: All outcomes (e.g., results comprised of performance and impacts) are the consequence of a process. It is nearly impossible for even competent and highly motivated people to consistently extract ideal results from poor processes. Most inconsistencies or failures in outcomes can be traced to sources associated with process inadequacies. As such, it is advisable to work on process improvement.

**Assure Quality at the Source**: Perfect quality can only be achieved when every element of work is performed perfectly the first time and every time. When and if errors occur, it is best to detect and correct the error as close in time and as close to the source of the error as possible. This better enables investigation and understanding of the circumstances birthing the error and hence development of more apt solutions. In general, this requires routine use of the "go and observe" approach, that is, direct observations of where and how work is done by the people performing the work.

**Flow and Pull Value**: Value for customers and other stakeholders is maximized when it is created in response to real demand and is produced via continuous and uninterrupted flow. Anything that disrupts the continuous flow of value is waste. This is perhaps the least understood and least practiced principle within the *Shingo Model*. Value is created through a series of activities, that is, through processes. In most processes, some process activities or steps create value while others do not. The goal is to eliminate all value-detracting and non-value-adding activities and hence to create purely value-adding processes. In general, flow can be thought of as the continuous forward progress of products, services, or less tangible things such as information to the customer. Flow is improved by removing any barriers that impede this continuous forward movement and by identifying and implementing anything that simplifies this movement. The notion of pulling value is that nothing should be produced, no service performed, no information passed along until it is required, that is, in response to real demand. When the requirement emerges, an initiation signal should be sent upstream. The goal in terms of how to pull value is so-called "one-piece flow" or "make one, move one."

There are a significant number of tools and methods that are supportive of continuous and breakthrough improvement. Only a few such tools and methods are provided in the present work so that readers interested in such tools are referred to any of the many exceptional resources cited previously.

# HIERARCHICAL CONSIDERATION OF CONTINUOUS IMPROVEMENT PRINCIPLES

When integrated into a comprehensive enterprise-wide context, continuous improvement has been documented to serve as a dynamic organizational ability (Anand et al., 2009). Such a structure can be established, although the five continuous improvement principles included among the larger set of ten guiding principles embedded in the *Shingo Model* are typically stated without reference to any hierarchical or priority structure. One such structure proceeds from the more esoteric or strategic level to the tactical level and is explained as follows.

## Pursue Excellence

Restatement of the *Shingo Guiding Principle* of "seek perfection" in an alternative form—pursue excellence—has two motivations.

One motivation is to decouple the principle from the use of the term "perfection," as it is commonly used in the clinical literature, that is, to decouple it from the notion of narcissistic focus on appearance or performance to the neglect of other important considerations. These forms of narcissism have been seen to result in, e.g., addiction to surgically delivered perfection around some personal or cultural ideal, and in performance anxiety that manifests in many actors, musicians, and others in performance-oriented careers (Joosten, Bongers, and Janssen, 2009). It can be inferred from this that unhealthy fixation on perfection may in fact lead to "perfection paralysis" that can narrow enterprise focus to a hopelessly thin line and cripple productivity.

More importantly, the thrust of seeking perfection is really one of chasing after optimal value with minimal (zero) waste. This is grounded in the mindset that "only the best is good enough, and that only temporarily so." The word "temporarily" is emphasized here to communicate that what is "best" is in constant development as technologies and methods yield ever new understanding and manifestations of best. Similarly, real and perceived needs can change, so that what is best today may come to be regarded as archaic, irrelevant, or even harmful tomorrow.

As such, the pursuit of excellence drives both the strategic intent and tactical activities that support continuous improvement, wherever on the spectrum of incremental through breakthrough improvement is needed or desired. Pursuit of excellence is central to continuous improvement since the main idea of continuous improvement is to achieve ever-improving performance, at ever-improving value, at an ever-increasing rate of change that outpaces the competition and that delivers viable, desirable solutions to key challenges faced by the enterprise on behalf of its varied stakeholders.

In other words: achieving perfection is an ill-stated expression for pursuing excellence.

## Embrace Critical and Scientific Thinking: Knowledge Confirmation and Generation

How is excellence pursued? It begins with the acquisition of knowledge and further development thereof (Ackermann, 1965).

Though there are multiple paths to knowledge, embracing critical and scientific thinking is key to this effort. Critical and scientific thinking form the crucible through which thinking and acting systemically, and focus on processes, are tested in the effort to create new or better solutions to enterprise challenges.

"Critical thinking" has been added to the *Shingo Guiding Principle* that is both more commonly and more briefly stated as "embrace scientific thinking." This addition has been introduced as a means of emphasizing the full intent of the principle, while also noting that, although scientific thinking and critical thinking have similarities, there are also distinctions between them.

Critical and scientific thinking demand rigorous, systematic exploration of the impacts of changes. Changes of greatest interest are ordinarily ones that are intentionally introduced and small changes can yield big results, although often, the areas where enacting change delivers the most positive difference in results are not obvious. These changes are typically made for one of two primary reasons, both of which are driven by the quest to better satisfy stakeholder needs or interests, or to address a specific enterprise concern.

One reason that one or more changes are made is to identify or establish cause-and-consequence relationships. The term *consequence* is synonymous with "results and impacts," where these range from internal consequences to external ones, and from trivial to monumental in magnitude. In common language, use of the term consequence often connotes negative outcomes, but that is not the intended meaning here. Instead, consequence should be interpreted as a result of specific actions, whether the result is good, bad, or indifferent or is small or large.

Cause-and-consequence relationships may be expressed as functional relationships. That is:

$$Y = f\left(X_1, X_2, ..., X_p\right) + \varepsilon$$

where Y is a response variable of interest and is often referred to as a critical to quality characteristic (CTQ), $X_1$, $X_2$, ... $X_p$ are predictor or control variables, and $\varepsilon$ is a so-called random error term that simultaneously addresses several issues, among which are:

- The functional form of the relationship will almost certainly be incorrectly specified,
- Some "vital" control variables will fail to be identified, and
- Both the CTQ and control variables will be imprecisely measured.

Referral to Y as a *critical to quality characteristic* or CTQ makes use of language that is common to the field of Six Sigma (Goetsch and Davis, 2014). The idea behind this is that the outcome, Y, is of import to fulfillment of customer/stakeholder needs, whether the customer or stakeholder in question is an internal or external one. That is, it is critical to quality from the customer/stakeholder perspective.

Delivery of ideal CTQ (Y) values is important to fulfillment of stakeholder needs, whereas the X's are process variables or elements that are under the direct control or—at least—influence of the enterprise. Y itself, however, is only determined through actions undertaken by the enterprise, where these actions represent the X's so that these "control" the outcome, Y.

As such, an initial goal is that of identification of control variables that *may* influence the CTQ. In identifying variables that *may* influence the CTQ, it is ordinarily the case that some of these *may not* influence the CTQ, but that some subset of these variables *do* influence the CTQ. The control variables that *do* influence the CTQ are commonly divided into two categories that, as previously noted, may be referred to as the *vital few* and the *trivial many*. Further, control variables may be *quantitative* or *qualitative* in nature. Quantitative variables are variables that change in amount and are sometimes referred to as *operating parameters*, whereas qualitative variables are factors that change in type or kind and are sometimes referred to as *critical elements* (Linderman et al., 2003).

Fundamentally, these variables are the design factors that the enterprise must manipulate as necessary to deliver the best solution to stakeholder needs. Of particular interest then is determination of the vital few control variables that most influence the CTQ.

Once the vital few control variables or design factors that most influence the CTQ have been identified, the second motivation behind establishing cause-and-consequence relationships comes into play. This second motivation is to identify the best or optimal combination of control variable values that will yield the best CTQ outcome. In some cases, there will be multiple combinations of control variable settings that will deliver the same best CTQ value. In such cases, it is necessary to determine the explicit combination of control variable values that will be chosen from among the multiple combinations delivering the same best CTQ value. Given that each of the multiple combinations delivers the same best CTQ value, the determination of which combination to choose is made by appealing to a secondary decision criterion, such as choosing the combination of control variables that leads to the best CTQ value at lowest cost, or with lowest associated equipment maintenance, or that does so most quickly.

But what is critical thinking? What is scientific thinking?

Critical thinking is the ability to think clearly and rationally about what to do or not do, or what to believe or disbelieve. This involves the ability to engage in reflective and independent thinking, and hence to successfully accomplish the following:

- Understand logical connections between ideas;
- Identify, form, and assess arguments;
- Detect common mistakes and inconsistencies in reasoning;
- Systematically solve problems;
- Identify the relevance and importance of ideas; and
- Scrutinize and reflect on the justification of one's own beliefs and values.

Critical thinking will assess evidence, but it is not in the main a matter of accumulating information or evidence for accumulation's own sake. Instead, a skilled critical thinker is able to deduce consequences from what is known, and to seek information relevant to the solution of extant problems, while also prioritizing the problems to be attacked. While critical thinking can be used to expose fallacious arguments or poor reasoning, it can equally aid cooperative reasoning and improve work processes. These are all reasons why critical thinking is important to continuous improvement.

Scientific thinking is a manner of thinking about various subjects, contents, or problems of interests in ways that improve the quality of thinking. This is accomplished by skillfully seizing control of the structures inherent in thinking, and subsequently imposing rigorous intellectual standards upon those structures.

Improving the quality of thinking—in an enterprise context—is central to, but is not the primary goal of, practicing scientific thinking. Instead, the primary goal of scientific thinking is to spark subsequent action that improves the quality, applicability, and creativity of solutions to challenges faced by the enterprise and its stakeholders.

The three watchwords of critical and scientific thinking are empiricism, rationalism, and skepticism, and it is an appropriate blend of these that we seek.

The primary differences between empiricism and rationalism lie in what must be externally discovered and what is native or internally available to the individual or group engaged in critical and scientific thinking. In other words, the difference lies in what is perception and what is cognition (Allport, 1955).

Cognition is the mental action or process of acquiring knowledge and understanding through thought. Cognition is typically associated with thought processes believed to be the province of the central nervous system (brain and spinal cord). Cognition is responsible for rational or logical knowledge that is internally available, even if identifying and accessing this knowledge is not necessarily straight-forward.

In contrast, perception is experience-driven and is associated with empiricism in the forms of organizing and processing sensory data that is delivered to the central nervous system by the peripheral nervous system (everything else—taste, smell, sight, touch, and so on). Sensory data provides information from and about the external environment to the individual, group, or enterprise brain.

Empiricism is experientially rooted and hence anchored to data-driven decision making (Chesbrough, 2010), that is, it is *a posteriori* knowledge derived from observation. The enterprise intent of data-driven decision making is to transform data into knowledge, knowledge into strategy, strategy into activities, and activities into results (Davenport et al., 2001). Empirically acquired knowledge is often complemented by *a priori* knowledge gained through reason—or rationalism. In other words, perception and cognition, empiricism and rationalism can and should work in concert with one another.

To practice skepticism is to routinely challenge or confront one's own beliefs and conclusions. This requires routine and rigorous scrutiny of evidence, arguments, and reasons for belief as part of the larger effort of guarding ourselves from both self-deception and deception promulgated by others, whether the deception is intentional or unintentional. The process anticipates challenging the veracity and reliability of assumed (believed) facts, versus objective reality by predicting—better—observing the consequences or logical outcomes of beliefs and actions pursued relative to those beliefs. Comparison of predicted outcomes with actual ones will tend to generally either confirm or refute the value of those beliefs.

Contrary to what is commonly thought, the true skeptic is not closed-minded, but rather is undogmatic, holding beliefs tentatively that are open to challenge. They are open to changing their minds when confronted with sufficient and reliable information that is backed by sound argumentation.

Extraordinary claims require extraordinary evidence. The challenge is to be open-minded without being empty-headed. A healthy blend of empiricism, rationalism, and skepticism targets this objective.

How does this work? How do we know that a specific outcome is truly the result of a particular strategy, policy, partnership, or activity?

This is the issue of correlation vs. causality and it has long been a subject of debate since, generally, correlation is necessary to imply causality, but is not sufficient to establish causality. This debate is ordinarily couched in the language of cause-and-effect or cause-and-consequence relationships.

Complicating discovery and documentation of cause-and-consequence relationships is that many such relationships are partial in nature, that is, a single consequence, Y, may be rooted in many causes, $X_1, X_2, \ldots X_p$, that may or may not be coincident in time. Alternatively, a single cause, X, may contribute to, yet not be solely responsible for, any of multiple consequences, $Y_1, Y_2, \ldots Y_m$ that may or may not occur contemporaneously. Naturally occurring system or process variation or noise only adds to the vagaries of this discourse, further obscuring cause-and-consequence relationships.

Demonstration of causality ordinarily requires full or partial fulfillment of three requirements—the fuller the fulfillment, the more compelling the argument in favor of causality. The requirements are:

- Temporal precedence,
- Cause-and-consequence covariation, and
- Lack of plausible alternative explanations.

Temporal precedence implies that a cause precedes an effect, that is, the cause occurs beforehand so that consequences time-lag causes. While this is an easily understood concept, it is often less simple to demonstrate than to document temporal precedence. In fact, a consequence is often *significantly* time-lagged from its cause(s), making the detection of cause-and-consequence relationships more challenging still. This is often the case of interacting cycles where $X \leftrightarrow Y$ relationships may occur, that is where X implies or causes Y and, similarly, Y causes X.

Cause-and-consequence covariation is critical since, before a causal relationship between X and Y can be established, it is necessary to demonstrate that some type of relationship or covariation exists between X and Y. If X = cause and Y = consequence, then $X \rightarrow Y$ (cause implies consequence) suggests that if cause X occurs that consequence Y will manifest in whole or in part in the future. Conversely, if X is absent then Y will not fully manifest. Again, however, naturally occurring noise or variation adds complexity to the task of establishing cause-and-consequence covariation between X and Y.

Establishing that a relationship exists between X and Y does not of necessity imply that the relationship is a causal one. Indeed, the nature of any relationship involving X and Y may be causal, may reflect the influence of one or more intervening factors, or may be spurious. The no plausible alternative explanation requirement for establishing causality mandates that, through logical or otherwise compelling argumentation, all other alternative explanations for a relationship between X and Y can within reason be ruled out or marginalized.

Collectively, these three conditions set the burden of proof for cause-and-consequence relationships quite high, but such is the nature of critical and scientific thinking. Pursuit of excellence should generally be understood to entail consistent and significant effort, with much of that effort associated with the rigor and reward of critical and scientific thinking.

## Focus on Processes: Where Problems Arise, Solutions Reside, and Misunderstanding Abounds

Most work occurs as discrete acts or operations that—appropriately assembled—form a process. Linked processes, in turn, form a system and a single process may contribute to multiple systems. Connected or networked systems form larger entities still—systems of systems. Optimizing overall performance requires coordination of these systems; optimizing systems requires optimizing coordination of linked processes; optimization of any given process requires—at minimum—understanding of the role the process is intended to fulfill within the system to which it contributes. Optimizing a process requires each act that is part of the process, as well as the assembly of these acts.

Although the situation is clearly complex, it is not one devoid of hope. Rhetoric employed in operational excellence, quality management, Six Sigma, and related areas has long emphasized a focus on processes and this focus has been documented to deliver superior product designs when compared to the product designs that result from discrete jumps (Dertouzos, Lester, and Solow, 1989).

While acknowledging that this is important to process improvement, improvement generally, and excellence more pervasively, it cannot be too strongly argued that such focus should never be divorced from the following considerations:

- Enterprise culture,
- What the process is intended to deliver,
- The objective of improving the process,
- The greater systems context in which a process is carried out,
- The notion that optimizing a given process may in fact prove detrimental in the larger system perspective (Detert, Schroeder, and Mauriel, 2000).

The continuous improvement principle of focusing on processes and the enterprise alignment principle of thinking (and acting) systemically are inextricably linked and should hence be simultaneously addressed if they are to better deliver on their promise of operational excellence. Sadly, this is too rarely practiced with this deficiency owing in large part to tunnel vision relative to overemphasis and lack of understanding of what it means to practice a process focus. That is, too often there is an emphasis on processes without full understanding of how those processes relate to the larger systems and enterprise contexts.

## Assuring Quality at the Source: Correcting Problems Where and When They First Occur

Whether the specific values that follow are precise is questionable. The principle behind the figures is not in question. It is generally considered that every defect, every problem has an associated cost. Of course, different defects and different problems have different costs.

The longer a defect or problem goes undetected, the greater the cost. Not all costs are monetary in nature, nevertheless the costs of most defects or problems can ultimately be translated into monetary units, since most consequences will have monetary repercussions. As an example, reputational damage will almost always lead to monetizable losses, such as loss in share price or loss in market share, even if such losses prove temporary.

The figures typically reported that a defect that is detected and corrected at its source will have a cost of one monetary unit to the enterprise; a defect found downstream but still within the enterprise will have a cost of ten monetary units, and a defect that is passed along to and detected by the customer will cost the enterprise 100 monetary units. Again, these figures will clearly differ according to many factors such as the specific defect in question, the specific industry involved, and so on. But the point is obvious: while it is best not to make an error at all, if an error is made, the sooner the error is detected and corrected, the lower the cost to the enterprise.

Generally, Lean practices and principles seek to recover value sacrificed to poor processes, poor practices, poor policies, poor partnerships, and more. Relative to principle and associated practices of assuring quality at the source, the idea is to improve the performance of a process or—more holistically—a value stream, thus reducing the cost of a performance and provision, and in turn freeing up resources for other uses (Kohlbacher, 2010). This is akin to divesting the enterprise from poor processes and systems in ways similar to an enterprise divesting itself of poor acquisitions or unnecessary resources (Hayward and Shimizu, 2006).

This is the fundamental idea behind the principle of assuring quality at the source.

## Value of Flow and Pull: A Broader Stakeholder Perspective

Although stated as a single principle, flow and pull value are in fact closely correlated principles, each affecting the other. It is generally understood that what is of value and how much is determined by the customer. Value is a complex topic—so too is the concept of flowing and pulling value.

Value is created in "streams." Using the analogy of water flowing in a stream, the goal is to ensure smooth flow of value from one upstream activity to the next, to the next, to the next—removing all obstructions to flow. These obstructions are the equivalent of debris in a stream that hinders the free flow of water.

An example familiar to most experienced air travelers is provided by security screening. When there are relatively few passengers passing (flowing) through security, the process is generally simple with few delays. It begins with an initial check of a passenger's identification and boarding pass. Typically, this is followed by passenger removal of shoes, jackets, and belts and emptying of pockets, with these items placed in a separate bin that is passed through an electronic screening device. Similarly, fluids, laptop computers, and selected other electronic devices are separately screened, as are any carry-on baggage. Finally, the passenger will pass through a screening device. At this point, if all has gone without difficulty, screening will be complete and the passenger will repack items as needed, put on their shoes, belt, and so on and move along. Flow is slowed or interrupted however, when too few screening lanes are open and the passenger queues in open lanes begin to back-up. Passengers who are slow or ill-prepared to go through screening will cause delays. If a passenger fails to empty their pockets completely or fails to remove fluids from their baggage, or perhaps has a surgical pin that sets off a metal detector, screening is slowed. If screening devices raise any concerns, bags must be opened and inspected, and repacked and—again—screening is slowed. In short, there are many ways to interrupt the smooth flow of passengers through screening and much must go well to ensure smooth flow.

As may be surmised, ensuring smooth flow of value is largely dictated by two elements. One key element of flow is queue management— that is, management of the line of product or information that flows through the (value) stream, with the ultimate goal being one-piece flow. The idea of "one" in one-piece flow is that what the customer wants should be produced, in the quantity desired by the customer, provided in the timing needed by the customer, and with this flow of value in the form of a product, service, or information proceeding from beginning to end in an uninterrupted manner (Sekine, 1992).

Unlike a push system where production is initiated on the basis of a forecast that may be of questionable accuracy, pull systems initiate production or service or the flow of information in response to actual demand for the product, service, or information in question. Pull is a synonym for actual demand (Nemet, 2009), with the pull of value originating with customer demand and each step in the associated value stream pulling value in the form of product, service, or information from the immediately prior stage in the stream. The principle of pulling and flowing value is hence about value maximization, rather than maximizing production (Jensen, 2002; Leavy, 2012).

It must be noted that not all production, service provision, or information flow comes in response to customer-initiated demand. Indeed, there may be multiple initiators, including discovery-driven demand associated with research and development oriented invention and innovation that is sometimes called technology-push (Chidamber and Kon, 1994; Di Stefano, Gambardella, and Verona, 2012; Garcia-Quevedo, Pellegrino, and Savona, 2017), scientific discovery such as may occur in medical or pharmaceutical environments (Walsh, 1984), or—as previously noted—forecast or anticipated demand that sometimes equivocates to wishful thinking.

Before moving on from the principle of flow and pull value, the notion of value should be considered at a somewhat deeper level. The objective of the ensuing discussion is to stimulate the reader to develop enhanced consideration of what value is and what it means to pull and flow value within the complex systems context in which any enterprise operates.

A broader perspective regards value as determined by the voices of multiple stakeholders wherein it is not only the ability to fulfill customer needs and desires that is of import, but also the impact of doing so on society, the natural environment, reverberation throughout the supply chain, enterprise human ecology, and more.

The aforementioned broader perspective—referred to as value creation appropriation (VCA)—has gained momentum since the mid-1990s, with particular interest in the relationship between the dynamics of VCA and the strategic stakeholder view (Garcia-Castro and Aguilera, 2015) wherein stakeholders beyond the producer or service provider and the customer/consumer are also considered. In contrast, the historic view of (economic) value regards only two relevant stakeholders—the customer or consumer and the producer—wherein value is the sum of customer and producer surpluses. A consumer surplus is the difference between the amount a consumer is willing to pay for a product or service and the actual amount paid. Similarly, a producer or provider surplus is the difference between the amount that the producer or provider receives and the minimum amount that producer or provider is willing to accept in return for the product or service—a concept that has been extended beyond monetary value to include ecological and social considerations (Bagnoli and Watts, 2003; Devinney, 2009; Lenzen et al., 2007).

Introduction of additional stakeholders into value considerations, along with forms of value beyond monetary value, adds layers of complexity that demand redefinition of the notion of what constitutes a surplus. As such, a surplus will be defined as the difference between the minimal acceptable conditions of product or service provision and the actual conditions of delivery. Conditions are here regarded as including—at minimum—those of the triple top and bottom lines—that is, economic, social, and ecological conditions over appropriately determined time spans. Although the term surplus has been used, clearly it is possible that some or all stakeholders may experience deficit circumstances. In this sense, the total value created or surrendered by an enterprise must also include the value captured or surrendered by its stakeholders, in whatever forms that value assumes. This broader stakeholder-based view of VCA offers the theoretical foundation to a stakeholder approach to value where some stakeholders obtain positive net present value in their enterprise relationships, whereas other stakeholders obtain negative net present value.

It is at this juncture that the difference between shareholder value creation and total value created by the enterprise and its stakeholders must be addressed. Stakeholder value creation refers to the value generated on behalf of enterprise ownership. In contrast, value created by the enterprise and its stakeholders is the total economic value accumulated by all enterprise stakeholders. The total value created by an enterprise is simply the difference between willingness to pay and the opportunity cost (Brandenburger and Stuart, 1996). The enterprise acquires and expends resources such as capital, labor, and raw materials from suppliers. These resources are then transformed into products and services that are offered to enterprise customers. Customers capture more value when their willingness to pay for the product increases or when the price paid to the enterprise decreases. Similarly, suppliers capture more value when their opportunity costs decrease or by increasing the price paid by the enterprise for that which is supplied, or when their production or service provision costs decrease.

How is value measured? Traditional metrics of enterprise value creation use straight-forward measures such as profit ratios, net income, or of economic value added as the difference between economic profit and enterprise cost of capital (Davis and Kay, 1990). Such measures can be easily compared across the competitive landscape, hence their appeal. Though easily computed, these measures do not account for the stakeholder benefits created by the enterprise across all stakeholder segments, including benefits accrued by capital providers (Harrison, Bosse, and Phillips, 2010). Among significant benefits that are not directly observable in enterprise accounting statements are improved employee compensation and reduced consumer prices.

In the future, improved understanding of the principle of pulling and flowing value will almost certainly demand an evolving, deeper understanding of *value* in forms that extend beyond simple *monetary* value. Similarly, evolving understanding of pulling and flowing value will require consideration of stakeholders beyond the traditional ones of customers and producers only.

For other supporting concepts, systems, and tools relevant to this dimension please refer to the Shingo guidelines mentioned earlier and available to be downloaded from http://www.shingo.org/.

# 22

## *Shingo Model: Results Dimension Principle*

The *Results* dimension should be more broadly construed with both *performance and impacts*. While many will see these as synonymous or that any citation of differences between the two is equivalent to hairsplitting, the opinion herein is that separating one from the other is more akin to atom-splitting, or at least the consequence thereof which is the release of great power. In this sense, impacts are a consequence of results and may be of either intended or unintended nature.

The *Results* dimension has only one corresponding principle: *Create Value for the Customer.* The argument in favor of using "performance and impacts" as opposed to "results" derives from the concept of a chain reaction wherein the initial results spread the reaction or impacts, which under certain conditions may dramatically accelerate. Though often cast in a negative light, it is instructive to think of this in a way similar to the way that we might think of contagion or of something "going viral." Thinking of "results" as "performance and impacts" thus becomes akin to an extension of the S7 Structure beyond enterprise alignment into the realm of the intended beneficiaries of the enterprise (e.g., customers, but not only customers) . . . and the beneficiaries of their beneficiaries . . . and the beneficiaries of their beneficiaries of their beneficiaries . . . *ad infinitum.*

Use of *contagion* as an analogy for *impacts* from antecedent actions should serve to heighten our awareness that "what is good for the goose is *not always* good for the gander," and in fact that which is beneficial for one party may in turn create detrimental effects or impacts for a subsequent upstream or downstream party. This implies that an organization should strive to be cognizant of secondary and ancillary uses customers may have for products and services the organization provides and, in so far as possible, what may happen beyond those immediate uses. As an example, a pesticide or herbicide that improves both the yield and health of a crop so that more people can be fed more healthily may in turn become persistent in the soil or may penetrate an aquifer leading to illness resulting in lost workdays and productivity, disability or death, or other consequent tragedy. We see that despite good intentions associated with a product or service, the product or service may lead to both beneficial intended performance and impacts, as well as later unintended and detrimental performance and impacts.

Taking inspiration from wisdom literature that "where there is no guidance the people fall, but in abundance of counselors there is victory" (Proverbs 11:14, *New American Standard Bible*) underscores the potential value of interacting with various stakeholders. In this regard, crowdsourcing (Brabham, 2008) and citizen sourcing (Cobo, 2012) can provide valuable insight relative to the propagation of impacts through knowledge, insight, foresight, and wisdom that may not be resident in the enterprise, its supply chain, or among other intended enterprise beneficiaries. Similarly, approaches such as benchmarking may yield insights from internal sources or benchmarking partners (Drew, 1997; Vorhies and Morgan, 2005). In any case, each crowdsourcing, citizen sourcing, and benchmarking offer the possibility of garnering and hence of providing perspective beyond that directly implied by the *Shingo Guiding Principle* of create value for customers that is here more broadly stated in its future form of create value for stakeholders.

## CREATE VALUE FOR THE CUSTOMER

It is with the foregoing comments in mind that we refer to the *Shingo Guiding Principle* of *create value for the customer*, where customer value is regarded as the benefits received in exchange for the amount invested by the customer (Urbany and Davis, 2010). We note, in particular, that creating value for customers should always occur within the larger context of thinking, behaving, creating, and providing value not only legally, ethically, and morally, but also systematically, always with the awareness that an enterprise ecosystem may extend well beyond the organization, its suppliers, and its intended beneficiaries to unforeseen parties and that such parties may incur unintentional harm.

In other words, we take as a learning point that results and impacts must be concurrently considered, with full cognition that what is golden to one party or group may subsequently transform into fool's gold for another. As such, systematic thinking—previously cited as core to enterprise alignment—must occur with full cognizance of the relationships that exist between results and impacts.

Further, we must be fully aware that dynamic interactions are in play when the enterprise *creates value for the customer*. As such, when creating value for the customer, the larger context demands a more systemic construct that can be stated as *create value for stakeholders*, since creation of customer value devoid of consideration of other stakeholders may in fact create overall performance and impacts that are net negative.

**Create Value for Stakeholders**: Value must ultimately be determined through the lens of what customers want and for which they are willing to pay. Enterprises that fail to deliver effectively and efficiently on this fundamental outcome become unsustainable in the longer run. Extending this idea to the broader stakeholder perspective, stakeholder value is the sum of the real and perceived benefits accrued in exchange for the investment made by the stakeholder. When a single stakeholder is involved, that stakeholder will seek to optimize their benefits. Expansion to multiple stakeholders suggests that overall optimization may lead to situations where some stakeholders experience loss. In such instances, the enterprise must develop a broader stakeholder value strategy. Such strategies may focus on the benefits of one or a few stakeholders, may seek overall maximum benefit across relevant stakeholder segments, or may adopt a risk management stance that minimizes overall stakeholder losses or the number of stakeholders experiencing loss. Other possible stakeholder value strategies are a hybrid of the preceding ones. More generally, this principle can be stated as *create value for stakeholders*, with customers typically included among the collection of relevant stakeholders.

## A TREE IS KNOWN BY ITS FRUIT

Most readers will be familiar with the adage that a tree is known by its fruit. In the context of operational excellence, this adage is understood to mean that all enterprise strategy, activities, processes, and systems will ultimately be judged by the performance and impacts that result from these. Stated somewhat differently, the enterprise will be judged by the specific value it does and does not create for its stakeholders, by how it does so—and how it doesn't do so, and by trend in its performance.

If performance and impacts are inconsistent from year-to-year, sometimes up, sometimes down, if performance and impacts cannot clearly be connected to identified cause-and-consequence relationships in the enterprise or—worse—performance and impacts are consistently "rotten," then the enterprise cannot be considered operationally excellent, though it may have areas in which it excels. If, on the other hand, performance and impacts are consistently outstanding year-upon-year and can be demonstrably associated with cause-and-consequence relationships, then the enterprise will generally be understood to be on the path to operational excellence.

In keeping with the adage, the primary thrust of this book has been one of describing what the good fruit of operational excellence is like, the sorts of tree on which such fruit grows, and the planting and subsequent cultivation of such trees.

This is not, however, formulaic. Every enterprise has unique elements that must be considered. The implication is that while many common themes and approaches to operational excellence can be identified, each enterprise must become fully cognizant of its strengths and weaknesses, the threats in its environment as well as the opportunities resident in its competitive landscape, and must customize appropriately its path toward operational excellence.

## A HIERARCHY OF SHINGO GUIDING PRINCIPLES: SEEDS AND FRUIT

The ten guiding principles of the *Shingo Model* each hold value independently, but their true value is that they form a system of mutually enriching and interrelated principles. This system can be represented as in Figure 22.1, as a hierarchy represented in four layers, with the principles recorded in each layer proceeding in a clockwise direction from the top of the layer. Similar to principles, each layer holds value independently, but it is the exploitation of relationships among the principles and among the layers that unleashes the greatest power.

**FIGURE 22.1**
Hierarchy of Shingo guiding principles.

The layers of Figure 22.1 are intended to be read from the outside in, and in numeric order. Chapters 19 through 22 each correspond to a layer of this Figure and proceed from the exterior layer of Figure 22.1 to its core.

These principles have been discussed in relation to one another within each layer throughout Chapters 19 through 22 and have also been discussed relative to movement from one layer to the next, so that only selected final comments are in order.

Relative to the layers of Figure 22.1, cultural enablers facilitate enterprise alignment, enterprise alignment empowers continuous improvement, and continuous improvement leads to enhanced results. The outermost layer—cultural enablers—provides the seed for the fruit of enterprise alignment. Similarly, enterprise alignment principles become the seeds from which continuous improvement principles grow. In all, cultural enablers, enterprise alignment, and continuous improvement yield the fruit of operational excellence, the most crucial rendering of which is found in enterprise results, where results span many categories ranging from tactical to strategic in nature.

Within the cultural enabler layer, respect for each and every individual is prerequisite to leading with humility. The principles of the enterprise alignment layer of Figure 22.1 are perhaps the ones with least important specific order in the sense that each facilitates fulfillment of the other, but with the chosen order reflecting that creation of unity of purpose and shared vision should precede thinking systemically—a choice that follows from the notion that unity of purpose and shared vision frame or prioritize precisely what should be thought about systemically.

Within the continuous improvement layer of Figure 22.1, it is the pursuit of excellence that motivates embracing the principles and practices of critical and scientific thinking. In turn, critical and scientific thinking enhances the ability to productively focus on processes, the doing of which will inevitably push the assurance of quality closer and closer to the actual activity—e.g., source—that has the potential to create or detract from the value of a product or service. Accomplishing this enhances the ability of the enterprise to flow value to its stakeholders in response to pull, that is, in response to actual demand.

Collectively, these enable the enterprise to deliver tactically and strategically superior results—the holy grail of operational excellence.

For other supporting concepts, systems, and tools relevant to this dimension please refer to the Shingo guidelines mentioned earlier and available to download from http://www.shingo.org/.

# 23

## The Shingo Model

Integration of *Shingo Guiding Principles*, the *Three Insights of Enterprise Excellence*, and supporting systems and tools in relation to results (performance and impacts) yields the *Shingo Model*. Graphic representation of this model is provided in Figure 23.1 (ShingoPrize.org/model.html). Similarly, *Shingo Guiding Principles* in the graphical form in which they are ordinarily presented appear in Figure 23.2.

Figure 23.1 includes five interlocking elements with culture at its core, surrounded by guiding principles, systems, tools, and results. To this juncture, results and principles have been extensively discussed, some tools have been presented, and the importance of systems have been emphasized. It is important however, to understand the meaning of tools, systems, and results relative to the *Shingo Model*.

## SYSTEMS, TOOLS, AND RESULTS

In this model, a tool is regarded as a single device or item that accomplishes a specific task. Examples of tools that have been presented herein include the nominal group technique, Kano customer needs model, house of quality, interrelationship digraph, and affinity diagram.

Similarly, a system is a highly integrated collection of tools or tasks that work in concert to accomplish a specified outcome. Reward and recognition systems and customer complaint systems provide two familiar examples of systems, with product ideation providing another. The product ideation and deployment system might be considered to include the following elements:

- initial voice of the customer gathering that is followed by facilitation and seeding of a brainstorming activity,

- brainstorming itself,
- affinity diagram construction to categorize brainstormed ideas,
- followed by use of the nominal group technique to prioritize ideas, and
- an interrelationship digraph to determine where ideas are in conflict and where they are synergistic,
- followed by formal concept generation and selection that includes use of concept screening and scoring, then finally
- use of the house of quality and quality function deployment to move the product to market.

Some parts of the product ideation and deployment system can be grouped into clear subsystems. For example, concept generation and selection might be regarded as a subsystem that includes use of tools such as ideation to generate concepts that are then screened and scored to facilitate final concept selection.

Lastly, a result is a measurable outcome, whether that outcome is unsuccessful, neutral or successful. This measurable outcome results from implementation of tools and systems. Examples of results might include decreased error rates, faster changeover of a manufacturing setup, increased employee engagement, improved customer retention, increased market share, improved community relations, or a smaller carbon footprint.

We see then that tools are formed into systems that produce results. If the enterprise is to produce the best possible results for its stakeholders, it must optimize its systems, in part by appropriate choice, integration, and use of tools.

## REINFORCING CYCLES IN THE *SHINGO MODEL*

It is with this understanding of systems, tools, and results that we turn to Figure 23.1. Enterprise culture lies at the heart of Figure 23.1 and we here note that the whole of an enterprise's goings on are rooted in its culture—its purpose for and way of doing what it does. Fundamentally, culture is "the way we do things around here"—that is, the collection of all the behaviors in the enterprise wherein some behaviors will be positive, productive, or uplifting, whereas other behaviors may be negative, counterproductive, or corrosive. As such, it is important to recall that the *Shingo Guiding Principles* manifest in ideal behaviors. As such, systems become intentionally aligned to ideal behaviors by providing incentives for individuals functioning within a system to think and act in ways that move progressively closer to ideal behaviors. This comes with the caveat that—rather than a single leap from current behaviors to ideal ones—this progression may require a series of steps as systems are intentionally evolved. The reinforcing cycles in the *Shingo Model* as expressed in Figure 23.1 are intended to aid this progression, with one cycle presented as a clockwise rotation and its complementary one rotating in a counterclockwise direction.

Beginning at the top of Figure 23.1 with guiding principles that have been previously presented and are repeated in Figure 23.2 and moving in a clockwise direction, the *Shingo Model* indicates that guiding principles are used to align systems, the functioning of which are either enhanced or impeded by specific tools used to drive or achieve results, where results then affirm the guiding principles. This is what occurs when all is well, since of course poor alignment or poor choice and use of tools will lead to suboptimal results that—at least to an extent—fail to fully satisfy guiding principles. Similarly, beginning again at the top of Figure 23.1 and moving in a counterclockwise direction, the *Shingo Model* indicates that guiding principles drive results in the form of performance and impacts from which the enterprise can derive both insight and foresight that will aid refinement of the tools used to better enable the systems that, in turn, drive guiding principles that are anchored in enterprise core values deeper into the enterprise at both the individual and collective levels.

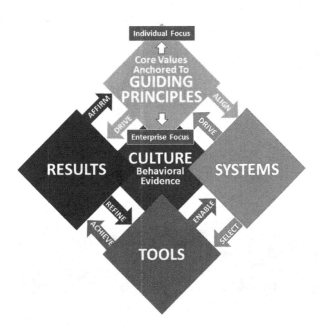

**FIGURE 23.1**
Shingo Model.

## CORRESPONDENCE WITH *THE TOYOTA WAY*

Given the broad familiarity of Lean-and-quality oriented professionals with the landmark book, *The Toyota Way*, by Jeffrey Liker (2003), it is of value to present an approximate correspondence between the guiding principles of the *Shingo Model* and those presented in *The Toyota Way*.

Liker identified 14 principles that can be distributed across four primary domains. These domains, their corresponding aims, and related principles are provided in Table 23.1 and appear on the right side of Figure 23.3 where the 14 management principles comprising *The Toyota Way* are positioned on its right side and the ten *Shingo Guiding Principles* are positioned on its left side. Extending from the bottom to the top of the left side of the triangle in Figure 23.3 and associated with the various domains are brief descriptions of each intent of each domain.

A high degree of agreement between the *10 Shingo Guiding Principles* and the *14 Toyota Way* principles identified by Liker is seen to exist. This result is not unexpected, given the seminal influence on the famed Toyota Production System that was exerted by Shigeo Shingo.

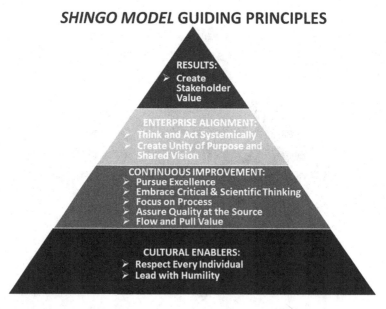

**SHINGO MODEL GUIDING PRINCIPLES**

**FIGURE 23.2**
The 10 *Shingo Guiding Principles*.

**TABLE 23.1**

Toyota Way 14 Management Principles

| Domain | Aim |
|---|---|
| **Problem-Solving** | **Continuous improvement and learning** |
| **Principles** | Continual organizational learning via relentless reflection (*hansei*) and continuous improvement (*kaizen*) |
| | Go to the place where the work is done to see and assess the situation and its nuances (*gemba genbutsu*) |
| | Make decisions by consensus, thoroughly considering all options, then implement rapidly |
| **People and Partners** | **Respect, challenge, and grow them** |
| **Principles** | Grow leaders who live the philosophy |
| | Respect, develop, and challenge your people and teams |
| | Respect your extended network of partners and suppliers by challenging them and helping them improve |
| **Process** | **Eliminate waste** |
| **Principles** | Create process flow to surface problems |
| | Avoid overproduction via pull systems |
| | Level out the workload (*heijunka*) |
| | Stop when or if quality problems arise (*jidoka*) |
| | Standardize tasks for continuous improvement |
| | Use visual control to reveal problems |
| | Use only reliable, thoroughly tested technology |
| **Philosophy** | **Long-term thinking** |
| **Principles** | Base management decisions on a long-term philosophy, even at the expense of short-term financial goals |

*Source:* Liker, J. (2003), *The Toyota Way: 14 Management Principles from the World's Greatest Manufacturer,* McGraw Hill Professional, New York, NY.

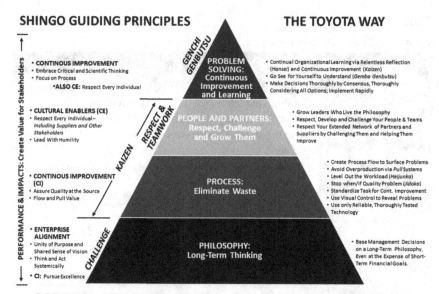

**SHINGO GUIDING PRINCIPLES**

**THE TOYOTA WAY**

PERFORMANCE & IMPACTS: Create Value for Stakeholders

GENCHI GENBUTSU

RESPECT & TEAMWORK

KAIZEN

CHALLENGE

**PROBLEM SOLVING:**
Continuous Improvement and Learning

**PEOPLE AND PARTNERS:**
Respect, Challenge and Grow Them

**PROCESS:**
Eliminate Waste

**PHILOSOPHY:**
Long-Term Thinking

- **CONTINOUS IMPROVEMENT**
  - Embrace Critical and Scientific Thinking
  - Focus on Process
  - **ALSO CE:** Respect Every Individual

- **CULTURAL ENABLERS (CE)**
  - Respect Every Individual— Including Suppliers and Other Stakeholders
  - Lead With Humility

- **CONTINOUS IMPROVEMENT (CI)**
  - Assure Quality at the Source
  - Flow and Pull Value

- **ENTERPRISE ALIGNMENT**
  - Unity of Purpose and Shared Sense of Vision
  - Think and Act Systemically
  - **CI:** Pursue Excellence

- Continual Organizational Learning via Relentless Reflection (*Hansei*) and Continuous Improvement (*Kaizen*)
- Go See for Yourself to Understand (*Gemba Genbutsu*)
- Make Decisions Thoroughly by Consensus, Thoroughly Considering All Options; Implement Rapidly

- Grow Leaders Who Live the Philosophy
- Respect, Develop and Challenge Your People & Teams
- Respect Your Extended Network of Partners and Suppliers by Challenging Them and Helping Them Improve

- Create Process Flow to Surface Problems
- Avoid Overproduction via *Pull* Systems
- Level Out the Workload (*Heijunka*)
- Stop when/if Quality Problem (*Jidoka*)
- Standardize Task for Cont. Improvement
- Use Visual Control to Reveal Problems
- Use only Reliable, Thoroughly Tested Technology

- Base Management Decisions on a Long-Term Philosophy, Even at the Expense of Short-Term Financial Goals.

## CORRESPONDENCE OF SHINGO GUIDING PRINCIPLES WITH THE TOYOTA WAY AND *TOYOTA TERMS*

**FIGURE 23.3**

Mapping principles: *Shingo Guiding Principles* and Liker's Toyota Way Principles.

# 24

## *The* Shingo Model *as a Complex Management Systems Model*

In many regards, culture can be thought of as the shadow behind much that does and does not occur in an enterprise. Although culture may be regarded as the way that the enterprise does things, it is more. Culture is also why the enterprise does what it does and how it does so. While enterprise culture may be tangibly expressed in terms of, for example, formal codes of conduct, it is also rife with intangible elements. A result of this perspective is that principles, processes, systems, activities, vision, strategy, and more are all embedded in enterprise culture. In this context, as before, we regard strategy as a description of how the enterprise intends to create value for its varied stakeholders (Kaplan and Norton, 2004). The enterprise, though, is part of a much larger picture, functioning within the larger ecology that is represented by the BEST environmental domains and interacting with its stakeholders.

In this broader enterprise context, guiding principles saturate its culture, vision and objectives, strategy and processes formulated to realize these, and the specific activities that represent the actual doing, that is, that generate consequent performance and impacts. This view is portrayed in Figures 24.1 and 24.2. Regardless, we see the importance of respecting not only every member of the enterprise, but also its stakeholders, the communities it serves, and even its "adversaries" that may include tangible members such as regulatory agencies or other cause-driven constraining forces such as environmental, social, or educational concerns. It is not until this level of respect exists that enterprise leadership demonstrates true humility. In this regard, respect every individual and lead with humility are "supra" principles that are fundamental to the enterprise as a whole, so that while evidence of each can be seen in each of the three inner

**FIGURE 24.1**
The *Shingo Model* as a complex management systems operational excellence model.

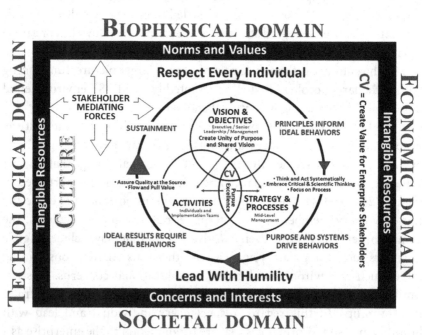

**FIGURE 24.2**
The *Shingo Model* in a complex management systems model context.

circles of Figures 24.1 and 24.2, they are nevertheless best represented as supra principles.

Leading with humility better enables the communication of vision and objectives because the humble leader is regarded as more authentic, and in that sense "more worthy" to lead creation of shared meaning. This is essential to formation of a collective identity and in turn to creation of unity of purpose and a common vision (Bennis and Thomas, 2002; Collins, 2005; Pierce et al., 1989). This is more than emotional and intellectual buy-in, it is also a collective will to move forward, collaboratively and with coordinated effort. This is an example of one of the *Three Insights of Enterprise Excellence* in action, namely, that principles inform (ideal) behaviors.

This collective will or drive must be mobilized or deployed and must be done so with maximum effectiveness. Effectiveness is advanced through enterprise-wide scientific and systematic thinking that critically examines relevant processes, but with a sense of priority that is aligned with vision and objectives. In this we see that purpose and systems drive behaviors, crucial among which is pursuit of excellence across a broad spectrum of areas that include, but are not limited to, enterprise operations, its supply chain, its innovation priorities and efforts, and analytics-driven decisions and actions.

In focusing on value creating and value detracting, processes or portions of optimization and/or renewal is supported by the search for root enablers of value creation or root causes of value destruction. This approach will progressively and inevitably drive efforts to assure quality at the source. The more successful these efforts are, the better the ability of the enterprise to flow and pull value that is delivered in its varied forms to enterprise stakeholders. In Shingo terminology, these are examples of ideal behaviors driving ideal results.

The small arrowheads on the vision and objectives, strategy and processes, and activities circles and the fact that the circles intersect one another indicate that these are interrelated and mutually reinforcing cycles—hence the wo-way arrows connecting these—so that none of these, nor even all of these considered independently, can deliver what the three considered collectively (e.g., as a system) can deliver.

Ultimately, the overall enterprise intent is to deliver value to its varied stakeholders, among which one stakeholder segment—often customers—is likely to be of greater concern than the others relative to any given change. Specific value delivered depends of course on many factors including how subtle or revolutionary the change is, how much risk is associated with the change, how much of that risk is shared risk, and the stakeholder segment that is of greatest concern. In some instances, some stakeholder segments will benefit from changes, some segments may remain more-or-less inoculated or bulletproof to effects of the same changes, and remaining segments may be called upon to make sacrifices as a means of attaining some greater good, whether that good is tangible or intangible.

In any instance, but especially in cases where significant sacrifice is called for, it is incumbent on the enterprise to make a clear and compelling case for change well before change is implemented, especially to those stakeholder segments bearing the brunt of the sacrifice. Not only must the benefits of change be made clear, but also the depth and duration of sacrifice. Change may be inevitable, but better buy in to change relies on how and how well change is approached and communicated.

Relative to the *10 Shingo Guiding Principles* upon which the *Shingo Model* is built, the outermost circle of Figure 24.1 is intended to reveal the enabling nature of the *Three Insights of Enterprise Excellence* that emerged somewhat later. The increasing size of the arrowheads on the outer circle as it proceeds clockwise are intended to communicate improving understanding and adeptness of the enterprise as the cycle is repeated over and over, and hence enterprise advancement.

This latter concept is analogous to application of a Plan–Do–Study–Act (PDSA) approach to overall enterprise optimization and renewal, and serves to enable both the enterprise's quest for excellence and its ability to sustain itself. This latter claim is based not only on cycles of conscious improvement, but on the mutually reinforcing nature of the enterprise's vision, systems, processes, practices, and policies in relation to its culture and the hard work of understanding and interacting in mutually beneficial ways with its stakeholders. These observations assume an appropriately high level of enterprise alignment. Equally important is clear awareness of the positioning of the enterprise within the portion of the external environment represented by the BEST environmental domains, and with respect to mediating forces, as portrayed in Figure 24.2.

It is at this juncture that Figure 24.2 and Figure 10.1 may be combined. Recall that Figure 10.1 provided a representation of a complex management systems operational excellence model. Combining the two figures provides a unifying view of the *Shingo Model* and an operational excellence model, as seen through a complex management systems lens. This is represented in Figure 24.3.

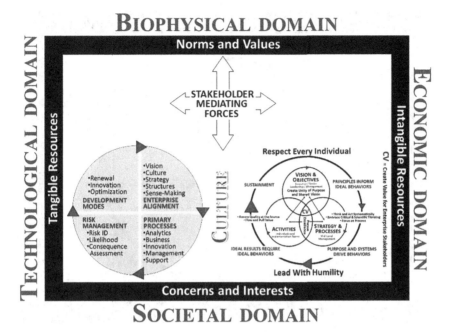

**FIGURE 24.3**

Combining the *Shingo Model* with the complex management systems operational excellence model.

## DEEPER INTEGRATION OF THE *SHINGO MODEL* AND THE COMPLEX MANAGEMENT SYSTEMS MODEL

We now see the fit of the *Shingo Model* in a complex management systems context.

With advance apologies for what will prove to be a complex graphic, Figure 24.4 has been developed with the aim of making this fit more explicit.

This figure provides one possible set of logical correspondences between the areas into which the *Shingo Guiding Principles* of Figure 22.2 are divided — Results, Enterprise Alignment, Continuous Improvement, and Cultural Enablers — and the main enterprise "bricks" identified in Figures 5.1, 7.1, 8.1, and 9.1—that is, Enterprise Alignment, Primary Enterprise Processes, Enterprise Risk Management, and Enterprise Advancement Means is displayed in Figure 24.4. Explanation of this figure requires description of its logic, as well as discussion aimed at harmonizing the differing "dialects" of the *Shingo Model* and of complex management systems modeling.

**FIGURE 24.4**
Correspondence of the organization with the *Shingo Model*.

## The Outer Circle and Its Core

Prior to examining the perimeter of Figure 24.4, consider the outer circle of the figure and the three arrowheads positioned on this circle. This circle is used to denote the sustainment of the enterprise. The rightmost arrowhead indicates that culture drives alignment. This is followed by the arrowhead on the lower portion of the outer circle wherein alignment drives activities that will ultimately advance the enterprise. The arrowhead on the left side of the circle indicates that activities (behaviors) drive results that aid enterprise advancement. Advancement of the enterprise through relentless pursuit of excellence is enabled by key strategy, including strategy aimed at innovation or renewal or optimization and key processes or activities including, for example, social-ecological innovation-oriented ones contribute to enterprise sustainability, both in the short-term (survival) and long-term (prosperity). Most if not all strategies and actions aimed at ensuring the health and prosperity of the enterprise—its sustainability— can be regarded as having risk management components that are mixed with creation and delivery of value to enterprise stakeholders—the two elements at the core of Figure 24.4. This latter assertion leads to the association of risk management, value creation, and pursuit of excellence with sustainment in Figure 24.4.

Some elements can be integrated throughout the model or, more accurately, throughout the enterprise via its purpose, vision, strategy, processes, and activities and reflected in its results and sustainability. As an obvious example, innovation is often a key element of enterprise strategy that may contribute to an enterprise purpose of being more socially and environmentally responsible, while at the same time delivering financial results necessary to the health and sustainability of the enterprise. To deliver innovative products or services that accomplish this, it is likely important to routinize—that is, make procedural—innovative thinking, processes, and actions. In such cases, depending on the context or scope of the conversation, innovation is key to continuous and breakthrough improvement, is a process, is critical to enterprise advancement, and hence also to its sustainability. This implies that some elements—innovation providing a case in point—may be included in multiple locations in the model and play multiple roles in the enterprise.

## Members of the Inner Circle and Pointing Fingers

Note first that the three small circles and three arrows at the interior of Figure 24.4 reside with the outer enterprise sustainment circle. This relative positioning is intended to communicate that all enterprise strategy, activities, and results should contribute to its sustainability.

Beginning with the top, inner circle and moving in a clockwise direction we see that culture drives alignment, which in turn drives activities and— as seen at the core of Figure 24.4—these, together with relentless pursuit of excellence, collectively drive creation of value for enterprise stakeholders. In a similar way, the three arrows or fingers forming a triangle at the core of Figure 24.4 can be read as alignment drives choice and sequencing of actions, which in turn drive results, with results including the creation of value for stakeholders.

## Probing the Perimeter

The top and bottom borders of Figure 24.4 link the principles of the Cultural Enablers dimension of respecting every individual and leading with humility with enterprise alignment. These are intended to address the inextricable linkage of culture with strategic and operational alignment of the enterprise. As such, we see that realization of the initial enterprise excellence insight that principles inform the ideal behaviors necessary to strategy execution contributes to enterprise alignment (Figure 5.1).

More full alignment requires unified intellectual, emotional, and physical commitment to a shared enterprise-level vision, as well as systemic or holistic understanding of the purpose behind the vision. Rather than pure emotion however, optimizing the level at which purpose and vision are fulfilled requires the sort of strategic (intellectual) and analytic engagement that is advanced through sound scientific thinking (logic) and subsequent action that produces results.

This suggests that some continuous and breakthrough improvement principles supporting the *Shingo Model* are fundamentally more cerebral and critical to enabling the delivery of results. Such continuous and breakthrough improvement principles include systemic thinking and rigorous practice of scientific thinking. Action-oriented continuous and breakthrough improvement principles such as process focus, assurance of quality at the source, and flowing and pulling value in response to actual demand. These deliver results arrived at through execution of various processes and activities.

Delivery of results require translation of purpose and vision into systems and of systems into constituent processes, leading to the second enterprise excellence insight, that purpose and systems drive behaviors—and it is those behaviors that form the core of the various primary processes (and other) enterprise processes. These processes and activities are driven by ideal behaviors leading to ideal results, with the intended byproduct being enterprise advancement.

The right border of Figure 24.4 is, in the end, about the "ultimate" result of creating value for enterprise stakeholders. This ultimate result concerns creating value for the enterprise stakeholder, with the typical preeminent stakeholder being enterprise customers. Such value creation is complex and stems from enterprise strategy yet should be systemic throughout essentially all enterprise processes and activities. Given the importance of value creation, emphasis is placed on identification and execution of ideal behaviors and a means of producing this ultimate result at its most extreme level, while noting that this level is subject to the sorts of constraints associated with multiple stakeholders that have been previously addressed.

Finally, in addressing the left border of Figure 24.4, it is reiterated that all strategies, actions, and results represented in the interior of Figure 24.4 are intended to result in good enterprise health and prosperity and hence

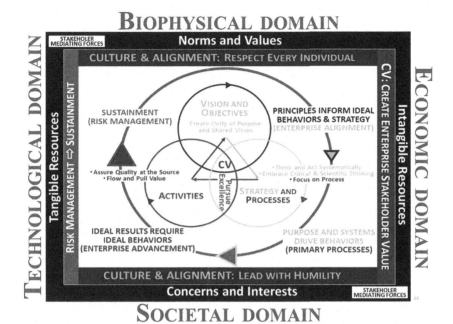

**FIGURE 24.5**
Complex management systems-based expression of the *Shingo Model*.

sustainability of the enterprise. Using health as an analogy, this is true even in instances where the primary aim of enterprise leadership is to develop the enterprise for divestment purposes, wherein greater health will ordinarily attract more attractive divestment opportunities.

Figure 24.4 can now be embedded at the heart of Figure 24.2 to yield Figure 24.5. This latter figure provides the full expression of the *Shingo Model* in a complex management systems modeling context. All that remains is consideration of how this model is used on a practical level to aid enterprises in their onward journeys toward operational excellence. In doing so, we will first turn to the most public face of this model, the Shingo Prize for Operational Excellence.

# 25

## Enterprise Assessment Using Shingo Assessment Criteria

At the time of this writing, Shingo Prize applicants are assessed on a 1,000-point possible scale relative to the four dimensions of the *Shingo Model*: Cultural Enablers (250 points), Continuous Improvement (350 points), Enterprise Alignment (200 points), and Results (200 points). As previously noted, future rebalancing of these is anticipated, with a shift toward greater emphasis on results and key systems. That being said, it is the long-standing perspective of the Shingo Institute that systems within cultural enablers, continuous process improvement, and enterprise alignment drive behaviors and results, that is, that these drive performance and impacts. As such, rebalancing is aimed at making the importance of results more overt. It is the intent of the Shingo Institute that the model and guidelines continue to evolve as new insights and learnings are gained. To this end, the Institute continues in its research efforts. It should also be noted that the Institute is fortunate to have access to resources beyond its walls and is grateful to many who participate in the development of and support its work.

As represented in Figure 25.1, the intent of an assessment is to evaluate the entire applying entity to determine the degree to which the principles of operational excellence are embedded into the culture of an organization. How close to ideal behavior are the current behaviors observed? How mature is the culture? Results are also evaluated. Behaviors are evaluated using behavior assessment scales, and results are evaluated using the results assessment scale. Scales are presented below.

The difference between observed behavior and ideal behavior is the gap. The assessment will provide a gap analysis that can be used to focus improvement activities. It will provide a baseline of cultural reality

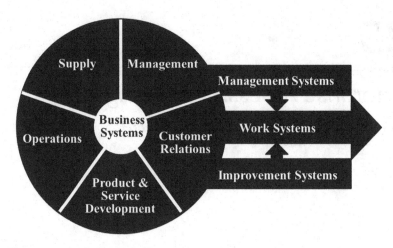

**FIGURE 25.1**
Assessing the systems in an enterprise.

that will enable an organization to move forward on its journey toward building a culture of operational excellence.

Tables provided in this section can be found in the *Shingo Application Guidelines* (https://shingo.org/assets/Application_Guidelines.pdf). Note that while belief in operational excellence has not diminished within the Shingo Institute or other advocates of its model, a transition is in process toward usage of the term "enterprise excellence" that many perceive as more encompassing and as perhaps more representative of non-manufacturing-oriented enterprises. The application guidelines containing the same or similar tables are available at the Shingo Institute website: www.shingo.org.

Table 25.1 provides the standard scoring matrix used in the assessment of applicant enterprises. In this matrix, it should be noted that with respect to Cultural Enablers, Continuous Process Improvement, and Enterprise Alignment that the current assessment process allocates differing percentages of points to senior leadership, operations managers, operations associates, support service managers, and support service associates. As we continue to improve, it is anticipated the adjustments to weighting will also be made.

The Cultural Enablers dimension is associated with the principles of "lead with humility" and "respect every individual." Similarly, the Continuous (and breakthrough) Improvement dimension is related to the principles of "seek perfection," "embrace scientific thinking," "focus on process," "assure quality at the source," and "flow and pull value."

**TABLE 25.1**

Shingo Prize Applicant Assessment Scoring Matrix

| Scoring Matrix | | Senior Leadership | Operations | | Support | |
|---|---|---|---|---|---|---|
| | | | Managers | Associates | Managers | Associates |
| Cultural Enabler (250 pts.) | *Cultural Enablers Weight* | 40% | 20% | 10% | 20% | 10% |
| Continuous Improvement (350 pts.) | *Continuous Improvement Weight* | 15% | 35% | 15% | 25% | 10% |
| Enterprise Alignment (200 pts.) | *Enterprise Alignment Weight* | 50% | 20% | 5% | 20% | 5% |
| Results (200 pts.) | *Quality* 20% | | | | | |
| | *Cost/Productivity* 20% | | | | | |
| | *Delivery* 20% | | | | | |
| | *Customer Satisfaction* 20% | | | | | |
| | *Safety/Environment/Morale* 20% | | | | | |

*Source:* Shingo Institute (2017), *The Shingo Model Book*, Shingo Institute, Utah State University, Logan, UT.

The Enterprise Alignment dimension is related to the principles of "think systemically" and "create constancy of purpose." Finally, the Results Dimension is associated with "creating value for the customer."

The first three of these dimensions—Cultural Enablers, Continuous Improvement, and Enterprise Alignment—are assessed using the behavioral assessment scale provided in Table 25.2. The Results dimension is assessed using the measures assessment scale provided in Table 25.3.

The *Results* dimension assesses enterprise performance and impacts relative to the five categories of:

- Quality,
- Cost/productivity,
- Delivery,
- Customer satisfaction, and
- Safety/environment/morale.

Each of these results categories are equally weighted. It should be noted, however, that in assessment of enterprise results there is no differentiation with respect to leaders, managers, and associates in the way that there is for other categories.

In delineating scoring as we have described, each dimension is associated with specific principles emphasized in the *Shingo Model*. As such, assessment seeks to identify the presence, practice, and relative effectiveness of these principles in the enterprise at behavioral and performance levels. Simultaneously, however, this is done through examination of key systems that are contextually relevant to the enterprise.

Turning to Table 25.1, the percentages provided therein represent a "level playing field" in the sense that enterprises applying for a prize are assessed in a consistent manner for comparability purposes. Very much worth noting, however, is that many enterprises using excellence models never formally pursue a prize or award such as the Shingo Prize, Baldrige National Quality Award, or EFQM Excellence Award or the recognition that comes with being named as a recipient. Instead, many enterprises use such models as a self-assessment tool and do so routinely, typically annually, in their pursuit of ongoing improvement.

In cases where a given enterprise excellence model is used only for self-assessment and self-improvement, it is often reasonable for an organization to focus an assessment more narrowly on specific systems being changed and those being assessed for sustainability. This might be viewed as scaling down a given assessment. This can be helpful in understanding more rapidly if a gap is actually being closed by the changes being made. It is important, however, to stay aligned with the original design and methodology of the assessment being scaled. In the case of the Shingo assessment, this would mean that, although the scale may be narrower and could even be scored differently, the assessment would still evaluate the behaviors and results being driven by a system and the maturity of each. By staying aligned with an assessment methodology and model, an organization is able to scale up and down while retaining the integrity of a given assessment. In simple terms, if aligned appropriately, moving the maturity levels of behaviors and results in enough systems should move the maturity level of the organization as a whole when an organizational assessment is taken.

The primary approach used to assess enterprises against a given model and associated set of criteria is to employ carefully crafted graduated maturity scales. This approach is reflected in Tables 25.2 and 25.3. Maturity scales are descriptive with each step in the scale providing representative findings of behaviors or performance at progressively more mature or advanced levels. With both scales, fully matching the descriptors within a level would be associated with a score at the top of the level. The top of level 5 or 100 percent is ideal. Development and effective subsequent use of maturity scales requires significant expertise in the area being assessed. This is the case because expert judgment is needed to expand reasonably beyond non-contextualized and relatively generic examples of behavior or performance at specific maturity levels. In any case, there is always a degree of judgment or subjectivity that is necessary when such an assessment approach is used, since maturity scales are qualitative in nature. Obviously enough then, the value of any judgment depends on the expertise of the judge.

There are several components to be evaluated when using the following behavior assessment scale. The first is how closely behaviors observed match ideal behaviors. Second, how embedded the behavior is into the culture; this is also referred to as maturity. Note that good or bad behaviors can be embedded, and an assessor should consider both in the assessment process. A bad behavior that is deeply embedded in a culture is very difficult to change and will take significant intervention to do so. To assess how embedded/mature a behavior is in an organization's culture, the following lenses are evaluated: frequency, intensity, duration, scope, and role.

**TABLE 25.2**

Behavior Assessment Scale

| Lenses | Level 1 0% to 20% | Level 2 21% to 40% | Level 3 41% to 60% | Level 4 61% to 80% | Level 5 81% to 100% |
|---|---|---|---|---|---|
| **Role** | Leaders are focused mostly on fire-fighting and largely absent from improvement efforts. | Leaders are aware of other's initiatives to improve but are largely uninvolved. | Leaders set direction for improvement and support efforts of others. | Leaders are involved in improvement efforts and support the alignment of principles of enterprise excellence with systems. | Leaders are focused on ensuring that enterprise excellence principles are driven deeply into the culture and regularly assessed for improvement. |
| | Managers are oriented toward getting results "at all costs." | Managers mostly look to specialists to create improvement through a project orientation. | Managers are involved in developing systems and helping others to use tools effectively. | Managers focus on driving behaviors through the design of systems. | Managers are primarily focused on continuously improving systems to drive behavior that is more closely aligned with enterprise excellence principles. |
| | Associates focus on doing their jobs and are generally treated like an expense. | Associates are occasionally asked to participate on an improvement team that is usually led by someone outside their natural work team. | Associates are trained and participate in improvement projects. | Associates are routinely involved in using tools to drive continuous improvement in their own areas of responsibility. | Associates understand principles, the "why" behind the tools, and are leaders for improving their own work systems and other systems within their value stream. |

*(Continued)*

**TABLE 25.2 (CONTINUED)**

Behavior Assessment Scale

| Lenses | Level 1<br>0% to 20% | Level 2<br>21% to 40% | Level 3<br>41% to 60% | Level 4<br>61% to 80% | Level 5<br>81% to 100% |
|---|---|---|---|---|---|
| **Frequency** | Infrequent or rare. | Event-based and irregular. | Frequent and common. | Consistent and predominant. | Constant and uniform. |
| **Duration** | Initiated or undeveloped. | Experimental and formative. | Repeatable and predictable. | Established and stable. | Culturally integrated and mature. |
| **Intensity** | Apathetic or indifferent. | Apparent with individual commitment. | Moderate local commitment. | Persistent, wide commitment. | Tenacious with full commitment. |
| **Scope** | Isolated with point solutions. | Silos, internal value stream only. | Predominantly in operations with functional value stream consideration. | Multiple business processes with integrated value stream consideration. | Enterprise-wide with extended value stream consideration. |

**TABLE 25.3**

Results Assessment Scale

| Lenses | Level 1<br>0 to 20% | Level 2<br>21 to 40% | Level 3<br>41 to 60% | Level 4<br>61 to 80% | Level 5<br>81 to 100% |
|---|---|---|---|---|---|
| **Stability** | Little or no evidence of stability.<br>Little to no predictability.<br>Beginning to implement.<br>Unpredictable.<br>0–1 year. | | Has begun to stabilize.<br>Initiating predictability.<br>Building maturity.<br>All levels have become comfortable with measures.<br>2 to 3 years. | | Stable.<br>Predictable.<br>Long-term.<br>Mature.<br>4+ years. |
| **Trend/Level** | Level is low.<br>Trend is poor.<br>Little to no evidence of goals.<br>Little to no evidence of benchmarking. | | Moderate improvement in level.<br>Trends are mostly positive to flat with some backsliding.<br>Benchmarking is industry-focused. | | High level of attainment considered world-class.<br>Benchmarks constantly raise the bar and are a function of process, not industry.<br>Positive trend with very few anomalies to explain.<br>Trend is well above expectations. |
| **Alignment** | Isolated with inconsistent usage of measures.<br>Little alignment.<br>Strong silos. | | Some areas are aligned.<br>Performance measures aligned in operations.<br>Silos are beginning to fall.<br>Working toward enterprise-wide alignment. | | All measures align to corporate goals and down to the lowest level.<br>Enterprise-wide extended value stream.<br>No silos. |

*(Continued)*

**TABLE 25.3 (CONTINUED)**

Results Assessment Scale

| Lenses | Level 1<br>0 to 20% | Level 2<br>21 to 40% | Level 3<br>41 to 60% | Level 4<br>61 to 80% | Level 5<br>81 to 100% |
|---|---|---|---|---|---|
| **Improvement** | Little to no systematic feedback.<br>Sporadic feedback.<br>Little evidence of goal setting, some evidence in operations. | | Regular feedback in some areas.<br>All areas do not address feedback systematically.<br>Many areas beyond operations have a process to set goals. | | Routine feedback to appropriate party.<br>Evidence of feedback in all areas.<br>Almost all areas have realistic and challenging goals. |

- **Frequency**: how often do we see the behavior?
- **Duration**: are we seeing the behavior for the first time or have we seen this behavior for years?
- **Intensity**: is there a sense of passion and importance for the behavior (i.e., to deviate would signal problems)?
- **Scope**: do we see the behavior in just a few cells/areas or is it widespread throughout the organization?
- **Role**: who exhibits the behavior and is it exhibited at the appropriate level—leader, manager, or associate?

## PRESENTATION OF SHINGO ASSESSMENT RESULTS

Shingo assessment results are provided in two separate and distinct formats after each site visit. The first is a representation of the scores received in each dimension of the model. This is done by taking the assessment team score and equating it with either low-level (LL), mid-level (ML), or high-level (HL) of the level achieved on the behavioral maturity scale or the results assessment scale. This results in an organization knowing their relative score within a narrow range but not an exact numerical score. Reporting in this manner is intentional to keep the attention of an organization on the gap for improvement and away from specifically how many points they may have missed or fallen short on. Table 25.3 illustrates how this would look.

The second format is an assessment feedback report written by the entire assessment team; on average, five examiners make up a team. The feedback report once again follows the format of the model and its dimensions. It provides the detail behind the score and is where examiners describe behaviors observed, results achieved, and comparisons to the ideal. The report typically becomes a tool used to focus improvement efforts moving forward.

## ALTERNATIVE PRESENTATION METHODS

Assessment results may be reported in many ways with perhaps no single way best for every enterprise. The format suggested below is a relatively generic one that combines familiar graphic and narrative approaches, so that the format itself is one that lends itself to being easily understood, in some cases, more easily prioritized and made actionable as well. Those approaches are radar charts (Sokovic et al., 2010) adapted to Shingo Assessment Criteria, and SWOT Plot Narratives where SWOT is an acronym for *strengths, weaknesses, opportunities,* and *threats* (Helms and Nixon, 2010; Jackson, Joshi and Erhardt, 2003). Strategic integration of these approaches as a means of assessing both social-ecological innovation and sustainable enterprise excellence, resilience, and robustness has previously been actively applied in recent years (Edgeman, 2013; Edgeman and Eskildsen, 2014b).

As with each of the following graphical assessment summaries, it is of value to form a "SWOT Plot Narrative" companion to Figure 25.2, such as the one provided in the lower half of Figure 25.3. The purpose of companion narratives is to provide in standardized formats a more holistic or integrated summary of the respective graphical representation, with the combined graphic and narrative forms providing a powerful dual assessment approach. Many such formats can be suggested, with the SWOT Plot (Strengths—Weaknesses—Opportunities—Threats) being

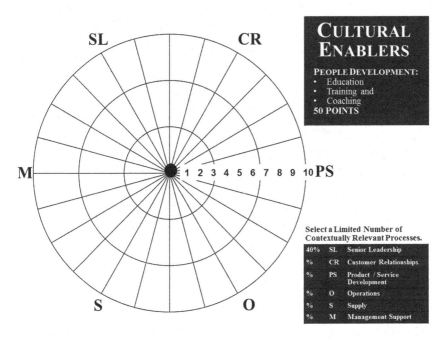

**FIGURE 25.2**
Education, training, and coaching area of *Shingo Model* People Development category within Cultural Enablers.

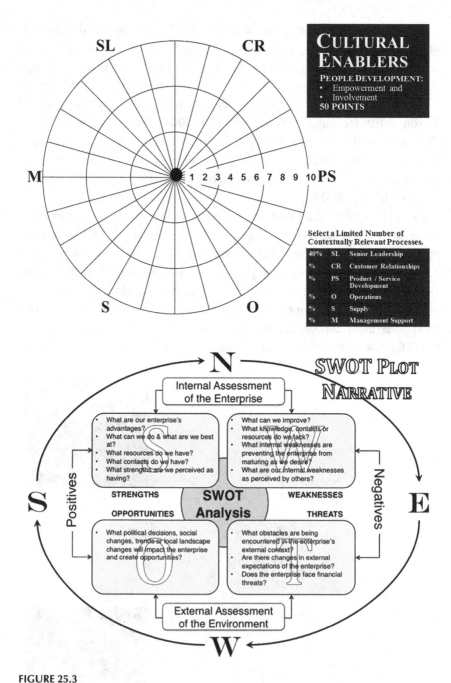

**FIGURE 25.3**
Radar chart for empowerment and involvement area of Shingo Cultural Enablers Dimension together with an accompanying generic SWOT Plot Narrative.

**TABLE 25.4**

Generic SWOT Plot Narrative Questions

| N | | |
|---|---|---|
| ⇦ **Internal Assessment of the Enterprise** ⇨ | | |
| **Strengths** | **Weaknesses** | |
| • What are our enterprise's advantages? <br> • What can we do and what are we best at? <br> • What resources and contacts do we have? <br> • What strengths are we perceived as having? | • What can we improve? <br> • What knowledge, contacts, or resources do we lack? <br> • What internal weaknesses are preventing the enterprise from maturing as we desire? <br> • What are our internal weaknesses as perceived by others? | |
| **Opportunities** | **Threats** | |
| • What political decisions, social changes, trends, or local landscape changes will impact the enterprise and create opportunities? | • What obstacles are being encountered in the enterprise's external context? <br> • Are there changes in external expectations of the enterprise? <br> • Does the enterprise face financial threats? | |
| ⇦ **External Assessment of the Environment** ⇨ | | |
| W | | |

(Left margin: S — ⇧ Positives ⇩) (Right margin: ⇧ Negatives ⇩ — E)

only one of these, albeit one having the advantages of both simplicity and widespread familiarity.

A generic SWOT Plot Narrative format is provided in the lower half of Figure 25.3. Within a given SWOT Plot Narrative, the questions posed in each of the S, W, O, and T categories of Figure 25.3 and repeated in Table 25.4 are ones commonly addressed in SWOT analysis. There is, however, no magic list or number of questions that should be asked as part of a given SWOT Plot assessment, implying that the specific content of any question asked can and should be customized as needed.

The N–E–W–S rotating around the SWOT Plot Narrative perimeter provided in the lower half of Figure 25.3 is intended to communicate two goals. The first of these goals is that the combination of the narrative and the radar chart should communicate direction (North—East—West—South) or insight into the current (or recent) state of that which is being assessed. The second goal we have for such assessments is that the *NEWS* (news)

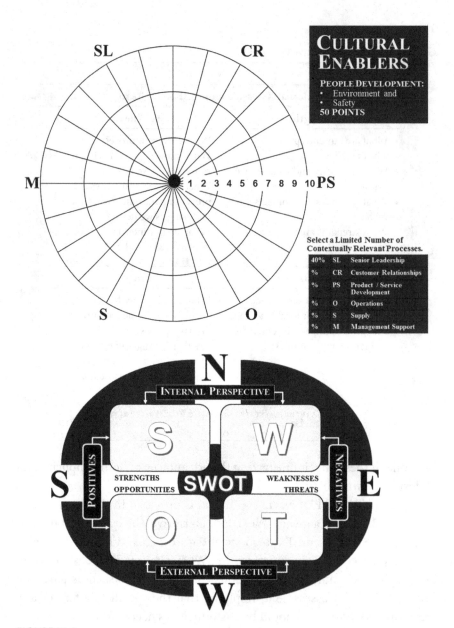

**FIGURE 25.4**
Combined Cultural Enablers radar chart and SWOT Plot for environment and safety.

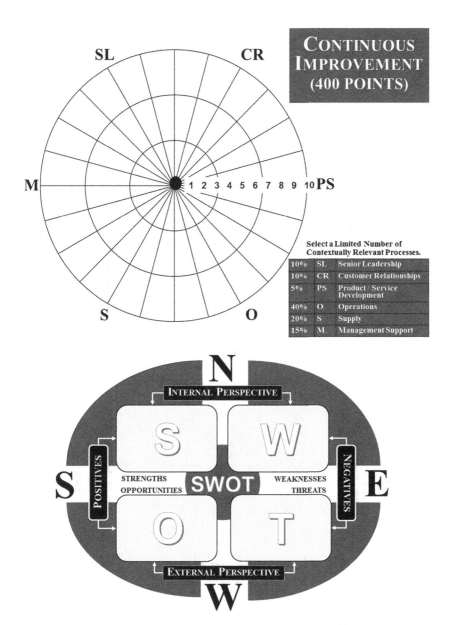

**FIGURE 25.5**

Combined continuous improvement radar chart and SWOT Plot.

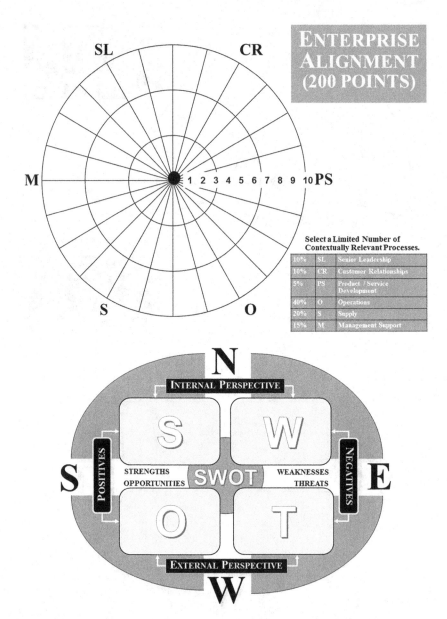

**FIGURE 25.6**

Combined enterprise alignment radar chart and SWOT Plot.

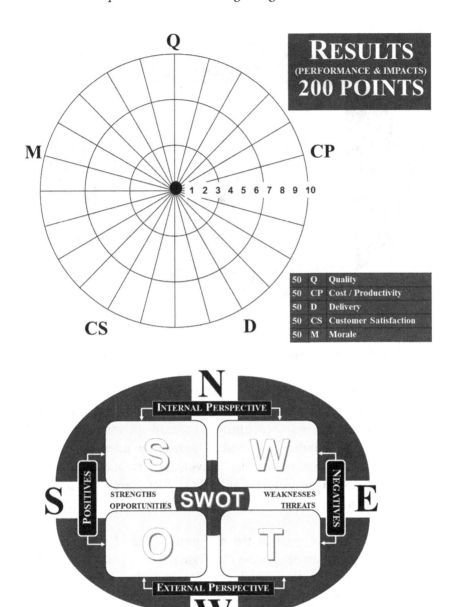

**FIGURE 25.7**

Combined results (performance and impacts) radar chart and SWOT Plot.

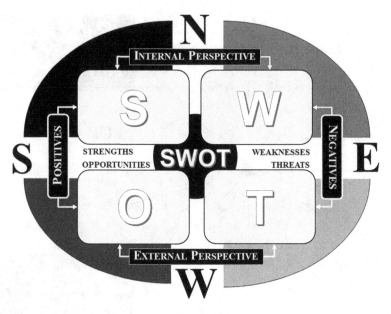

**FIGURE 25.8**
Integrated SWOT Plot Narrative across *Shingo Model* assessment areas.

aspect of the SWOT Plot Narrative should provide foresight that suggests the sorts of changes that need to be made to advance the enterprise in the area that is being assessed—hence progress toward operational excellence.

Given that some individuals find it simpler to interpret graphical assessment information, while other individuals relate more comfortably to narrative assessment information, SWOT Plot Narratives should be augmented by a graphical analog, with a common analog form provided by a radar chart.

While radar charts, such as the one provided in the upper half of Figure 25.3, derive their name from their visual resemblance to radar (and sonar) echolocation graphs, it is also the case that the content of a given radar chart is intended to "echo" or report the "location" or performance of an enterprise relative to the dimensions represented along its axes or arms. The performance along a given dimension is typically represented by positioning a dot on a 1-to-10 or 1-to-100 scale for the dimension, with "bigger" being "better" or, consistent with prior discussion, more mature. As such, when the dots on each arm of a radar chart are connected, patterns forming larger envelopes represent better or more mature performance relative to assessed elements, hence progression toward operational excellence.

Figures 25.4 through 25.7 represent combined radar chart and SWOT Plot Narratives for the remaining assessment areas. Figure 25.8 is intended to represent an overall SWOT Plot Narrative assessment across the entirety of the enterprise, relative to that which is assessed by the *Shingo Model*. In forming an overall or integrated narrative, it is important to remember that not all assessed areas are of equal importance, both from the perspective of relevance to the enterprise, and relative to the model itself.

The various radar charts and SWOT Plot Narratives can be combined into a single dashboard to provide an overall assessment in a highly accessible and informative format.

# 26

## *The Shingo Prize: Recognizing Exceptional Enterprises*

The most well known of Shingo Institute activities is the challenge for the Shingo Prize, an award—unlike the Baldrige Award or the EFQM Excellence Award—that is global in scope. Equally, the Shingo Institute publicly recognizes enterprises at various stages of their journey toward enterprise excellence, employing differing award levels: Shingo Bronze Medallion, Shingo Silver Medallion, and Shingo Prize.

Further differentiating the Shingo Prize from the Baldrige Award and EFQM Excellence Award are its emphases on Lean culture (behaviors), principles, systems, tools, and results. These factors have contributed to relatively less (overt) consideration of performance and impacts during assessments of Shingo Prize applicant enterprises than either America's Malcolm Baldrige Award or Europe's EFQM Excellence Award. Although this has been the historical case, greater emphasis on performance and impacts—results—is rapidly evolving. Similarly, the Shingo Prize differs from other awards in that there is no specific limitation on the number of recipients during a given year or for any of the award levels. Organizations are not in competition with other applicants, rather, they are assessed to a standard. A list of 2010 through mid-2017 recipients for each of the Shingo Prize, Shingo Silver Medallion, Shingo Bronze Medallion is provided in Tables 26.1 through 26.3.

In addition to companies cited in the preceding tables, an archived list of prior Shingo Prize, Shingo Silver Medallion, and Shingo Bronze Medallion recipients can be found online at www.shingo.org/awards.

*Shingo Prize* recipient enterprises can be characterized as follows. They are recognized as world-class for successful establishment of a culture anchored on principles of enterprise excellence that are deeply embedded

**TABLE 26.1**

Shingo Prize Recipients: 2010 through Mid-2018

| Level | Year | Enterprise/Location |
|---|---|---|
| Shingo Prize | 2018 | • Ball Beverage Packaging Europe, Naro Forminsk Cans—Naro Forminsk, Russia<br>• AbbVie Ballytivnan—Sligo, Ireland |
| | 2017 | • Abbott Nutrition Supply Chain Facility, Sligo—Sligo, Ireland<br>• Ball Beverage Packaging Europe, Naro Forminsk Ends—Naro Forminsk, Russia<br>• Thermo Fisher Scientific, Vilnius—Vilnius, Lithuania |
| | 2016 | • Boston Scientific Cork—Cork, Ireland<br>• Rexam Querétaro—Querétaro, Mexico |
| | 2015 | • Abbott Diagnostics Longford—Longford, Ireland<br>• Envases Universales Rexam de Centroamerica, S.A.—Amatitlan, Guatemala |
| | 2014 | • NewsUK–Newsprinters Ltd—Holytown, Motherwell, UK<br>• Barnes Aerospace OEM Strategic Business—Ogden, Utah, USA<br>• DePuy Synthes Ireland—Cork, Ireland<br>• Abbott Vascular—Clonmel, Tipperary, Ireland |
| | 2013 | • *No Shingo Prize Recipients in 2013* |
| | 2012 | • Ethicon Inc.—Jaurez, Chihuahua, Mexico<br>• Rexam Beverage Can, Águas Claras Cans—Águas Claras, Rio Grande do Sul/Viamão, Brazil |
| | 2011 | • Goodyear do Brasil Produtos de Borrach Ltda.—São Paulo, Brazil<br>• US Synthetic—Orem, Utah, USA |
| | 2010 | • John Deere Power Products—Greeneville, Tennessee, USA<br>• Lycoming Engines—Williamsport, Pennsylvania, USA |

into the thinking and behavior of all leaders, as well as attainment of world-class results. Performance and impacts are measured both in terms of business results and the degree to which business, management, improvement, and work systems are driving appropriate and ideal behavior at all levels. Enterprise leadership is strongly focused on ensuring that enterprise excellence principles are deeply embedded in enterprise culture and that this is routinely assessed and subject to improvement. Managers are focused on continuous improvement of systems to drive behaviors that are well aligned with enterprise excellence principles. Associates actively assume responsibility for improving not only their own work systems but other systems within their value stream. Understanding of why things are done in the way they are has saturated the associate level of the enterprise.

## TABLE 26.2

Shingo Silver Medallion Recipients: 2010 through Mid-2018

| Level | Year | Enterprise/Location |
|-------|------|---------------------|
| **Shingo Silver Medallion** | 2017 | • MassMutual, CFO and MMUS Operations—Springfield, Massachusetts, USA<br>• Visteon Electronics Tunisia, Bir El Bey Plant—Bir El Bay, Tunis, Tunisia |
| | 2016 | • Hospira Limited, a Pfizer Company—Haina, San Cristobal, Dominican Republic<br>• Meda Rottapharm Ltd., a Mylan Company, Dublin, Ireland |
| | 2015 | • Commonwealth Bank of Australia, Collections & Customer Solutions—Sydney, New South Wales, Australia |
| | 2014 | • Rexam Beverage Can South America, Jacareí—Jacareí, São Paulo, Brazil<br>• PyMPSA Plásticos y Materias Primas—Guadalajara, Jalisco, Mexico<br>• Rexam Healthcare, Neuenburg—Neuenburg am Rhein, Germany<br>• Rexam Beverage Can, Enzesfeld—Enzesfeld, Vienna, Austria<br>• Boston Scientific, Maple Grove—Maple Grove, Minnesota, USA<br>• Vale Europe Ltd., Clydach Refinery—Clydach, Swansea, UK |
| | 2013 | • MEI Queretaro—El Marques, Querétaro, Mexico<br>• Pentair Water Pool and Spa—Moorpark, California, USA<br>• Rexam Beverage Can South America, Manaus Ends—Manaus, Amazonas, Brazil<br>• Rexam do Brasil Ltda Extrema Can Plant—Extrema, Minas Gerais, Brazil<br>• Visteon Climate Systems India Ltd.—Bhiwadi, Alwar, Rajasthan, India<br>• Visteon Electronica Mexico, Saucito Plant—Chihuahua, Chihuahua, Mexico |
| | 2012 | • Pentair Technical Products—Reynosa, Tamaulipas, Mexico<br>• Tobyhanna Army Depot, COMSEC—Tobyhanna, Pennsylvania, USA<br>• Visteon Electronica Mexico, Carolinas Plant—Chihuahua, Chihuahua, Mexico |
| | 2011 | • Autoliv (China) Steering Wheel Co., Ltd.—Shanghai, China<br>• Barnes Aerospace OEM Strategic Business—Ogden, Utah, USA<br>• dj Orthopedics de Mexico S.A. de C.V.—Tijuana, Baja California, Mexico<br>• Lundbeck, Supply Operation & Engineering (Valby and Lumsas site)—Valby, Copenhagen, Denmark<br>• Remy Componentes, S. de R.L. de C.V.—San Luis Potosi, SLP, Mexico<br>• Rexam Beverage Can South America, Recife Ends—Cabo Sto Agostinho, Brazil<br>• Tobyhanna Army Depot (AN/MST-T1(V))—Tobyhanna, Pennsylvania, USA |

*(Continued)*

**TABLE 26.2 (CONTINUED)**

Shingo Silver Medallion Recipients: 2010 through Mid-2018

| Level | Year | Enterprise/Location |
|---|---|---|
| | **2010** | • Autoliv Steering Wheels Mexico AQW S. de R.L. de C.V.—El Marqués, Mexico |
| | | • Goodyear Tire & Rubber—Lawton, Oklahoma, USA |
| | | • Hi-Tech Gears Ltd.—Manesar, India |

Improvement activity has begun to focus on the enterprise as a whole and the enterprise scorecard has clearly defined performance measures that include behavioral ones. Key measures are stable, predictable, and mature, and demonstrate positive trends and only rare anomalies. Challenging yet realistic goals are present in most areas and there is solid understanding of what constitutes world-class performance and how nearly it is approximated by enterprise performance. Most measures are clearly aligned with corporate goals and cascade to the lowest levels of the enterprise. Functional silos are difficult to identify so that value streams are instead emphasized.

*Shingo Silver Medallion* recipient enterprises are ones that consistently demonstrate strong use of appropriate tools and techniques. Silver Medallion winning enterprises also have mature systems that drive improvement. These enterprises are beginning to align their thinking and behavior with guiding principles of enterprise excellence. Enterprise leadership is involved in improvement efforts and supports the alignment of enterprise excellence principles with systems. Managers are deeply involved and focused on driving behaviors through the design of systems. Associates are routinely involved in use of improvement tools to drive both continuous and breakthrough improvement in their areas of responsibility. Understanding of why this is done has begun to penetrate the associate level of the enterprise. Improvement activity is focused on multiple business systems. The business scorecard uses a broad and flexible portfolio of measures that is beginning to incorporate behavioral elements. Key measures are stable and trending in mostly positive directions and people at all levels of the enterprise understand how to affect the measures appropriately for their areas of responsibility. Relevant performance goals are being set for most business systems and alignment is clear and obvious in most of these systems, with plans in place to align the remaining ones.

*Shingo Bronze Medallion* recipient enterprises are ones demonstrating strong use of tools and techniques for business improvement and progress

**TABLE 26.3**

Shingo Bronze Medallion Recipients: 2010 through Mid-2018

| Level | Year | Enterprise/Location |
|---|---|---|
| **Shingo Bronze Medallion** | 2018 | • Forest Tosara Limited—Dublin, Ireland |
| | 2017 | • Cardinal Health, Quiroproductos de Cuauhtemoc, S. de R.L. de C.V.—Cuauhtemoc, Chihuahua, Mexico |
| | | • LEAR Corporation Silao—Silao, Guanajuato, Mexico |
| | | • Letterkenny Army Depot, PATRIOT Launcher New Build Program—Chambersburg, Pennsylvania, USA |
| | | • Land Apparel S.A.—Puerto Cortés, Honduras |
| | 2016 | • *No Shingo Bronze Medallion Recipients in 2016* |
| | 2015 | • Lake Region Medical—New Ross, Wexford, Ireland |
| | | • Boston Scientific, Costa Rica—El Coyol, Alajuela, Costa Rica |
| | | • Carestream Health, Yokneam—Yokneam, Israel |
| | 2014 | • Lundbeck Pharmaceuticals Italy S.p.A.—Padova, Italy |
| | | • Vistaprint Deer Park Australia—Derrimut, Victoria, Australia |
| | | • Corporation Steris Canada—Québec, QC, Canada |
| | | • Autoliv Inflator Co., Ltd.—Shanghai, China |
| | | • Rexam Beverage Can South America—Rio de Janeiro, Brazil |
| | 2013 | • Covidien—Athlone, Ireland |
| | | • Letterkenny Army Depot, Force Provider—Chambersburg, Pennsylvania, USA |
| | | • Regeneron Pharmaceuticals Inc. (IOPS)—Rensselaer, New York, USA |
| | | • Rexam Beverage Can South America, Cuiabá Cans—Cuiabá, Mato Grosso, Brazil |
| | | • Starkey de Mexico S.A. de C.V.—Matamoros, Tamaulipas, Mexico |
| | 2012 | • Johnson Controls Lerma Plant—Lerma, Mexico |
| | | • Lake Region Medical Limited—New Ross, Co. Wexford, Ireland |
| | | • Remy Automotive Brasil Ltda.—Brusque, Santa Catarina, Brazil |
| | | • State Farm Life Insurance Company, Operations Center—Bloomington, Illinois, USA |
| | 2011 | • Denver Health, Community Health Services—Denver, Colorado, USA |
| | | • Letterkenny Army Depot Aviation Ground Power Unit—Chambersburg, Pennsylvania, USA |
| | | • Leyland Trucks, Ltd.—Leyland, Lancashire, United Kingdom |
| | | • Rexam Plastic Packaging do Brasil—Jundiaí, São Paulo, Brazil |
| | | • US Army Armament Research, Development & Engineering Center— Picatinny Arsenal, New Jersey, USA |
| | 2010 | • Letterkenny Army Depot, PATRIOT Missile—Chambersburg, Pennsylvania, USA |
| | | • Tobyhanna Army Depot, AIM-9M Sidewinder Missile—Tobyhanna, Pennsylvania, USA |

is being made toward developing effective systems to create continuous and consistent use of relevant tools on an enterprise-wide basis. Enterprise leadership is actively and visibly setting the direction for improvement and supports the efforts of others. Similarly, managers are involved in developing systems and helping others to use tools and techniques effectively. Associates are trained and actively participate in improvement projects. Not fully mature at the associate level is understanding of why things are being done the way they are so that improvement activity is generally focused heavily at the operations level and has only begun in support level. Measures are beginning to communicate cause-and-effect relationships and consequences with key measures that have begun to stabilize and that are trending in mostly positive directions.

# 27

## *The Challenge to Change*

A map is an abstraction of the landscape that is intended to capture selected relevant features, thereby enabling its users to better navigate the mapped landscape. The landscape may be as tangible as that for some physical geography, or less so, as in the case of enterprise strategy (Burton and Pennotti, 2003). Selection of those features considered relevant by the mapmaker, omission of other features, and understanding of both are critical to the efficacy of a given map.

Enterprise excellence models—and there are many—are essentially maps, with each model having aspects in common with alternative ones, as well as aspects that are unique. We began with an examination of a complex systems management model and examined critical elements thereof.

Subsequently, the *Shingo Model* was considered. The *Shingo Model* is a globally recognized one against which numerous enterprises assess their performance. Insight gained from assessment results enables subsequent remedy of identified problem areas, whereas foresight generated from the assessment can be used to shape future enterprise strategy. Such use of insight and foresight from regular assessment—usually on an annual basis—forms part of an enterprise's overall enterprise effort to speed its advance along a path toward operational excellence. Note the intentional phrasing of "*a* path toward operational excellence," as opposed to "*the* path toward operational excellence"—a choice informed by the knowledge that multiple such paths will ordinarily exist, with some of those paths being more or less severe, some more or less obvious, some more or less controversial, and so on.

This *Shingo Model* was then positioned within the larger perspective of the BEST environmental domains and in relation to relevant mitigating factors. BEST is an acronym where B, E, S, and T correspond to biophysical (ecological), economic (financial), societal, and technological elements that exert influence on and interact with the enterprise and its strategies, activities, and results. These four primary external domains are ones over which enterprises often have little or no control. The result was a more highly specified, more realistic complex systems model, the aim of which is to aid enterprise progress toward a sustainable and balanced blend of resilience, robustness, and excellence.

Among elements distinguishing the *Shingo Model* from other enterprise excellence models, such as those supporting America's Malcolm Baldrige National Quality Award and Europe's EFQM Excellence Award, is a distinct focus on interrelated guiding principles and the sort of enterprise culture those principles engender. In conjunction with the *Three Insights of Enterprise Excellence*—namely that ideal results require ideal behavior, principles inform ideal behavior, and that systems drive behavior—these insights are integral to the assessment process. It is with a review of the specific approach that the Shingo Institute employs to assess applicant enterprises that our exploration ends.

What can be deduced from our exploration process is that the *Shingo Model* is well positioned as a sound complex systems-based management model, with the weight of established theory and practice behind it. This deduction is further authenticated by the continuing success of organizations experienced in the implementation of and continued adherence to the guiding principles that underscore the *Shingo Model*. This combination of elements suggests that enterprises employing the model can do so with confidence and that—should things go awry— the enterprise can look to the model, its theory, and its *Shingo Guiding Principles* to aid enterprise pursuit of corrective action.

This should be comforting in environments where it is often difficult to establish direct cause-and-consequence relationships between, for example, pursuit of operational excellence and financial returns. Such relationships are themselves often more complex, with varied mediating factors that are not always obvious, but that are always of import.

Irrespective of the level of confidence an enterprise chooses to invest in the model and its application, it is likely that only those enterprises willing to exercise substantial patience will be able to build and sustain a culture that delivers positive performance and impacts year-upon-year. The call for patience is warranted by the sheer number of variables involved, and the time required by most enterprises to understand the subtleties of the variables and the sometimes synergistic, sometimes antagonistic ways in which they interact.

This suggests that enterprises looking for a quick fix to their woes may be disappointed. Too often such enterprises engage only superficially in understanding and implementing such models, attempting to do so without undertaking the sort of deep and often gradual cultural transformation that is required. Enterprises of this sort often place emphasis on tools and the impacts that tool use can create. To be sure, wise selection and use of tools is to be encouraged, but tool use alone will advance enterprises only to a point—a point that to travel beyond requires supporting systems and culture.

As such, there are several challenges to successful change that can be easily identified. Some challenges are more tangible and can be more mechanistically approached, with progress in conquering those challenges more readily identifiable. For example, providing appropriate education and training is tangible and its impacts often visible. In contrast, less tangible and more difficult barriers or challenges include exercise of appropriate levels of patience and the usually slow and hard but necessary work of cultural transformation.

Any organization desiring to travel the path toward operational excellence will need to regularly and vigorously confront these and other challenges.

# Afterword: Multiplying the Treasure

Before treasure can be multiplied, it must first be found. The tools of treasure hunting include but are not limited to those presented in this tome—tools such as voice of the customer methods, ideation, concept generation and selection, and quality function deployment. While these will help to "dig up the treasures" of operational excellence, it is the map itself that serves as the guide to adventure.

A common theme found in the wisdom literature is that of stewardship (e.g., Luke 19:11–27, Christian Bible). Stewardship is a broad concept, but it is generally acknowledged that a "good and faithful steward" will multiply the resources with which they have been entrusted. Enterprise leadership is entrusted with many resources, including the time and activities of enterprise human ecology, money, the authority to form relationships of many sorts, and the power to make decisions concerning the priorities and direction of the enterprise.

Multiplication may assume many forms, but always involves investment and investment involves sharing of resources. In turn, voluntary sharing requires divestiture of control in favor of trust. Implicit in this sequence is that, properly exercised, its execution will deliver improved results across the enterprise stakeholder spectrum.

Critical to navigating our map in a way that finds more of the hidden treasure, and subsequently multiplies that treasure, is making the knowledge and skill associated with "treasure hunting" more widespread. Knowledge and skill in themselves are insufficient to sustain the treasure reaping process, and must be augmented by creation, cultivation, and maintenance of a culture in which treasure hunting is safely and pervasively practiced and appropriately rewarded. Accomplishing this is hard work, the goal of which is not solely treasure hunting, or treasure finding, or even treasure multiplication, but rather the acceleration and perpetuation of each of these. Well done, this proliferates much like a drug-resistant contagion—albeit a beneficial contagion.

Though enterprises are to an extent shaped by their circumstances or context, in the longer run the issue is one of how an enterprise anticipates and navigates circumstances beyond its control, while shaping its direction and destiny through its decisions and accompanying actions relative to those things it influences or controls. In other words, the enterprise is more a product of these decisions and actions than of the circumstances in which those decisions are made and actions taken.

The questions are ones of which decisions are made, how they are made, and what actions are taken, and these depend on the culture of the enterprise. Given that enterprise advancement occurs through renewal, optimization, or innovation, the sort of culture needed is one that will more rapidly renew, better stimulate performance that approaches optimal, and more successfully innovates. This trajectory demands engendering an enterprise culture that encourages informed, intelligent, and careful yet decisive risk-taking throughout the enterprise, at both individual and collaborative levels. Enterprises able to create and maintain such cultures harness a formidable force for change with change being one of three constants in life, together with principles and choices (Covey, 1989): principles govern the decisions or choices we make and hence the direction that change takes—and, in turn, the direction of the enterprise.

Noting that the enterprise does not exist in a vacuum, but generally participates in multiple supply chains, the enterprise may well have opportunities to influence other supply chain members and begin the process of heaping good-upon-good, in non-proprietary fashion.

In these and other ways, an enterprise can share its operational excellence treasure map and multiply not only their own fortunes but those of others. Properly executed, these benefits will extend to society in the forms of improved products and services that are simultaneously more socially and environmentally responsible.

# References

Ackermann, F. and Eden, C. (2011), "Strategic management of stakeholders: theory and practice", *Long Range Planning*, 44, 3, 179–196.

Ackermann, R.J. (1965), *Theories of Knowledge: A Critical Introduction*, McGraw-Hill, New York, NY.

Ackoff, R.L. (1981), *Creating the Corporate Future*, John Wiley & Sons, New York, NY.

Ackoff, R.L. (1994), "Systems thinking and thinking systems", *System Dynamics Review*, 10, 2–3, 175–188.

Adams, C. and Petrella, L. (2010), "Collaboration, connections and change: The UN Global Compact, the Global Reporting Initiative, and Principles for Responsible Management Education and the globally responsible leadership initiative", *Sustainability Accounting, Management and Policy Journal*, 1, 2, 292–296.

Ahmed, S.U., Islam, Z., Mahtab, H. and Hasan, I. (2014), "Institutional investment and corporate social performance: Linkage towards sustainable development", *Corporate Social Responsibility and Environmental Management*, 21, 1, 1–13.

Akao, Y. (1994), "Development history of quality function deployment", in Mizuno, S. and Akao, Y. (Eds.), *QFD: The Customer Driven Approach to Quality Planning and Deployment*, 339–351, Asian Productivity Association, Minato, Tokyo.

Akao, Y. and Mazur, G.H. (2003), "The leading edge in QFD: past, present and future", *International Journal of Quality & Reliability Management*, 20, 1, 20–35.

Allport, F.H. (1955), *Theories of Perception and the Concept of Structure: A Review and Critical Analysis with an Introduction to a Dynamic-Structural Theory of Behavior*, John Wiley & Sons, Inc., Hoboken, NJ.

Anand, G., Ward, P.T., Tatikonda, M.V. and Schilling, D.A. (2009), "Dynamic capabilities through continuous improvement infrastructure", *Journal of Operations Management*, 27, 6, 444–461.

Andreadis, N. (2009), "Learning and organizational effectiveness: A systems perspective", *Process Improvement*, 48, 1, 5–11.

Antunes, P. (2011), "BPM and exception handling: Focus on organizational resilience", *IEEE Transactions on Systems, Man, and Cybernetics*, 41, 3, 383–392.

Bacon, F. and Montagu, B. (1854), *The Works of Francis Bacon, Lord Chancellor of England, Vol. 1*, Parry & McMillan, Philadelphia, PA.

Bagnoli, M. and Watts, S.G. (2003), "Selling to socially responsible consumers: Competition and the private provision of public goods", *Journal of Economics & Management Strategy* 12, 3, 419–445.

Barak, M.E.M. (2013), *Managing Diversity: Toward a Globally Inclusive Workplace*, Sage Publications, Los Angeles, CA.

Bendell, T., Boulter, L. and Kelly, J. (1993), *Benchmarking for Competitive Advantage*, Financial Times/Pitman Publishing, London, UK.

Bennis, W.G. and Thomas, R.J. (2002), "Crucibles of leadership", *Harvard Business Review*, 80, 1, 60–69.

Bens, I. (2012), *Advanced Facilitation Strategies: Tools and Techniques to Master Difficult Situations*, John Wiley & Sons, New York, NY.

Berlin, L. (2005), *The Man Behind the Microchip: Robert Noyce and the Invention of Silicon Valley*, Oxford University Press, New York, NY.

Berry, L.L., Zeithaml, V.A. and Parasuraman, A. (1990), "Five imperatives for improving service quality", *MIT Sloan Management Review*, 31, 4, 29–38.

Bessant, J., Caffyn, S. and Gallagher, M. (2001), "An evolutionary model of continuous improvement behaviour", *Technovation*, 21, 2, 67–77.

Bevan, D. and Werhane, P. (2015), "The inexorable sociality of commerce: The individual and others in Adam Smith", *Journal of Business Ethics*, 127, 2, 327–335.

Bhuiyan, N. and Baghel, A. (2005), "An overview of continuous improvement: From the past to the present", *Management Decision*, 43, 5, 761–771.

Block, P. (2013), *Stewardship: Choosing Service over Self-Interest*, Berrett-Koehler Publishers, San Francisco, CA.

Boer, H. and Gertsen, F. (2003), "From continuous improvement to continuous innovation: A (retro)(per)spective", *International Journal of Technology Management*, 26, 8, 805–827.

Boland Jr., R.J., Collopy, F., Lyytinen, K. and Yoo, Y. (2008), "Managing as designing: Lessons for organization leaders from the design practice of Frank O. Gehry", *Design Issues*, 24, 1, 10–25.

Bond, M.A. and Haynes, M.C. (2014), "Workplace diversity: A social-ecological framework and policy implications", *Social Issues and Policy Review*, 8, 1, 167–201.

Box, G.E.P. and N.R. Draper (1987), *Empirical Model-Building and Response Surfaces*, John Wiley and Sons, New York, NY.

Box, G.E.P. and N.R. Draper (1998), *Evolutionary Operation: A Statistical Method for Process Improvement*, Vol. 67, Wiley-Interscience, New York, NY.

Brabham, D.C. (2008), "Crowdsourcing as a model for problem solving: An introduction and cases", *Convergence: The International Journal of Research into New Media Technologies*, 14, 1, 75–90.

Brandenburger A. and Stuart H. (1996), "Value-based business strategy", *Journal of Economics and Management Strategy*, 5, 1, 5–24.

Brassard, M. (1989), *The Memory Jogger + Featuring the Seven Management and Planning Tools*, GOAL/QPC, Methuen, MA.

Brown, A. (2014), "Organisational paradigms and sustainability in excellence: From mechanistic approaches to learning and innovation", *International Journal of Quality and Service Sciences*, 6, 2–3, 181–190.

Browning, T.R. (2009), "The many views of a process: Toward a process architecture framework for product development processes", *Systems Engineering*, 12, 1, 69–90.

Burt, D.N. (1989), "Managing product quality through strategic purchasing", *Sloan Management Review*, 30, 3, 39–48.

Burton, H.O. and Pennotti, M.C. (2003), "The enterprise map: A system for implementing strategy and achieving operational excellence", *Engineering Management Journal*, 15, 3, 15–20.

Burton, R.M., Obel, B. and DeSanctis (2011), *Organizational Design: A Step-by-Step Approach*, Cambridge University Press, Cambridge, UK.

Camillus, J.C. (2008), "Strategy as a wicked problem", *Harvard Business Review*, 86, 5, 98–106.

Camp, R.C. and Camp, Robert C. (1989), *Benchmarking: The Search for Industry Best Practices that Lead to Superior Performance*, ASQ Press, Milwaukee, WI .

Carbone, T.A. and Tippett, D.D. (2004), "Project risk management using the project risk FMEA", *Engineering Management Journal*, 16, 4, 28–35.

Carroll, A.B. (1991), "The pyramid of corporate social responsibility: Toward ethical management of organizational stakeholders", *Business Horizons*, 34, 4, 39–48.

Carvalho, V.M., Nirei, M., Saito, Y.U. and Tahbaz-Salehi, A. (2016), "Supply chain disruptions: Evidence from the Great East Japan Earthquake", Working Paper 2017-01, *Becker Friedman Institute for Research in Economics at the University of Chicago*, Chicago, IL.

Caudron, S. (1991), "How Xerox won the Baldrige", *Personnel Journal*, 70, 4, 98–102.

Chakravorty, S.S. (2009), "Process improvement: Using Toyota's A3 reports", *The Quality Management Journal*, 16, 4, 7–26.

Chang, G. and Diddams, M. (2009), "Hubris or humility: Cautions surrounding the construct and self-definition of authentic leadership", *Academy of Management Proceedings*, 1, 1–6.

Checkland, P. (1994), "Systems theory and management thinking", *American Behavioral Scientist*, 23, 5, 705–708.

Chen, H., Chiang, R.H. and Storey, V.C. (2012), "Business intelligence and analytics: From big data to big impact", *MIS Quarterly*, 36, 4, 1165–1188.

Chen, Y.S., Lai, S.B. and Wen, C.T. (2006), "The influence of green innovation performance on corporate advantage in Taiwan", *Journal of Business Ethics*, 67, 4, 331–339.

Chesbrough, H. (2010), "Business model innovation: Opportunities and barriers", *Long Range Planning*, 43, 2, 354–363.

Chidamber, S.R. and Kon, H.B. (1994), "A research retrospective of innovation inception and success: The technology–push, demand–pull question", *International Journal of Technology Management*, 9, 1, 94–112.

Choi, T.Y. (1995), "Conceptualizing continuous improvement: Implications for or ganizational change", *Omega*, 23, 6, 607–624.

Churchman, C. (1967), "Wicked problems", *Management Science*, 14, 4, B141–B1142.

Clarke, H.E. and Mayer, B. (2017), "Community recovery following the Deepwater Horizon oil spill: Toward a theory of cultural resilience", *Society & Natural Resources*, 30, 2, 129–144.

Claxton, J.D., Ritchie, J.R.B, and Zaichkowsky, J. (1980), "The nominal group technique: its potential for consumer research", *Journal of Consumer Research*, 7, 3, 308–313.

Coates, J.C. (2007), "The goals and promises of the Sarbanes–Oxley Act", *The Journal of Economic Perspectives*, 21, 1, 91–116.

Cobo, C. (2012), "Networks for citizen consultation and citizen sourcing of expertise", *Contemporary Social Science*, 7, 3, 283–304.

Collins, J.C. (2005), "Level 5 leadership: The triumph of humility and fierce resolve", *Harvard Business Review*, 83, 4, 136–146.

Collins, J.C. and Porras, J.I. (1996), "Building your company's vision", *Harvard Business Review*, 74, 5, 65–77.

Contu, D.L. (2002), "How resilience works", *Harvard Business Review*, 80, 3, 46–52.

Cooke, R.A. and Rousseau, D.M. (1988), "Behavioral norms and expectations: A quantitative approach to the assessment of organizational culture", *Group & Organization Studies*, 13, 3, 245–273.

Cooper, R.G. and Dreher, A. (2010), "Voice-of-customer methods", *Marketing Management*, 19, 4, 38–43.

Cooper, R.G. and Edgett (2008), "Ideation for product innovation: What are the best methods", *PDMA Visions Magazine*, 1, 1, 12–17.

Corbera, E. (2015), "Valuing nature, paying for ecosystem services and realizing social justice: A response to Matulis (2014)", *Ecological Economics*, 110, 154–157.

Covey, S.R. (1989), *Seven Habits of Highly Effective People*, Simon and Schuster, New York, NY.

Covey, S.R. (1992), *Principle Centered Leadership*, Simon and Schuster, New York, NY.

Crossan, M.M., Lane, H.W. and White, R.E. (1999), "An organizational learning framework: From Intuition to Institution", *Academy of Management Review*, 24, 3, 522–537.

Darling, J.R., Keeffe, M.J. and Ross, J.K. (2007), "Entrepreneurial leadership strategies and values: Keys to operational excellence", *Journal of Small Business & Entrepreneurship*, 20, 1, 41–54.

Davenport, T.H., Harris, J.G., David, W. and Jacobson, A.L. (2001), "Data to knowledge to results: Building an analytic capability", *California Management Review*, 43, 2, 117–138.

Davis E. and Kay J. (1990), "Assessing corporate performance", *London Business School Review*, 1, 2, 1–16.

DeFeo, J.A. (2017), *Juran's Quality Handbook*, 7th Edition, McGraw Hill Education, New York, NY.

Deming, W.E. (1985), "Transformation of western style of management", *Interfaces*, 15, 3, 6–11.

Deming, W.E. (1994), *The New Economics*, 2nd edition, MIT Press, Cambridge, MA.

Deo, N. (2017), *Graph Theory with Applications to Engineering and Computer Science*, Courier Dover Publications, North Chelmsford, MA.

Dertouzos, M.L., Lester, R.K. and Solow, R.M. (1989), *Made in America: Regaining the Productive Edge*, MIT Press, Cambridge, MA.

Desmarchelier, B., Djellal, F. and Gallouj, F. (2013), "Environmental policies and eco-innovations by service firms: An agent-based model", *Technological Forecasting and Social Change*, 80, 7, 1395–1408.

Detert, J.R., Schroeder, R.G. and Mauriel, J.J. (2000), "A framework for linking culture and improvement initiatives in organizations", *Academy of Management Review*, 25, 4, 850–863.

Devinney, T.M. (2009), "Is the socially responsible corporation a myth? The good, the bad, and the ugly of corporate social responsibility", *The Academy of Management Perspectives* 23, 2, 44–56.

Dewan, S. and Mendelson, H. (1998), "Information technology and time-based competition in financial markets", *Management Science*, 44, 5, 595–609.

Dewar, R.D. and Dutton, J.E. (1986), "The adoption of radical and incremental innovations: An empirical analysis", *Management Science*, 32, 11, 1422–1433.

Di Stefano, G., Gambardella, A. and Verona, G. (2012), "Technology push and demand pull perspectives in innovation studies: Current findings and future research directions", *Research Policy*, 41, 8, 1283–1295.

Doggett, A.M. (2005), "Root cause analysis: A framework for tool selection", *Quality Management Journal*, 12, 4, 34–45.

Doz, Y.L. and Kosonen, M. (2010), "Embedding strategic agility: A leadership agenda for accelerating business model renewal", *Long Range Planning*, 43, 2, 370–382.

Drew, S.A.W. (1997), "From knowledge to action: The impact of benchmarking on organizational performance", *Long Range Planning*, 30, 3, 427–441.

Drucker, P.F. (1988), "The coming of the new organization", *Harvard Business Review*, 66, 1, 4–11.

Earley, P.C., Connolly, T. and Ekegren, G. (1989), "Goals, strategy development, and task performance: Some limits on the efficacy of goal setting", *Journal of Applied Psychology*, 74, 1, 24–33.

Edgeman, R. (2000), "BEST business excellence: An expanded view", *Measuring Business Excellence*, 4, 4, 15–17.

Edgeman, R. (2011), "SIPOC and COPIS: Business flow – business optimization in a six sigma context", in M. Lovric (ed.), *International Encyclopedia of Statistical Science*, Vol. 4, 1337–1338, Springer, Berlin, Heidelberg.

Edgeman, R. (2015a), "Strategic resistance for sustaining enterprise relevance: A paradigm for sustainable enterprise excellence, resilience and robustness", *International Journal of Productivity and Performance Management*, 64, 3, 318–333.

Edgeman, R. (2015b), "Wicked global challenges: Sustainability in the enterprise crosshairs", *Measuring Business Excellence*, 19, 1, 13–23.

Edgeman, R. and Eskildsen, J.K. (2012), "C4 model of people-centered innovation: Culture, consciousness, and customer-centric co-creation", *Journal of Innovation Best Business Practice*, 2012, DOI: 10.5151/2012.932564.

Edgeman, R. and Eskildsen, J.K. (2014a), "Modeling and assessing sustainable enterprise excellence", *Business Strategy and the Environment*, 23, 3, 173–187.

Edgeman, R. and Eskildsen, J. (2014b), "Social-ecological innovation", in J. Wang (ed.), *Encyclopedia of Business Analytics & Optimization*, Vol. 5, 532–543, IGI Global, Hershey, PA.

Edgeman, R., Eskildsen, J. and Neely, A. (2015), "Translating triple top line strategy into triple bottom line performance", *Measuring Business Excellence*, 19, 1, 1–12.

Edgeman, R. and Hensler, D.A. (2005), "QFD and the BEST paradigm: Deploying sustainable solutions", *World Review of Science, Technology and Sustainable Development*, 2, 1, 49–59.

Edgeman, R. and Scherer, F. (1998), "Systemic leadership via core value deployment", *Leadership & Organization Development Journal*, 20, 2–3, 94–97.

Edgeman, R. and Williams, J.A. (2014), "Enterprise self-assessment analytics for sustainability, resilience & robustness", *TQM Journal*, 26, 4, 368–381.

Edgeman, R. and Wu, Z. (2015), "Anthropocene age wicked challenges: Yin, yang and sustainable enterprise excellence", in Stentoft, J., Paulraj, A. and Vastag, G. (eds.), *Research in the Decision Sciences for Global Supply Chain Networks*, 273–294, Pearson Education, Inc., New York, NY.

Edmondson, A.C. (2008), "The competitive imperative of learning", *Harvard Business Review*, 86, 7/8, 60–67.

Elkington, J. (1997), *Cannibals with Forks: The Triple Bottom Line of 21st Century Business*, Capstone Publishing, Oxford, UK.

Evans, J.R. and Lindner, C.H. (2012), "Business analytics: The next frontier for decision sciences", *Decision Line*, 43, 2, 4–6.

Fang, C., Lee, J. and Schilling, M.A. (2010), "Balancing exploration and exploitation through structural design: The isolation of subgroups and organizational learning", *Organization Science*, 21, 3, 625–642.

Farjoun, M. (2010), "Beyond dualism: Stability and chance as a duality", *Academy of Management Review*, 35, 2, 202–225.

Fassin, Y. (2012), "Stakeholder management, reciprocity and stakeholder responsibility", *Journal of Business Ethics*, 109, 1, 83–96.

Ford, M.W., Evans, J.R. and Masterson, S.S. (2014), "An information processing perspective of process management: Evidence from Baldrige Award recipients", *The Quality Management Journal*, 21, 1, 25–41.

Freeman, R.E. (2010), *Strategic Management: A Stakeholder Approach*, Cambridge University Press, Cambridge, UK.

Friedman, S.M. (2011), "Three Mile Island, Chernobyl, and Fukushima: An analysis of traditional and new media coverage of nuclear accidents and radiation", *Bulletin of Atomic Scientists*, 67, 5, 55–65.

Fullerton, R.R., Kennedy, F.A. and Widener, S.K. (2014), "Lean manufacturing and firm performance: The incremental contribution of lean management accounting practices", *Journal of Operations Management*, 32, 7, 414–428.

Gallo, A. (2014), "The value of keeping the right customers", *Harvard Business Review*, 92, 8, 29.

Gallupe, R.B. and Cooper, W.H. (1993), "Brainstorming electronically", *MIT Sloan Management Review*, 35, 1, 27–36.

Garcia-Castro, R. and Aguilera, R.V. (2015), "Incremental value creation and appropriation in a world with multiple stakeholders", *Strategic Management Journal*, 36, 1, 137–147.

Garcia-Quevedo, J., Pellegrino, G. and Savona, M. (2017), "Reviving demand-pull perspectives: The effect of demand uncertainty and stagnancy on R&D strategy", *Cambridge Journal of Economics*, 41, 4, 1087–1122.

Garvin, D.A. (1987), "Competing on the 8 dimensions of quality", *Harvard Business Review*, 65, 6, 101–109.

Gausemeier, J., Fink, A. and Schlake, O. (1998), "Scenario management: An approach to develop future potentials", *Technological Forecasting and Social Change*, 59, 2, 111–130.

George, B. (2003), *Authentic Leadership: Rediscovering the Secrets to Creating Lasting Value*, John Wiley & Sons, New York, NY.

George, G., McGahan, A.M. and Prabhu, J. (2012), "Innovation for inclusive growth: Towards a theoretical framework and a research agenda", *Journal of Management Studies*, 49, 4, 661–683.

Gerst, R. (2001), *The Performance Improvement Toolkit: The Guide to Knowledge-Based Improvement*, Converge Consulting Group, Inc., Alberta, Canada.

Gharajedaghi, J. and Ackoff, R.L. (1984), "Mechanisms, organisms and social systems", *Strategic Management Journal*, 5, 3, 289–300.

Gibson-Graham, J.K., Cameron, J. and Healy, S. (2013), *Take Back the Economy: An Ethical Guide for Transforming our Communities*, University of Minnesota Press, Minneapolis, MN.

Gilchrist, W. (1993), "Modelling failure modes and effects analysis", *International Journal of Quality & Reliability Management*, 10, 5, 16–23.

Gloor, P.A. (2005), *Swarm Creativity: Competitive Advantage through Collaborative Innovation Networks*, Oxford University Press, Oxford, UK.

Goetsch, D.L. and Davis, S.B. (2014), *Quality Management for Organizational Excellence*, Pearson Publishing, Upper Saddle River, NJ.

Goodman, J. (2006), "Manage complaints to enhance loyalty", *Quality Progress*, 39, 2, 28–34.

Greenwood, R.G. (1981), "Management by objectives: As developed by Peter Drucker, assisted by Harold Smiddy", *The Academy of Management Review*, 6, 2, 225–230.

Gregory Stone, A., Russell, R.F. and Patterson, K. (2004). "Transformational versus servant leadership: A difference in leader focus", *Leadership & Organization Development Journal*, 25, 4, 349–361.

Griffin, A. and Hauser, J.R. (1993), "The voice of the customer", *Marketing Science*, 12, 1, 1–27.

Grunig, J.E. (1992), "What is excellence in management", in J.E. Grunig (ed.), *Excellence in Public Relations and Communication Management*, 219–250, Routledge, London, UK.

Haimes, Y.Y. and Schneiter, C. (1996), "Covey's seven habits and the systems approach: A comparative analysis", *IEEE Transactions on Systems, Man and Cybernetics*, 26, 4, 483–487.

Hamel, G. and Prahalad, C.K. (1994), *Competing for the Future*, Harvard Business Press, Boston, MA.

Hammer, M. (2002), "Process management and the future of six sigma", *MIT Sloan Management Review*, 43, 2, 26–32.

Hannah, S.T., Avolio, B.J. and Walumbwa, F.O. (2011), "Relationships between authentic leadership, moral courage, and ethical and pro-social behaviors", *Business Ethics Quarterly*, 21, 4, 555–578.

Harris, V. (1982), *A Book of Five Rings* by Miyamoto Musashi (1645), translated by V. Harris, Overlook Press, Woodstock, NY.

Harrison J.S., Bosse, D.A. and Phillips R.A. (2010), "Managing for stakeholders, stakeholder utility functions, and competitive advantage", *Strategic Management Journal*, 31, 1, 58–74.

Hauser, J.R. (1993), "How Puritan-Bennett used the house of quality", *MIT Sloan Management Review*, 34, 3, 61–70.

Hauser, J.R. and Clausing, D. (1988), "The house of quality", *Harvard Business Review*, 66, 3, 63–73.

Haynes, K.T., Josefy, M. and Hitt, M.A. (2015), "Tipping point: Manager's self-interest, greed, and altruism", *Journal of Leadership & Organizational Studies*, 22, 3, 265–279.

Hayward, M.L. and Shimizu, K. (2006), "De-commitment to losing strategic action: Evidence from the divestiture of poorly performing acquisitions", *Strategic Management Journal*, 27, 6, 541–557.

Hegel, G.W.F. (1807), *The Phenomenology of the Mind*, Republished by Dover Publications (2003), Mineola, NY.

Helms, M.M. and Nixon, J. (2010), "Exploring SWOT analysis—where are we now? A review of academic research from the last decade", *Journal of Strategy and Management*, 3, 3, 215–251.

Herstatt, C. and Von Hippel, E. (1992), "From experience: Developing new product concepts via the lead user method: A case study in a lot-tech field", *Journal of Product Innovation Management*, 9, 3, 213–221.

Hines, P., Holweg, M. and Rich, N. (2004), "Learning to evolve: A review of contemporary lean thinking", *International Journal of Operations & Production Management*, 24, 10, 994–1011.

Hines, P. and Rich, N. (1997), "The seven value stream mapping tools", *International Journal of Operations & Production Management*, 17, 1, 46–64.

Hoffman, E. (2012), *User Integration in Sustainable Product Development: Organisational Learning through Boundary-Spanning Processes*, Greenleaf Publishing, Sheffield, UK.

Hogeveen, J., Inzlicht, M. and Obhi, S.S., 2014. "Power changes how the brain responds to others", *Journal of Experimental Psychology: General*, 143, 2, 755–762.

Homburg, C. and Fürst, A. (2005), "How organizational complaint handling drives customer loyalty: an analysis of the mechanistic and the organic approach", *Journal of Marketing*, 69, 3, 95–114.

Hull, C.E. and Rothenberg, S. (2008), "Firm performance: The interactions of corporate social performance with innovation and industry differentiation", *Strategic Management Journal*, 29, 7, 781–789.

Hurley, R.F. and Hult, G.T.M. (1998), "Innovation, market orientation, and organizational learning: An integration and empirical examination", *Journal of Marketing*, 62, 3, 42–54.

Hutchins, D. (2008), *Hoshin Kanri: The Strategic Approach to Continuous Improvement*, Gower Publishing Limited, Hampshire, UK.

Imai, M. (1986), *Kaizen: The Key to Japan's Competitive Success*. McGraw-Hill Publishing, New York, NY.

Imai, M. (2012), *Gemba Kaizen: A Commonsense Approach to a Continuous Improvement Strategy*, McGraw Hill Professional, New York, NY.

Jackson, M.C. (2003), *Systems Thinking: Creative Holism for Managers*, Wiley, Chichester, UK.

Jackson, S.E., Joshi, A. and Erhardt, N.L. (2003), "Recent research on team and organizational diversity: SWOT analysis and implications", *Journal of Management*, 29, 6, 801–830.

Jahromi, A.T., Stakhovych, S. and Ewing, M. (2014), "Managing B2B customer churn, retention and profitability", *Industrial Marketing Management*, 43, 7, 1258–1268.

Jap, S.D. and Anderson, E. (2007), "Testing a life-cycle theory of cooperative interorganizational relationships: Movement across stages and performance", *Management Science*, 53, 2, 260–275.

Jenner, R.A. (1998), "Dissipative enterprises, chaos, and the principles of lean organizations", *Omega*, 26, 3, 397–407.

Jensen, M.C. (2002), "Value maximization, stakeholder theory, and the corporate objective function", *Business Ethics Quarterly*, 12, 2, 235–256.

Joosten, T., Bongers, I. and Janssen, R. (2009), "Application of lean thinking to health care: Issues and observations", *International Journal for Quality in Health Care*, 21, 5, 341–347.

Joskow, P.L. and Parsons, J.E. (2012), *The Future of Nuclear Power after Fukushima*, MIT Center for Energy and Environmental Policy Research, Working Paper WP 2012-001, Cambridge, MA, USA.

Juran, J.M. (2005), "Pareto, Lorenz, Cournot, Bernoulli, Juran and others", *Joseph M. Juran: Critical Evaluations in Business and Management*, 1, 4, 47.

Kahneman, D., Lovallo, D. and Sibony, O. (2011), "Before you make that big decision", *Harvard Business Review*, 89, 6, 50–60.

Kano, N. (1993), "A perspective on quality activities in American firms", *California Management Review*, 35, 3, 12–31.

Kaplan, R.S. and Norton, D.P. (1996), *The Balanced Scorecard: Translating Strategy into Action*, Harvard Business School Press, Boston, MA.

Kaplan, R.S. and Norton, D.P. (2004), "The strategy map: Guide to aligning intangible assets", *Strategy and Leadership*, 32, 5, 10–17.

Kaplan, R.S. and Norton, D.P. (2015), *Balanced Scorecard Success: The Kaplan-Norton Collection*, Harvard Business Review Press, Boston, MA.

Karimi, A., Safari, H., Hashemi, S.H. and Kalantar, P. (2014), "A study of the Baldrige Award framework using the applicant scoring data", *Total Quality Management & Business Excellence*, 25, 5–6, 461–477.

Katzenbach, J.R. (2000), *Peak Performance: Aligning the Hearts and Minds of Your Employees*, Harvard Business Press, Boston, MA.

Kellar, N.M., Speakman, T.R., Smith, C.R., Lane, S.M. Balmer, B.C., Trego, M.L., Catelani, K.N. et al. (2017), "Low reproductive success rates of common bottlenose dolphins Tursiops truncatus in the northern Gulf of Mexico following the Deepwater Horizon disaster", *Endangered Species Research*, 33, 143–158.

Keltner, D., 2017. *The Power Paradox: How We Gain and Lose Influence*, Penguin Publishing, London, UK.

Kessler, F. (1995), "Team decision making: Pitfalls and procedures", *Management Development Review*, 8, 5, 38–40.

Kesterson, Randy K. (2015), *The Basics of Hoshin Kanri*, CRC Press, Taylor and Francis Group, Boca Raton, FL.

Ketokivi, M. and Choi, T. (2014), "Renaissance of case research as a scientific method", *Journal of Operations Management*, 32, 5, 232–240.

Kim, W.C. and Mauborgne, R. (2005), *Blue Ocean Strategy: How to Create Uncontested Market Space and Make the Competition Irrelevant*, Harvard Business School Press, Boston, MA.

Kiss, A.N., Danis, W.M. and Cavusgil, S.T. (2012), "International entrepreneurship research in emerging economies: A critical review and research agenda", *Journal of Business Venturing*, 27, 2, 266–290.

Koenigsaecker, G. (2012), *Leading the lean enterprise transformation*, CRC Press, Boca Raton, FL.

Kohlbacher, M. (2010), "The effects of process orientation: A literature review", *Business Process Management Journal*, 16, 1, 135–152.

Kondo, Y. (1998), "Hoshin kanri: A participative way of quality management in Japan", *The TQM Magazine*, 10, 6, 425–431.

Koomey, J. (2012), *Cold Case, Cool Climate: Science-Based Advice for Ecological Entrepreneurs*, Analytics Press, Burlingame, CA.

Kreander, N., Gray, R.H., Power, D.M. and Sinclair, C.D. (2005), "Evaluating the performance of ethical and non-ethical funds: A matched pair analysis", *Journal of Business Finance & Accounting*, 32, 7–8, 1465–1493.

Kukihara, H., Yamawaki, N., Uchiyama, K. Arai, S. and Horikawa, E. (2014), "Trauma, depression, and resilience of earthquake / tsunami / nuclear disaster survivors of Hirono, Fukushima, Japan", *Psychiatry and Clinical Neurosciences*, 68, 7, 524–533.

Kunsch, P.L., Theys, M. and Brans, J.P. (2007). "The importance of systems thinking in ethical and sustainable decision-making", *Central European Journal of Operations Research*, 15, 3, 253–269.

Kurtz, C.F. and Snowden, D.J. (2003), "The new dynamics of strategy: Sense-making in a complex and complicated world", *IBM Systems Journal*, 42, 3, 462–483.

Larsson, R., Bengtsson, L., Henriksson, K. and Sparks, J. (1998), "The interorganizational learning dilemma: Collective knowledge development in strategic alliances", *Organization Science*, 9, 3, 285–305.

Leavy, B. (2012), "Collaborative innovation as the new imperative—design thinking, value co-creation, and the power of pull", *Strategy & Leadership*, 40, 2, 25–34.

Leavy, B. and Sterling, J. (2010), "Think disruptive! How to manage in a new era of innovation", *Strategy & Leadership*, 38, 4, 5–10.

Lee, R.G. and B.G. Dale (1998), "Policy deployment: An examination of the theory", *International Journal of Quality and Reliability Management*, 15, 5, 520–540.

Lee, S.M., Olson, D.L. and Trimi, S. (2012), "Co-innovation: Convergenomics, collaboration, and co-creation for organizational values", *Management Decision*, 50, 5, 817–831.

Lencioni, P.M. (2012), *The Advantage, Enhanced Edition: Why Organizational Health Trumps Everything Else In Business*. John Wiley & Sons, Hoboken, NJ.

Lenzen, M., Murray, J., Sack, F. and Wiedmann, T. (2007), "Shared producer and consumer responsibility—Theory and practice", *Ecological Economics*, 61, 1, 27–42.

Leonard-Barton, D. (1992), "Core capabilities and core rigidities: A paradox in managing new product development", *Strategic Management Journal*, 13, S1, 111–125.

Lewis, R.C. and Booms, B.H. (1983), "The marketing aspects of service quality", in L. Berry, G. Shostack, and G. Upah (eds.), *Emerging Perspectives on Services Marketing*, 99–107, American Marketing, Chicago, IL.

Liker, J. (2003), *The Toyota Way: 14 Management Principles from the World's Greatest Manufacturer*, McGraw Hill Professional, New York, NY.

Lillrank, P. (1995), "The transfer of management innovations from Japan", *Organization Studies*, 16, 6, 971–989.

Limnios, E.A.M., Mazzarol, T., Ghadouani, A. and Schilizzi, S.G. (2014), "The resilience architecture framework: Four organizational archetypes", *European Management Journal*, 32, 1, 104–116.

Linderman, K., Schroeder, R.G., Zaheer, S. and Choo, A.S. (2003), "Six Sigma: A goal-theoretic perspective", *Journal of Operations Management*, 21, 2, 193–203.

Liu, Y.C., Chakrabarti, C. and Bligh, T. (2003), "Towards an 'ideal' approach for concept generation", *Design Studies*, 24, 4, 341–355.

Llywelyn, M. (1992), *Strongbow: The Story of Richard and Aoife*. O'Brien Press Ltd., Dublin, Ireland.

Lycett, M. (2013), "Datafication: Making sense of (big) data in a complex world", *European Journal of Information Systems*, 22, 4, 381–386.

Maier, A.M., Moultrie, J. and Clarkson, P.J. (2012), "Assessing organizational capabilities: Reviewing and guiding the development of maturity grids", *IEEE Transactions on Engineering Management*, 59, 1, 138–159.

Matulis, B.S. (2014), "The economic valuation of nature: A question of justice?" *Ecological Economics*, 104, 155–157.

Matzler, K. and Hinterhuber, H.H. (1998), "How to make product development projects more successful by integrating Kano's model of customer satisfaction into quality function deployment", *Technovation*, 18, 1, 25–38.

McDonough, W. and Braungart, M. (2002a), "Design for the triple top line: New tools for sustainable commerce", *Corporate Environmental Strategy*, 9, 3, 251–258.

McDonough, W. and Braungart, M. (2002b), *Cradle to Cradle: Remaking the Way We Make Things*, North Point Press, New York, NY.

McKenna, S.D. (1996), "The darker side of the entrepreneur", *Leadership & Organization Development Journal*, 17, 6, 41–45.

McVea, J.F. and Freeman, R.E. (2005), "A names-and-faces approach to stakeholder management: How focusing on stakeholders as individuals can bring ethics and entrepreneurial strategy together", *Journal of Management Inquiry*, 14, 1, 57–69.

Miles, R.E., Snow, C.C., Meyer, A.D. and Coleman, H.J. (1978), "Organizational strategy, structure, and process", *Academy of Management Review*, 3, 3, 546–562.

Milne, M.J. and Gray, R. (2013), "W(h)ither ecology? The triple bottom line, the global reporting initiative, and corporate sustainability reporting", *Journal of Business Ethics*, 118, 1, 13–29.

Moen, R.D. and Norman, C.L. (2010), "Circling back: Clearing up myths about the Deming cycle and seeing how it keeps evolving", *Quality Progress*, 43, 11, 22–28.

Morris, J.A., Brotheridge, C.M. and Urbanski, J.C. (2005), "Bringing humility to leadership: Antecedents and consequences of leader humility", *Human Relations*, 58, 10, 1323–1350.

Murray, A., Skene, K. and Haynes, K. (2017), "The circular economy: An interdisciplinary exploration of the concept and application in a global context", *Journal of Business Ethics*, 140, 3, 369–380.

Nemet, G.F. (2009), "Demand-pull, technology-push, and government-led incentives for non-incremental technical change", *Research Policy*, 38, 5, 700–709.

Nidumolu, R., Prahalad, C.K. and Rangaswami, M.R. (2009), "Why sustainability is now the key driver of innovation", *Harvard Business Review*, 87, 9, 57–64.

Nonaka, I. (2008), *The Knowledge-Creating Company*, Harvard Business Review Press, Boston, MA.

Ohno, T. (1982), "How the Toyota production system was created", *Japanese Economic Studies*, 10, 4, 83–101.

Ohno, T. (1988), *Toyota Production System: Beyond Large-Scale Production*, CRC Press, Orlando, FL.

Oliver, C. (1997), "Sustainable competitive advantage: Combining institutional and resource-based views", *Strategic Management Journal*, 18, 9, 697–713.

Orlikowski, W.J. (2010), "The sociomateriality of organizational life: Considering technology in management research", *Cambridge Journal of Economics*, 34, 1, 125–141.

Parasuraman, A., Zeithaml, V.A. and L.L. Berry (1985), "A conceptual model of service quality and its implications for future research", *Journal of Marketing*, 49, 3, 41–50.

Parmenter, D. (2007), *Key Performance Indicators: Developing, Implementing and Using Winning KPIs*, John Wiley & Sons, Hoboken, NJ.

Peifer, J.L. (2014), "Fund loyalty among socially responsible investors: The importance of the economic and ethical domains", *Journal of Business Ethics*, 121, 4, 635–649.

Pentland, B.T. and Feldman, M.S. (2007), "Narrative networks: Patterns of technology and organization', *Organization Science*, 18, 5, 781–795.

Peppers, D. and Rogers, M. (2016), *Extreme Trust: Turning Proactive Honesty as a and Flawless Execution into Long-Term ProfitsCompetitive Advantage*, Penguin Publishing, London, UK.

Peters, T.J. and Waterman, R.H. (1982). *In Search of Excellence: Lessons from America's Best-Run Companies*, Harper& Row, New York, NY.

Petrakis, P.E. and Konstantakopoulou, D.P. (2015), *Uncertainty in Entrepreneurial Decision Making*, Palgrave Studies in Democracy, Innovation, and Entrepreneurship for Growth, Palgrave Macmillan, London, UK.

Pierce, J.L., Gardner, D.G., Cummings, L.L. and Dunham, R.B. (1989), "Organization-based self-esteem: Construct definition, measurement, and validation", *Academy of Management Journal*, 32, 3, 622–648.

Plenert, Gerhard (2012), *Driving Strategy to Execution Using Lean Six Sigma: A Framework for Creating High Performance Organizations*, CRC Press, Taylor and Francis Group, Series on Resource Management, Boca Raton, FL.

Poortinga, W., Aoyagi, M. and Pidgeon, N.F. (2013), "Public perceptions of climate change and energy futures before and after the Fukushima accident: A comparison between Britain and Japan", *Energy Policy*, 62, 1204–1211.

Porter, M.E. (1985), *Competitive Advantage*, Free Press, New York, NY.

Prahalad, C.K. and Hamel, G. (1990), "The core competences of the corporation", *Harvard Business Review*, 68, 3, 79–91.

Quiggin, J. (2012), *Zombie Economics: How Dead Ideas Still Walk Among Us*, Princeton University Press, Princeton, NJ.

Rasche, A., Waddock, S. and McIntosh, M. (2013), "The United Nations Global Compact is retrospect and prospect", *Business & Society*, 52, 1, 6–30.

Ratick, S., Meacham, B. and Aoyama, Y. (2008), "Locating backup facilities to enhance supply chain disaster resilience", *Growth and Change*, 39, 4, 642–666.

Reinke, S.J. (2004), "Service before self: Towards a theory of servant-leadership", *Global Virtue Ethics Review*, 5, 3, 30–57.

Reiss, S. (2004), "Multifaceted nature of intrinsic motivation: The theory of 16 basic desires", *Review of General Psychology*, 8, 3, 179–193.

Revelli, C. and Vivian, J.L. (2014), "Financial performance of socially responsible investing (SRI): What have we learned? A meta-analysis", *Business Ethics—A European Review*, 24, 2, 158–185.

Ribstein, L.E. (2002), "Market vs. regulatory responses to corporate fraud: A critique of the Sarbanes-Oxley Act of 2002", *Journal of Corporate Law*, 28, 1, 1–67.

Rogow, A.A. and Lasswell, H.D. (1963), *Power, Corruption, and Rectitude*, Prentice-Hall Publishing, Englewood Cliffs, NJ.

Rohrbeck, R. and Gemünden, H.G. (2011), "Corporate foresight: Its three roles in enhancing the innovation capacity of a firm", *Business Ethics: A European Review*, 21, 1, 100–114.

Rueda-Manzanares, A., Aragón-Correa, J.A. and Sharma, S. (2008), "The influence of stakeholders on the environmental strategy of service firms: The moderating effects of complexity, uncertainty and munificence", *British Journal of Management*, 19, 2, 185–203.

Rüegg-Stürm, J. (2005), *The New St. Gallen Management Model*, Palgrave Macmillan, New York, NY.

Rybka, Z. (2013), *Principles of the Bata Management System*, 3rd edition, Georg Publishers, Žilina, Slovak Republic.

Saaty, T.L. (2008), "Decision making with the analytic hierarchy process", *International Journal of Services Sciences*, 1, 1, 83–98.

Sabeti, H. (2011), "The for-benefit enterprise", *Harvard Business Review*, 89, 11, 98–104.

Salvato, C. (2009), "Capabilities unveiled: The role of ordinary activities in the evolution of product development processes", *Organization Science*, 20, 2, 384–409.

Sanford, C. (2011), *The Responsible Business: Reimagining Sustainability & Success*, Jossey-Bass, San Francisco, CA.

Santos-Vijande, M.L., López-Sánchez, J.Á. and Trespalacios, J.A. (2012), "How organizational learning affects a firm's flexibility, competitive strategy, and performance", *Journal of Business Research*, 65, 8, 1079–1089.

Sarkis, J. (2001), "Benchmarking for agility", *Benchmarking: An International Journal*, 8, 2, 88–107.

Schonberger, R.J. (1986), *World Class Manufacturing: The Lessons of Simplicity Applied.* The Free Press, New York, NY.

Schroeder, R.G., Kinderman, K., Liedtke, C. and Choo, A.S. (2008), "Six sigma: Definition and underlying theory", *Journal of Operations Management*, 26, 4, 536–554.

Schwartz, M.S. and Carroll, A.B. (2008), "Integrating and unifying competing and complementary frameworks: The search for a common core in the business and society field", *Business & Society*, 47, 2, 148–186.

Sekine, K. (1992), *One-Piece Flow: Cell Design for Transforming the Production Process.* Productivity Press, New York, NY.

Senge, P. (1990), *The Fifth Discipline: The Art and Practice of the Learning Organization.* Doubleday Currency, New York, NY.

Senge, P.M. and Sterman, J.D. (1992), "Systems thinking and organizational learning: Acting locally and thinking globally in the organization of the future", *European Journal of Operational Research*, 59, 1, 137–150.

Seyfang, G. and Smith, A. (2007), "Grassroots innovation for sustainable development: Towards a new research and policy agenda", *Environmental Politics*, 16, 4, 584–603.

Shabana, K.M., Buchholtz, A.K. and Carroll, A.B. (2016), "The institutionalization of corporate social responsibility reporting", *Business & Society*, 1–29.

Shahin, A. (2004), "Integration of FMEA and the Kano model: An exploratory examination", *International Quality of Quality & Reliability Management*, 21, 7, 731–746.

Sharma, R., Mithas, S. and Kankanhalli, A. (2014), "Transforming decision-making processes: A research agenda for understanding the impact of business analytics in organisations", *European Journal of Information Systems*, 23, 4, 433–441.

Shetty, Y.K. (1993), "Aiming high: Competitive benchmarking for superior performance", *Long Range Planning*, 26, 1, 39–44.

Shin, J., Taylor, M.S. and Seo, M.G. (2012), "Resources for change: The relationships of organizational inducements and psychological resilience to employee's attitudes and behaviors toward organizational change", *Academy of Management Journal*, 55, 3, 727–748.

Shingo, S. (1981), *The Toyota Production System*, Japanese Management Association, Tokyo, Japan.

Shingo, S. (1985), *A Revolution in Manufacturing: The SMED System*, Productivity Press, New York, NY.

Shingo, S. (1986), *Zero Quality Control: Source Inspection and the Poka-Yoke System*, Productivity Press, New York, NY.

Shingo, S. (2007), *Kaizen and the Art of Creative Thinking: The Scientific Thinking Mechanism*, Enna Products Corporation, Bellingham, WA.

Shingo, S. and Dillon, A.P. (1989), *A Study of the Toyota Production Systems: From an Industrial Engineering Viewpoint*, Productivity Press, New York, NY.

Shingo Institute (2017), *The Shingo Model Book*, Shingo Institute, Utah State University, Logan, UT.

Shook, J. (2009), "Toyota's secret: The A3 report", *MIT Sloan Management Review*, 50, 4, 30–33.

Simons, R. (1994), "How new top managers use control systems as levers of strategic renewal", *Strategic Management Journal*, 15, 3, 169–189.

Skaržauskienė, A. (2010), "Managing complexity: systems thinking as a catalyst of the organization performance", *Measuring Business Excellence*, 14, 4, 49–64.

Smith, B.N., Montagno, R.V. and Kuzmenko, T.N. (2004), "Transformational and servant leadership: Content and contextual comparisons", *Journal of Leadership & Organizational Studies*, 10, 4, 80–91.

Sokovic, M., Pavletic, D. and Pipan, K.K. (2010), "Quality improvement methodologies—PDCA cycle, RADAR matrix, DMAIC and DFSS", *Journal of Achievements in Materials and Manufacturing Engineering*, 43, 1, 476–483.

Sosik, J.J. and Jung, D.D. (2011), *Full Range Leadership Development: Pathways for People, Profit and Planet*, Taylor & Francis, Oxford, UK.

Soyka, P.A. (2012), *Creating a Sustainable Organization: Approaches for Enhancing Corporate Value through Sustainability*, FT Press, Upper Saddle River, NJ.

Spencer, B.A. (1994), "Models of organization and total quality management: A comparison and critical evaluation", *Academy of Management Review*, 19, 3, 446–471.

Stamatis, D.H. (2003), *Failure Mode and Effect Analysis: FMEA from Theory to Execution*, ASQ Quality Progress, Milwaukee, WI.

Sussland, W.A. (2002), "Connecting the planners and the doers", *Quality Progress*, 35, 6, 55–61.

Teece, D.J. (2010), "Business models, business strategy and innovation", *Long Range Planning*, 43, 2, 172–194.

Tennant, C. and Roberts, P. (2001), "Hoshin kanri: Implementing the catchball process", *Long Range Planning*, 34, 3, 287–308.

Tushman, M. and Nadler, D. (1986), "Organizing for innovation", *California Management Review*, 28, 3, 74–92.

Tushman, M.L. and O'Reilly, C.A. (1996), "The ambidextrous organizations: Managing evolutionary and revolutionary change", *California Management Review*, 38, 4, 8–30.

Ulrich, K.T. and Eppinger, S.D. (2015), *Product Design and Development*, 6th edition, McGraw-Hill Publishing, New York, NY.

Urbany, J.E. and Davis, J.H. (2010), *Growth by Focusing on What Matters: Competitive Strategy in 3 Circles*, Business Expert Press, New York, NY.

Useem, J. (2017), "Power causes brain damage", *The Atlantic*, June–July 2017, https://www.theatlantic.com/magazine/archive/2017/07/power-causes-brain-damage/5 28711/ (Accessed: 3 July 2017).

Vairaktarakis, G.L. (1999), "Optimization tools for design and marketing of new / improved products using the house of quality", *Journal of Operations Management*, 17, 6, 645–663.

Van Dijck, J. (2014), "Datafication, dataism and dataveillance: Big Data between scientific paradigm and ideology", *Surveillance & Society*, 12, 2, 197–208.

Van Wassenhove, L.N. (2006), "Humanitarian aid logistics: Supply chain management in high gear", *Journal of the Operational Research Society*, 57, 5, 475–489.

Vidaver-Cohen, D. and Altman, B.W. (2000), "Corporate citizenship in the new millennium: Foundation for an architecture of excellence", *Business and Society Review*, 105, 1, 145–168.

Voegtlin, C., Patzer, M. and Scherer, A.G. (2012), "Responsible leadership in global business: A new approach to leadership and its multi-level outcomes", *Journal of Business Ethics*, 105, 1, 1–16.

Voegtlin, C. and Pless, N.M. (2014), "Global governance: CSR and the role of the UN Global Compacts", *Journal of Business Ethics*, 122, 2, 179–191.

Voehl, F. Harrington, H.J., Mignosa, C. and Charron, R. (2014), *The Lean Six Sigma Black Belt Handbook*, CRC Press, Boca Raton, FL.

Vorhies, D.W. and Morgan, N.A. (2005), "Benchmarking marketing capabilities for sustainable competitive advantage", *Journal of Marketing*, 69, 1, 80–94.

Walsh, V. (1984), "Invention and innovation in the chemical industry: Demand-pull or discovery-push?" *Research Policy*, 13, 4, 211–234.

Wang, T. and Ji, P. (2010), "Understanding customer needs through quantitative analysis of Kano's model", *International Journal of Quality & Reliability Management*, 27, 2, 173–184.

Waters, D. (2007), *Supply Chain Risk Management: Vulnerability and Resilience in Logistics*, Kogan Page Ltd., London, UK.

Watson, G.H. (2003), "Policy deployment: Consensus method of strategy realization", in T. Conti Y. Kondo and G.H. Watson (Eds.), *Quality into the 21st Century: Perspectives on Quality and Competitiveness for Sustained Performance*, 191–218, ASQ Quality Press, Milwaukee, WI.

Welford, R. (2013), *Hijacking Environmentalism: Corporate Responses to Sustainable Development*, Routledge, London, UK.

Wenger, E.C. and Snyder, W.M. (2000), "Communities of practice: The organizational frontier", *Harvard Business Review*, 78, 1, 139–146.

Werther Jr., W.B. and Chandler, D. (2010), *Strategic Corporate Social Responsibility: Stakeholders in a Global Environment*, Sage Publications, Los Angeles, CA.

Wiens, J.A. (2013), *Oil in the Environment: Legacies and Lessons of the Exxon Valdez Oil Spill*, Wiens, J.A. (Ed.), Cambridge University Press, Cambridge, UK.

Wildman, J.L., Shuffler, M.L., Lazzara, E.H., Fiore, S.M., Burke, C.S., Salas, E. and Garven, S. (2012), "Trust development in swift starting action teams: A multilevel framework", *Group & Organization Management*, 37, 2, 137–170.

Wills, G. (2002), *Inventing America: Jefferson's Declaration of Independence*, Houghton Mifflin Harcourt, Boston, MA.

Witcher, B.J. (2003), "Policy management of strategy (hoshin kanri)", *Strategic Change*, 12, 2, 83–94.

Witcher, B.J. and Butterworth, R. (1999), "Hoshin kanri: How Xerox manages", *Long Range Planning*, 32, 3, 323–332.

Witcher, B.J. and Butterworth, R. (2000), "Hoshin kanri at Hewlett-Packard", *Journal of General Management*, 75, 4, 70–85.

Witcher, B.J. and Chau, V.S. (2007), "Balanced scorecard and hoshin kanri: Dynamic capabilities for managing strategic fit", *Management Decision*, 45, 3, 518–538.

Witcher, B.J., Chau, V.S. and Harding, P. (2008), "Dynamic capabilities: Top executive audits and hoshin kanri at Nissan South Africa", *International Journal of Operations & Production Management*, 28, 6, 540–561.

Womack, J.P. and Jones, D.T. (2010), *Lean Thinking: Banish Waste and Create Wealth in Your Corporation*, Simon and Schuster, New York, NY.

Womack, J., Jones, D.T. and Roos, D. (1990), *The Machine that Changed the World*. Simon and Schuster, New York, NY.

World Health Organization (2013), *Health Risk Assessment from the Nuclear Accident after the 2011 Great East Japan Earthquake and Tsunami*, World Health Organization, Geneva, Switzerland.

Wry, T., Lounsbury, M. and Glynn, M.A. (2011), "Legitimating nascent collective identities: Coordinating cultural entrepreneurship", *Organization Science*, 22, 2, 449–463.

Xie, M., Goh, T.N. and Tan, K.C. (2003), *Advanced QFD Applications*, ASQ Quality Press, Milwaukee, WI.

Yan, Q., Shaukat, A. and Tharyan, R. (2016), "Environmental and social disclosures: Link with corporate financial performance", *The British Accounting Review*, 48, 1, 102–116.

Zairi, M. (2000), "Managing customer dissatisfaction through effective complaints management systems", *The TQM Magazine*, 12, 5, 331–337.

Zeithaml, V.A., Parasuraman, A. and Berry, L.L. (1990), *Delivering Service Quality: Balancing Customer Perception and Expectations*, The Free Press, New York, NY.

Zhang, X., Tong, S., Eres, H., Wang, K. and Kossman, M. (2015), "Towards avoiding the hidden traps in QFD during requirements establishment", *Journal of Systems Science and Systems Engineering*, 24, 3, 316–336.

Zwetsloot, G.I. (2003), "From management systems to corporate social responsibility", *Journal of Business Ethics*, 44, 2–3, 201–208.

# Index

Printed in the United States
by Baker & Taylor Publisher Services